Murder
in the Heartland

Other books by M. William Phelps:

Perfect Poison
Lethal Guardian
Every Move You Make
Sleep in Heavenly Peace

Murder
in the Heartland

M. WILLIAM PHELPS

KENSINGTON BOOKS
Kensington Publishing Corp.
www.kensingtonbooks.com

Some names have been changed to protect the privacy of individuals connected to this story.

For Mom

A NOTE TO READERS

Murder in the Heartland was written during an ongoing murder investigation. An arrest has been made, a confession of the crime made public, but the investigation is still active as we go to press. The book does not attempt to solve any portion of the crime or taint the investigation and/or prosecution of the accused. Any allegations made by parties in the book against the accused are brought forth under their own opinions, thoughts, and judgments. The author does not, in any way, make conclusions about the case but aims to unravel this complicated true story and offer some sort of understanding (and insight) about the events herein.

PREFACE

My own introduction to murder came years ago when a family member was slain by a drug-crazed serial killer who preyed on helpless, vulnerable women in the Hartford, Connecticut, region. She was my oldest brother's wife, five months pregnant when her assailant reportedly put a pillowcase over her head and strangled her with a telephone cord. He was a large man, a professional-football-player type. An average-sized woman herself, she had no chance.

Although I wasn't writing about true crime then, I didn't realize how significant her murder would be to my work later on in life. Her death showed me that painful events such as murder carry over into everyday life in subtle ways, and hover, like guilt, over many of the things we do. Through the years, I've often sat and thought about this as I interviewed victims of murder: relatives, loved ones, friends, spouses, community members close to a case.

Soon after I finished investigating the Bobbie Jo Stinnett murder case, however, I realized the exclusive information I had uncovered while researching the book you are about to read had tested everything I thought I knew about life, loss, community, and dealing with unexpected tragedy.

As I was finishing my last book in December 2004, the Bobbie Jo Stinnett murder became front-page news. For about a week during the Christmas holiday, I couldn't turn on the television or open a newspaper without hearing something about the case. Everyone wanted to know what had driven a woman to cut another woman's child from her womb, killing the mother of the child. It became one of the most high-profile crime stories of the year.

I followed the case, made a few calls, interviewed some of the people involved, and began gathering anything I could find related to the case, with the thought I might one day pursue it as a book. I often juggle about ten to twelve cases before I decide on a book subject. I write dozens of letters to the people involved, send them, and see what happens. Who calls or writes back. A litmus test, to see how many people will talk on record.

The first letter I wrote pertaining to the Stinnett case was addressed to Carl Boman, the alleged perpetrator's ex-husband. I figured, if I could get Mr. Boman to come forward, I would have a powerful story to tell. He knew the accused perpetrator better than anyone; he could tell me things about her no one else could, and, more importantly, he could help me understand the psychology behind her possible motives, which fascinated me more than anything else.

I wrote Mr. Boman a letter, printed it out, placed it in an envelope, and put it in the out-box I have on my desk—but, for whatever reason, never sent it. *Wait*, something told me.

One afternoon a few months later, I was working at my desk when a little dialogue box on the bottom corner of my computer screen alerted me an e-mail had just arrived.

Then the name of the sender appeared in the box: *Carl Boman*.

"I want you to write this story," he wrote. "I need to get the truth out. There's way too much speculation and rumor out in public right now."

I was pleasantly shocked, to say the least, that Carl Boman had reached out to me. Still a bit skeptical, however, during our first telephone conversation, I said, "Let's talk about this. Tell me a little bit about what you know."

"Well, I have known her," Mr. Boman said first, referring to the alleged perpetrator, "for twenty years, and fathered four of her children. I've been right in the middle of everything for two decades. My life—my kids' lives—have been torn apart by all of this. Two of my children held Bobbie Jo's baby on the night she was murdered."

"Why me, though?" I asked.

"You seem very thorough. Like you can tell this story and put aside the rumor and speculation."

"I can't pay you," I said. "I never pay sources."

"I don't want money. I only want the truth."

Thus began my quest. Through Carl Boman and my own garrulous way of reaching out to people, I've been introduced to scores of sources for this book. Mr. Boman's children, all of whom have spoken to me in one form or another, are incredibly tough kids. They have been through a lot and lost more than most might assume; they are victims, too. Not that Bobbie Jo Stinnett and her immediate family haven't lost the most. But I've learned in the years of writing true-crime books, along with a tragedy of similar scope in my own family, the pain involved in the aftermath of murder—that is, if it is to be weighed on a scale of emotion—is equal, no matter which side you're on.

People suffer.

No pain is greater than any other.

Fundamentally, this is a story of loss, life, and being able to move forward in the face of an immeasurable tragedy. The accused killer's children still love their mother. But more than that, as Mr. Boman said to me once, "This is a tragic death that should have never happened—and that's one of the main reasons why I want to get this story out. The whole story. Everything that led up to this senseless murder needs to be told as a cautionary tale so people understand how mentally ill people who don't get professional help are potential time bombs. In this country, we need to take the issue of mental health more seriously."

While writing this book, I was amazed by the candor and honesty of some, while appalled by the lies of others. Especially flattering was that Sheriff Ben Espey, the law enforcement hero of this book, opened up and told me his story.

In the end, I found a story of two towns, two mothers, several children, one "miracle" child, an ex-husband left to clean up twenty years of family dysfunction, a sheriff determined to find a missing child, and a telling look into the heart of America.

I've written a number of true-crime books now and have seen and described the most depraved people in society. I thought I had become hardened by all the murder in my professional life, and nothing could break me. But this story turned me inside out. To understand why this crime happened is one thing; yet to sit and digest this material for as long as I did made me realize that people *truly* are capable of just about anything, especially when driven by desperation.

This, then, is not your typical, straightforward true-crime account: body, investigation, background of victim and perpetrator, trial, verdict, sentence. Some of those elements will appear, certainly. But this story encompasses two families, many victims, and two towns coming to terms with a senseless, incredibly hideous murder. Here, I give you the entire story as it played out from day one—but also, most important, the all-inclusive backstory of the alleged perpetrator, which explains why she did what she did and how she, her immediate family, and the two towns are coping with the aftermath today.

—M. WILLIAM PHELPS
Vernon, CT

PROLOGUE

Desperation

On December 13, 2004, Lisa Montgomery e-mailed her ex-husband, Carl Boman, about picking up their children. Carl and Lisa had been divorced (a second time) for five years. They lived hundreds of miles apart, in different states. Weekend visitations had become a tangled mess of changed times and dates, failed promises, and heated arguments—all brought on, Carl insisted, by his ex-wife.

"You can pick the kids up at 7am on Christmas morning," wrote Lisa.

She wanted the children home by eight o'clock on Christmas night, she then demanded. On top of that, Lisa didn't want her mother, Judy Shaughnessy, to see the children. She was adamant: "They are *not* to go out to [her] house."

Carl Boman had never intended to stop by his ex-mother-in-law's. The stipulation was, he said, just one more way for Lisa to wield some sort of control over the situation, as she, reluctantly, handed the kids over to him.

Throughout the e-mail, Lisa ranted and raved about the children's wants and needs, what Carl could and could *not* do. Looking at the e-mail later that night, it occurred to Carl that Lisa was doing the same thing she had done for the past ten years: manipulating and controlling the situation. In his opinion, all she had ever done was "spread hate and lies," said Carl, "and cause problems by making up stories." About him. Her current husband. The kids. Her mothers. Sisters.

Even herself.

Lately, she had been fabricating a story about her being pregnant. She had been telling people she was carrying twins, but had lost one child the previous month. The second child, she claimed, was healthy and due on December 13. To prove it, she had an ultrasound photograph and a nursery set up in her house. She'd gone to doctor appointments. Bought the child clothing and toys.

What Lisa didn't know then, however, was two days before receiving her e-mail, Carl had filed for permanent custody of the children. Lisa would be summoned into court on January 15, 2005, where her lies—"every single one of them"—would then be exposed. There had been four other instances in recent years when Lisa claimed to be pregnant, yet she had not produced a child. There was always an excuse, followed by another set of lies. Carl had known her for twenty years. They'd had four children together. There was no way she could be pregnant; medically speaking, it was impossible. Carl was there the day she'd had her tubal ligation surgery. They'd talked about it beforehand, and both had agreed it was the best thing for the family.

"She was actually relieved after the procedure," he said. "We didn't want any more children."

In court, Carl was going to prove Lisa was a fraud. He was planning on providing evidence of how she had perjured herself recently during a custody hearing over her nephew. During the hearing, Lisa said she'd given birth to a baby in her doctor's office, but it was stillborn. Because it had died, she told the court, she donated it to science.

The story was a total invention. Carl was going to produce an affidavit detailing the truth. In turn, he was sure the court would award him permanent custody of their children. Lisa's new husband, mother, sisters, the children, not to mention the town where she lived, would soon know she had been lying about being pregnant all along. Those five pregnancies—including the current tale of losing one of her twins—existed only in her mind.

"There was no way out of it for Lisa," said Carl. "She was being backed into a corner."

"I think she was in desperation," added Lisa's mother, Judy, "to get a baby one way or another—she ran out of options."

What nobody knew, as Carl sat there absorbing Lisa's latest

e-mail tirade, shaking his head in disgust, was that she was making plans of her own.

When Lisa found out a day later Carl had filed an injunction seeking permanent custody of two of their four children, she had one of the kids call him.

"Mom wants to know what you have planned, Dad," his son asked while she sat by the phone, staring at him.

"How are you, son?" Carl asked. His children mattered more than anything to Carl at that point. His son had just turned fifteen.

With Lisa by his side, Carl's son continued speaking for her. "She says she's considering allowing me to live with you but wants to know if you're taking me out of school." Then, after a moment of whispering in the background, "She's very upset, you know, that you filed those papers with the court."

"Put her on the phone."

"You have no chance of getting the kids," said Lisa as soon as she put the receiver to her mouth. "I'm going to prove *you* are the liar, Carl."

. . . impulses may be from below,
not from above . . .
but if I am the Devil's child,
I will live then from the Devil.

—Ralph Waldo Emerson

I

THE RUSE

1

It was five days before the winter solstice. December 16, 2004, started off a bit abnormal—although, upon waking up to what was a magnificent sunrise, few would have guessed. The wind was blowing in across the Nebraska plains from the west at a steady pace of twelve miles per hour, which, by itself, was not so unusual. Yet the temperature capped out at around fifty degrees by midday, making it feel like a chilly evening in late September, or maybe a pleasant early-October morning: brusque, cool, effervescent.

In town, many of the women took advantage of the unseasonable weather. Wearing red-and-white aprons, some felt inspired to take out muddy throw rugs and floormats, hang them from clotheslines, and beat the dirt out of them with brooms. Others opened windows and aired things out a bit—the cool, fresh air casting a sparkle on everything it touched. Some men, unimpressed by such a scant spike in the mercury, donned customary black-and-red plaid flannel shirts, coveralls, leather gloves, and winter caps with earflaps. They were seen making repairs to property-line fences and timber corral posts, while others stood sipping coffee and "shootin' the breeze" near the center of town, framed by the cottonwoods, oaks, and maples, leafless and brittle, that stood in perfect rows along the gullies of Highway 113.

Before that Thursday afternoon, the town of Skidmore was but a black dot on the map of America's heartland. To say it was a small farming parish would understate how rural the countryside actually was. Skidmore, according to the green-and-white "city limit" sign on the edge of town, is home to a mere 342—"give'r take a few," noted one native—nestled in the northwestern corner of Missouri, a state named after a Siouan Native American tribe, which, translated, means "canoe."

To an outsider, the town resembles an eighteenth-century landscape painting hanging on a velvet saloon wall somewhere farther west, dusty and ignored, a bucolic setting, innocent of technology, infrastructure, big-city bureaucrats, and mundane problems.

But to townsfolk, Skidmore is Eden, a comfortable, intimate place to live *and* die. "Everybody knows everybody" is a reliable cliché there, evident in the way people greet each other with a nod and wave. In Missouri, where the state license plates proclaim "Show Me State," red, white, and blue are more than simply colors; and rolls of hay, coiled up like massive cinnamon buns as tall as street signs, dot the thousands of acres of gently sloping farmland.

In many ways, time has stood still in Skidmore. An old railroad line that carried cattle and grain a century ago marks a decomposing path through the countryside, subtly reminding folks that nothing ever truly goes away. All over town are remnants of another day and age: memories verifying how life, regardless of how it is elsewhere, moves at a slower pace, and how people still take the time to stop and shake hands, pat one another on the shoulder, ask about the kids, quote a passage from the Bible, or maybe just share a bottle of "pop" while sitting on a porch swing.

In their hearts, any one of them will gladly admit, with a snap of their suspenders, Skidmorians care about the place where they live and the people who make up their community. They don't bother anyone, and, in return, expect the same treatment from others.

"People there, well, it's a different sorta place," said one outsider. To which an acquaintance added, "If you don't belong in Skidmore, ya betta jus stay the hell outta there."

2

Nearly two hundred miles south, in eastern-central Kansas, the day hadn't started out so warm and inviting. When she awoke, a cold snap lingered in the house.

Getting dressed, she put on one of her oversized bulky sweaters, a pair of baggy blue jeans, sneakers, and glasses. She pulled her hair back in a ponytail. Her heavy winter coat was downstairs on a kitchen chair. She could grab it on the way out.

As usual, she sat by herself at the dining table, forgoing coffee for what many later agreed was an "addiction to Pepsi." Then, staring out the window, she lit a Marlboro, because she knew her husband had left for work already. Like a lot of things in her life, she'd been hiding her affair with nicotine from him.

Her two daughters and son slept upstairs. She had told her husband the night before she was "getting up early to go shopping" in Topeka, but the kids had no idea she was awake. It was close to five in the morning. If she wasn't working one of her three part-time jobs, there wasn't a chance she'd be up so early.

After stubbing out her cigarette, she walked upstairs into her oldest daughter's room and sat on the edge of the bed, as she did on most mornings. She and *Rebecca** were close, like best friends. They talked about things she wouldn't consider sharing with her other children, and unquestionably not her husband.

"What are you doing today, Mom?" asked Rebecca. She was muzzy and worn-out, having just awakened. Seventeen-year-old Rebecca and her mother had gone shopping for baby clothes sev-

---

*Italics on first use of proper names and locations represents pseudonym or author's replacement.

eral times over the past few months. Her mother was "excited" about being pregnant and wanted to share the experience with her oldest. "You'll have children of your own one day," she told Rebecca more than once as they browsed through racks of clothes, baby rattles, and toys.

Sitting quietly, she brushed Rebecca's hair away from her eyes with her right hand and stared at her for a brief time. In almost a whisper, "I'm going shopping in Topeka," she responded.

Everyone in the family was under the impression her due date had passed the previous Monday, December 13, and she was going to have the child any day now.

"Shopping might get things going," she continued when Rebecca didn't respond. "I need to pick up something for Kayla, anyway."

Kayla was the baby of the family. She didn't live at the house anymore. She was staying with a friend in *Georgia*.

At fourteen years old, Kayla was pretty much the free thinker of the four kids. She wasn't a submissive conformist, like so many children her own age, ready to accept anything anybody told her. Nor was she one of those kids that fell into, say, the "Goth" movement at school because it was the latest fad. Kayla thought about things thoroughly and made her own decisions. Her independent way of thinking had landed Kayla in Georgia, hundreds of miles away from her mother, stepfather, and siblings.

On August 25, 2004, exactly one week after her birthday, she bid farewell to everyone. First she went to Texas to stay with a fellow rat-terrier breeder for a couple days so she could attend a dog show there before traveling on.

Kayla referred to the woman she moved in with in Georgia as "Auntie," she said, out of "Southern respect," but *Mary Timmeny,* "Auntie M ," as Kayla and others referred to her, was a friend of the family, and had introduced Kayla to her passion: raising, breeding, and showing rat terriers. Mary had invited Kayla to spend a few weeks with her in Georgia during the summer of 2004 so she could teach her how to train her dogs and ready them for the dog show circuit. Kayla's father, Carl Boman, was amazed his ex-wife had agreed to it. As Carl viewed the situation, Mary was a stranger, someone Kayla's mother had met only a few times. Carl was beside himself with anger that his ex-wife had allowed Kayla to spend part of her summer with someone so far away.

Kayla's mother had custody, though. Carl couldn't do much about it, even if he wanted.

"So, in July," said Kayla, "I went out there for three weeks and got to go to two dog shows and showed dogs in both of those shows."

Kayla met her mother at a Lexington, Kentucky, dog show after the three-week sabbatical was over and went back home to Kansas.

A while later, Auntie Mary called. "I miss you," she said.

"I miss you, too."

"Would you like to come back and spend a few months with me here in Georgia?"

"Yes, yes, yes!" replied Kayla. She was "really excited" about it. It was all she had thought about since leaving.

"Don't tell your sisters, though, Kayla. Okay?" said Auntie Mary. She didn't want Kayla's mother to hear about it until she had a chance to talk to her herself.

"I won't," said Kayla.

"I'll talk to your mom soon about it. Okay?"

"Sure."

The plan was for Kayla to spend part of the school year with Mary in Georgia. She and Mary had hit it off during the three weeks that summer. Mary noticed a drive in Kayla and a natural reserve around the dogs she believed could be beneficial to Kayla on the dog show circuit, if only she had someone to keep her focused on the dynamics of training, which her mother, Kayla said, wanted no part of.

Kayla and Mary missed each other. Their feelings went beyond a mutual interest in the dogs to include love, affection, friendship. Kayla and Mary had bonded. For Kayla, it was like starting over. Her life had been filled with turmoil for a long time, what with the problems between her mother and father and between her mother and stepfather. Living in the structure of a solid family would allow her some much-deserved space and tranquillity. She wouldn't have to listen to her mother talk bad about her father. Or scream at her new husband when he failed to do what she wanted. Nor would she have to suffer when she felt torn between siblings siding with Mom or Dad. Not to mention Mom's obsession lately with having another child.

"You're going to miss Mom having her baby," one of Kayla's siblings said to her after hearing Kayla was leaving.

"I'll be back for it," promised Kayla.

Kayla was looking forward to the calming effect living with Mary would provide—something that had never existed in her short life.

At first, Kayla's mother didn't think it was a good idea for her to leave.

"Can I go, Mom?"

"I'll think about it," said her mother.

"When will you let me know?"

"You should probably forget it."

"Come on, Mom. Please?"

"I'll *think* about it, Kayla."

Then Rebecca stepped in, and "after much persuasion by her," recalled Kayla, "Mom finally agreed to it."

So, based on Rebecca's recommendation, shortly after the conversation, Kayla was sitting in her mom's car on her way to Georgia. Staying for "part of the school year," as Mary had suggested, turned into Kayla's spending the entire first quarter. But it was okay with Kayla; she was at ease with her new life. She enjoyed not being around the dysfunction and disorder back home. She was, one could say, her own person.

As Rebecca stretched, trying to pay attention, her mother got up off the bed and walked toward the door. Before opening it, she turned. "I want to get Kayla something special this Christmas. She's been gone so long. I miss her. Do you know what she wants?"

"No, not really, Mom," answered Rebecca.

"Okay, then. You go back to sleep. I'll call you later."

She took one last look at Rebecca and closed the door.

3

Outside the window where the woman who called herself *Darlene Fischer* lived, the temperature had dropped the previous night in Kansas. The prairie just beyond the driveway and the gray-shingled red-barn roof in the yard were dusted with frost; the windowpanes of the farmhouse down the road were fogged over; a rusted Ford pickup truck carcass sat on concrete blocks in the wheat field nearby and appeared as if someone had spray-painted the windshield white; and a shadow of smoke, rising from a woodstove chimney, coiled upward into a corkscrew, dancing in the sky.

Darlene had decided long ago, if this plan of hers was going to work, it would need to be set in motion today. Her husband had taken the following day, a Friday, off from work so he could go with her to her doctor's office and find out what was going on with the baby. He, along with her children and several people in town, were expecting her to go into labor any moment. She had been talking about having another baby for years—all the while, she claimed, contending with four miscarriages.

Part of her plan meant driving into Lyndon, just outside the town where she lived, and first stopping at Casey's General Store, where she worked part-time. It was her day off, but *Nancy*, a coworker, would be there.

She figured she'd walk in, tell Nancy what was happening, and word would soon spread throughout town she was in labor.

Before leaving the house, she took a paring knife from a kitchen

---

*Italics on first use of proper names and locations represents pseudonym or author's replacement.

drawer and put it in her pocket. She rarely carried a purse, or, for that matter, a knife. She needed rope, too. But she could purchase it later or pick up a bundle elsewhere. She had plenty of time.

At about 5:15 A.M., she pulled into Casey's parking lot. From the look of things, it was just Nancy sitting there behind the counter. She was probably half asleep, filing her nails, drinking coffee, maybe reading the morning paper. Her boss, the store manager, was there as well, a friend said later; but she was likely in the back office doing paperwork, getting ready for the day.

Leaning on the counter, Darlene looked at Nancy, put her hands around the bottom of her belly, and lunged her stomach forward to make it appear larger.

"My water's going to break today," she told Nancy, speaking "really quiet and softly," recalled a relative.

"I can feel it," she continued, looking at Nancy. "I'm having labor pains."

Nancy didn't believe her. She was one of several people in town starting to question her pregnancies. At the same time, a majority of the people in her close circle—all four of her kids and her husband—believed it was for real: she was going to have a baby.

"Well," she said to Nancy, "I'm going shopping in Topeka."

Minutes later, she took off.

While driving, she phoned home. Rebecca, up and about now, getting ready for school, answered.

"I'm on my way into town to go shopping. Any idea yet what I might get Kayla?"

"No, Mom. Sorry."

"Okay, we'll talk later."

"Right, Mom."

"I'll call you this afternoon."

"You okay?"

"I'm fine. My water is going to break. I can feel it."

4

Hours after Darlene Fischer left Casey's General Store in Lyndon, a few people spotted her in a Maryville, Missouri, Wal-Mart, about fourteen miles east of Skidmore, almost two hundred miles north of her home in Kansas. Those hours between the time she left Casey's and ended up in Maryville were unaccounted for. No one seemed to know what she did or where she went.

Back in Kansas, at home, she and her husband had turned a small upstairs room into a nursery for the approaching baby. The walls were painted a soft vanilla white; she pasted stickers from the Disney animated film *The Lion King* over the fresh paint: light purple elephants with yellow ears, yellow Simba lion cubs, green butterflies, green and purple dragonflies. It was cute. Comfortable. The perfect soft setting for a newborn. On one side of the room against the wall was an oak-railed crib with blankets and sheets matching the stickers. A nightlight sat on a table in the corner of the room next to a changing station packed with fresh T-shirts, blankets, sheets, and a brand-new bag of Pampers. A baby carrier was usually kept inside the crib, ready and waiting (in fact, she had it with her that afternoon in Maryville; it was sitting in the car beside her). Considering the neutral colors she chose, one might be inclined to think she didn't know if a girl or boy was forthcoming. She wanted a girl. There was no doubt about it. Having a daughter had become another obsession of hers lately. The only hint the nursery provided that a girl was imminent was a Minnie Mouse diaper holder hanging off one corner of the changing station. Other than that, the colors she chose would work for a girl or a boy.

Still, she had been showing off an ultrasound photograph of someone else's fetus she had downloaded from the Internet to her husband and kids, claiming it was an image of her "baby girl."

By 3:00 P.M., the chill of morning had yielded to a comfortable fifty-degree afternoon. Driving west from Maryville, making her way past the massive Kawasaki Motors plant outside downtown, and after possibly getting something to eat nearby, Darlene Fischer continued south on Highway 71 before taking a hard right onto the "A" road leading into Skidmore.

Just outside downtown Skidmore, about fifteen minutes later, she would have taken a right onto the 113, which became Elm Street in the center of town and West Elm, her ultimate destination, beyond that, past the town's one service station.

Sitting on the front seat beside her were directions to the house she'd printed off the Internet. As far back as Novemeber 17, 2004, Darlene had downloaded the directions and "mapped out" a route to this house. She had lived all over the Midwest and in New Mexico, San Diego, and Arkansas for a time, but found herself today driving into a town she had not been to before.

Following Elm Street down to the west end, Darlene heard the tires of her red Toyota Corolla crunch and pop against the gravel as she entered Bobbie Jo Stinnett's driveway, near the corner of Orchard and West Elm.

There it was on the right porch post column, exactly where Bobbie Jo had said it would be: the number *410*.

Bobbie Jo's home, like most in town, was small, just as Darlene had heard. It was a charming little place, though, with two large elm trees centered in front of the porch by the road, their branches weeping downward, brushing the ground.

Darlene had told Bobbie Jo she lived in Fairfax, Missouri, about twenty miles west of Skidmore.

Not true.

She also said she was interested in a few rat-terrier puppies one of Bobbie Jo's breeder studs had sired recently.

Like a lot of the pieces of Darlene's chaotic life, inquiring about the puppies was also a lie. The woman calling herself Darlene had her own terriers back home. She didn't need to travel over one hundred miles to buy one. In fact, she lived in Melvern, Kansas,

187 miles south of Skidmore, a three-hour drive. She was in Skidmore for the one thing Bobbie Jo Stinnett had that she couldn't have: a baby.

Bobbie Jo was a local rat-terrier breeder. Married, just twenty-three years old, she was in the last trimester of her first pregnancy, her due date about a month away. Looking at her, it was easy to see a woman beaming with the delight only a first-time mother can emit: a glow, incidentally, Darlene Fischer didn't have. The townsfolk of Skidmore adored Bobbie Jo. With her ebullient, smile, large brown eyes, wavy brunette-auburn hair, blemish-free skin as soft as silk, she personified the all-American girl.

"She was such a sweet person," recalled a friend. "She was so very smart. She would always give me advice when I needed it, and we would always talk about her pups. . . . She really knew her rat terriers."

That same friend, a teenager, spoke of Bobbie Jo as though she were her big sister; someone to whom she could turn for advice. "She was such a beautiful person, on the inside and out. My mentor, really."

It was around 3:15 P.M. when the woman who called herself Darlene Fischer pulled onto Bobbie Jo's street and parked in her driveway. The sun was burning warm and bright, illuminating a glorious holiday season. Christmas cards were in the mail. Invitations to New Year's Eve parties already out. Nativity scenes, cut from plywood and painted by hand, were propped up on front lawns. In Skidmore, people were, indeed, prepared to celebrate the birth of Jesus Christ and the Christmas holiday.

Greeting visitors, a welcome sign stood above a carved miniature birdhouse, a red cardinal and yellow finch buzzing around a black-eyed Susan, to the right side of Bobbie Jo's front door. This modest dwelling, set in a peaceful, middle-American suburb, was just like the dozen or so others around it.

As Bobbie Jo saw it, the afternoon meeting with Darlene had been brought on by chance. She and Darlene had made plans the previous day, after a mutual friend in the rat-terrier-breeding business had introduced them some time ago. From Bobbie Jo's point of view, the meeting was supposed to be just a routine, friendly business transaction.

Darlene was a woman of thirty-six years, sporting large-framed glasses with thin lenses that magnified her sunken dark green eyes. She was of average size and shape. She had natural reddish blond streaks throughout her brown hair, which hung down and nearly touched her small breasts. In most respects, Darlene looked no different from thousands of other women marching through their lives in the Midwest.

Mrs. Nobody.

To those who knew her more intimately, though, she seemed depressed, vacant, especially angry, the last few years. Just the other day, quite unexpectedly, she had expressed interest in buying one of Bobbie Jo's prized terrier pups. The two women had communicated via an online chat room, Annie's Rat Terrier Rest Area, where they seemed to share a common interest in the feisty canines. Maybe a new pup—or the baby she was telling everyone she was expecting—would cheer Darlene up, make her feel better about herself and her life.

The previous day, Darlene had e-mailed Bobbie Jo at 4:22 P.M. She logged on to Bobbie Jo's Happy Haven Farms Web site and, retrieving Bobbie Jo's e-mail address, wrote, "I was recommended to you by [a mutual friend]. . . ."

And so it began: a seemingly harmless electronic business proposition.

Using the e-mail address Fischer4kids at Hotmail, in that same brief note, Darlene said she had been "unable to reach" Bobbie Jo. She sounded somewhat panicky and impatient, perhaps worried the meeting the following day wouldn't take place as planned.

"Please get in touch with me soon," continued Darlene, "as we are considering the purchase of one of your puppies and would like to ask you a few questions."

Three hours later, Bobbie Jo responded. Under the subject line "Done and Done!," she wrote, "Darlene, I've e-mailed you with the directions so we can meet." To solidify her desire to get together, Bobbie Jo expressed her "hope" the e-mail would reach Darlene in time. "Great chatting with you on messenger," said Bobbie Jo, after explaining how much she was looking forward to "chatting with you tomorrow a.m.," before thanking their mutual friend for introducing them. "Talk to you soon, Darlene!" Bobbie Jo ended the e-mail. "Have a great evening."

Word of mouth: most great businesses, especially in a rural region like Skidmore, were built on the recommendations of others. Bobbie Jo counted on it. Save for paying a major Internet search engine to list her as a top search result, the only way to reach people interested in her pups was to keep customers happy, get word out through the Internet, and make contacts at the dog shows she attended.

Bobbie Jo hadn't been married two years yet. Eight months pregnant, she was happily going about her storybook life in Middle America. Happy Haven Farms had been Bobbie Jo's design. Zeb, her husband, worked full-time at a manufacturing plant in Maryville. He had helped his new bride out with the breeding business, but, for the most part, he allowed Bobbie Jo to maintain it herself. In just a few words, some of what Bobbie Jo had written on the home page of her Web site seemed to reflect not only her and Zeb's attitude toward breeding, but the way they viewed and valued life in general.

"Our puppies are placed in only the very best homes with the family that fits them best. Let us help you find your next pet, rat terrier or otherwise."

Bobbie Jo was meeting with Darlene to see if she met her stringent criteria for ownership. Bobbie Jo wasn't about to sell one of her pups to someone who couldn't be responsible enough to love and care for it. Bobbie Jo and Zeb were good people, concerned about the animals they had made a large part of their lives together.

"They were the type of people," said one former friend, "you could see growing old together . . . in their rocking chairs, watching their grandchildren play in the front yard. They minded their own business and didn't start any trouble."

Sitting in Bobbie Jo's driveway on Thursday afternoon, the woman who called herself Darlene Fischer turned off the ignition of her Corolla and looked up at Bobbie Jo's front door. Besides a paring knife from home, law enforcement later claimed she also had a home birthing kit, a bundle of rope she purchased that afternoon, and several blankets.

Grabbing her keys, Darlene opened her car door and walked toward Bobbie Jo's front porch. Looking in both directions as she made her way up the one step, pushing the nub of her glass frames back up the bridge of her nose, Darlene Fischer didn't see anyone around.

She and Bobbie Jo would be alone.

5

Brenda Standford was at her Lyndon, Kansas, home on the previous night, December 15, getting her children ready for bed, when Darlene Fischer—although Brenda knew her by another name—had phoned with some rather remarkable news. According to the time frame Brenda later gave, the phone call was made shortly after Darlene had been in touch with Bobbie Jo Stinnett online and made plans to meet with her the following day in Skidmore.

At one time, Brenda saw Darlene Fischer nearly every day. They were coworkers, even close friends.

Already preparing for bed, Brenda was startled by the phone call, she remembered, because "it was so darn late."

"Hi, Brenda," said Darlene. She sounded cheerful, upbeat.

"Darlene? That you?" Brenda was a busy woman: kids, husband, two jobs. "Why you calling me so late?"

"I had the baby," said Darlene in excitement. "Everyone's doing fine."

After a brief pause: "Wow," replied Brenda, "you're home from the hospital already?"

Brenda was under the impression Darlene had given birth earlier that morning, but she could tell she was calling her from home. It seemed strange the hospital would allow Darlene to leave so soon after giving birth.

"Yeah. You know, they ship you out of there so quick nowadays," said Darlene.

---

*Italics on first use of proper names and locations represents pseudonym or author's replacement.

Brenda was surprised. She knew insurance companies pushed new mothers out of hospital beds, if they were healthy, as soon as they could. *But in under twenty-four hours?*

"You and the baby are fine?" asked Brenda.

"Oh, yes. It went smooth."

"So what'd you have?"

"A girl. Can you believe it?"

"Just what you wanted."

"Yeah."

Over the past few months, Brenda had spoken to Darlene almost daily about the baby. She believed, "without a doubt in [her] mind," Darlene was pregnant. She would wear maternity clothes, or baggy shirts and sweaters, and talk about how excited she and her husband were about having the child.

"She would tell me that her ankles were swollen," recalled Brenda. "How she was having terrible bouts of morning sickness. 'My stomach is getting so hard,' she'd say. And it was . . . I felt it," added Brenda, before changing the subject slightly: "Up until the day everything happened, I believed her, because I watched her stomach grow. It was getting bigger, harder. She had me all the way."

6

Bobbie Jo Stinnett was under the impression she and Darlene Fischer had just met. But Darlene had met Bobbie Jo back in April 2004 at a dog show in Abilene, Kansas. Since that day, they had spoken online a number of times. Yet, she hadn't introduced herself as Darlene Fischer—instead, she went by her real name.

Lisa Montgomery.

The use of two names seemed to fit into what some later claimed was a "split personality" Lisa Montgomery had developed during the six months before she showed up at Bobbie Jo's house in Skidmore. "Lisa lied so much," recalled one family member, "she believed her own lies. This is why I feel she has a split personality: her other 'self'—or 'others'—took over at some point."

After the dog show in Abilene, Bobbie Jo had become friends with Lisa's youngest daughter, Kayla. Bobbie Jo and Kayla corresponded online through e-mail and instant messaging quite frequently. Kayla admired Bobbie Jo. Even loved her, she said.

"The last time I talked to Bobbie Jo," recalled Kayla, ". . . she was ecstatic about having her baby. She had a name picked out for quite some time. . . . She was telling me how [the baby] would sleep in their room (as they had a small house) until they could find a bigger house. I *know* Bobbie Jo would have been one awesome mother to that sweet little baby."

So why was Lisa Montgomery disguising herself as Darlene Fischer? Why hide behind a false identity? Wouldn't Bobbie Jo recognize Darlene as Lisa as soon as she answered the door? Wouldn't it put Lisa in an awkward position?

It was indeed an odd circumstance that Lisa Montgomery put herself in: one more piece of the puzzle that wouldn't make sense later when people learned of the unfathomable horror that was about to take place inside Bobbie Jo's little farmhouse.

The corn and soybean fields stretch along Highway 113 far beyond where any of Skidmore's 342 residents can see. In some areas, the vast flatness of the land runs adjacent to roadways made of gravel, cement, and blacktop, while rolling hills disappear into the horizon. Skidmore is a picturesque parcel of untarnished landscape, tucked in the corner of a state most locals feel blessed to call home.

"Skidmore ain't dun changed in, I dunno, a hundred years," said one local. "Same ol' town here'a."

The town is full of kind and generous people. Among the tumbleweeds, farmhouses, clapboard ranches, windmills, and one water tower, crime generally involves the theft of a John Deere tractor or a few kids popping out streetlights after lifting their daddy's shotgun. When the lights go out and the moon settles over the rolling meadows bordering the town, beyond the subtle hum of a chorus of crickets, the only sound coming from town might be the echo of a dog's lonesome bark or the drunken laughter of a local sippin' whiskey, swinging on a porch hammock, having a grand ol' time all by himself.

In the enormity of the Midwest, Skidmore is a flyover town many don't know exists. People in town like it that way, and they respect the privacy the region offers. The beauty of the landscape is a constant reminder that every part of life—ashes to ashes, dust to dust—is rooted in the rich black soil that breeds it. Traditions thrive in Skidmore: in the one Christian church, the one café, the pinewood rocking chairs on just about every porch, and the souls of the men and women who work the land. One would think here, in this serene, hush of a community, violence and murder would be unthought-of, if not for television crime shows piped into homes via satellite dishes.

But that has not been the case.

7

As Lisa Montgomery, posing as Darlene Fischer, made her way up to the Stinnetts' front door, Bobby Jo was inside the house talking on the phone to her mother, forty-four-year-old Becky Harper, who lived nearby and worked at the Sumy Oil Company, two blocks east of where Bobbie Jo lived.

"Can you pick me up from work?" asked Harper. Becky had a son, too, ten-year-old Tyler, Bobbie Jo's little brother.

"I'm expecting someone to come and look at a few dogs," responded Bobbie Jo.

"My truck is getting some work done. I need a ride to the garage."

There was a brief silence. Then, as Becky Harper was about to say something, Bobbie Jo must have been either startled by the slam of Lisa's car door or heard the creak of the porch steps as Lisa approached. Because next, Bobbie Jo said, "Oh, they're here, Mother. I've gotta go."

After a few more words between mother and daughter, Bobbie Jo ended the conversation.

It would be the last time Becky Harper ever spoke to her daughter.

Bobbie Jo Stinnett graduated from Nodaway-Holt Jr.-Senior High School. Located in nearby Graham, one of Skidmore's neighboring towns, the building itself was no larger than an elementary-sized school in most cities. In any given year, no more than 150 students are enrolled in the school.

Well-liked, Bobbie Jo was a cheerleader, involved in the 4-H Club, and worked on the school newspaper and yearbook. Her childhood friendship with Zeb blossomed into a high school romance (and, later, a dream marriage). Her academic work ethic made her not only an honor student, but one of the smarter kids in school. After graduation, one could easily assume, Bobbie Jo might have run away from Skidmore to find her place in a bigger city with more promise and a brighter future.

But that wasn't what Bobbie Jo wanted. She was content with what life had given her in Skidmore.

"She kind of blossomed in high school," a former teacher told reporters later. "She started to come out of her shell and [get] active in things [as she] gained popularity and friends."

Just out of high school, during the fall of 2000, Bobbie Jo went to work in Maryville at the Earl May Garden Center, which specialized in pets. There she turned what was a love she'd had as a child for animals into a passion for breeding and raising her own dogs.

Her ex-boss said she was "exceptionally sweet," adding, "She never had a bad thing to say about anyone."

"Bright" and "cheerful" were common adjectives attached to descriptions of Bobbie Jo. She loved all animals and, one coworker said, had a "knack for them."

"She loved horses, loved dogs; she adopted everything with a fuzzy face," said a friend of the family.

After Bobbie Jo quit her job at Earl May's, she started along one of her first career paths. Not because she didn't like the work at Earl May's, or the people. Instead, she felt the need to "earn more money" and be closer to her beau. She took a job at the Kawasaki Motors Manufacturing Corporation in Maryville, where Zeb, like hundreds of others in the region, sought employment after graduation. The Kawasaki plant opened in 1989 and focused on the production of general-purpose engines. Covering over 700,000 square feet on 113.7 acres of land, nearly the size of Skidmore itself, the factory employed well over six hundred people, many of whom lived in the immediate region.

"The pay is better," Bobbie Jo told one of her coworkers at Earl May's shortly before she quit. "Zeb and I are getting married soon. I need to make more money."

People who knew Zeb and Bobbie Jo admired how comfortable

they seemed around each other. Essentially, they were kids. Many high-school sweethearts who took the next step into marriage faltered later when they realized perhaps an important part of their lives had passed them by, and they had missed the chance to "sow some wild oats."

The Stinnetts were different. Friends and family saw them celebrating fifty years of marriage, grandkids laughing and playing all around them. "They were perfect for each other," recalled one friend.

Part of the bond they shared was knowing each other so well.

"[Zeb] is focused [on] car stereos and cars," Bobbie Jo wrote on her Web site. "I am focused mostly on rat terriers."

It was a loving jab, typical of Bobbie Jo's gentle sense of humor, directed at a man who had been berated by Bobbie Jo's aunt once for pulling up to her house with his stereo blaring so loud the porch windows rattled.

Bobbie Jo and Zeb lived their romance—that is, true romance—during a time when it seemed to exist only in Hollywood movies. Their relationship, some friends and family insisted, had been built on respect, companionship, friendship, and a storybook nuance missing in society today. It was evident in the way Zeb looked at Bobbie Jo and she at him. They could speak through a glance, a smile, or maybe just a hug.

In recent years, Bobbie Jo had been telling friends and fellow rat-terrier breeders on the Internet message board she frequented that she was planning on becoming a "Rat Terrier Breed Inspector."

"I want to be a licensed judge for the NKC [National Kennel Club] and . . . press secretary for a UKC [United Kennel Club]," she said one day. Obviously, Bobbie Jo had dreams and goals. Working in a manufacturing plant was a stepping-stone toward something bigger, something better.

Breeders and owners register dogs with both the NKC and the UKC. Bobbie Jo wanted to know everything she could about the business end of breeding. She wanted to be involved on every level in order to benefit her customers and dogs.

Bobbie Jo was serious about breeding. She wanted her customers to get exactly what they were paying for and took pride in the way she ran her business.

"We follow the . . . Breeder Code of Ethics," she wrote on her Happy Haven Farms Web site. "We are not a puppy mill and do not support puppy mills."

The same couldn't be said for Lisa Montgomery, who herself had been breeding rat terriers. Some had questioned the pedigree of Lisa's dogs, saying she had misrepresented her bloodline. One woman had even written a letter to Lisa's ex-husband, demanding access to any records he might have regarding one of Lisa's dogs, Lucky. The AKC, the woman wrote, "require a three-generation pedigree." As far as the woman knew, the terrier she purchased, Lucky's grandson, was only a "two-generation" dog. She felt duped and was rather upset because she felt she didn't get what she had paid for.

No one ever questioned Bobbie Jo or the pedigree of her dogs. She did things the right way—always. For example, when she showed her dogs, like the time in Abilene, back in April 2004, when she met Lisa Montgomery and Kayla Boman in person for the first time, she registered with the UKC because it was a UKC show.

"It's just the way she was: Bobbie Jo lived by the book. She was glowing and seemed really happy."

Soon after Bobbie Jo turned twenty-two, she and Zeb married. It was April 26, 2003, a peaceful, gorgeous spring afternoon at the Skidmore Christian Church, located about one hundred yards north of where Bobbie Jo and Zeb lived on West Elm. The Reverend Harold Hamon presided over the service. Friends and family, along with a "full-house church," one attendee said, watched as Bobbie Jo walked down the aisle on her grandfather's arm while Zeb waited at the foot of the altar for his bride-to-be. As Reverend Hamon recalled later, "And I asked, 'Who gives this woman to be married to this man?' And the grandfather said, 'I do.' She was a beautiful bride."

"They were kids in the neighborhood," added the reverend, "nice young kids. She was just a real nice girl, real pretty, quiet and reserved."

The wedding was a simple ceremony for two people who really didn't need, or expect, much out of life—the love they had for each other was enough.

With his buzz-cut brown hair and quiet demeanor, the groom,

Zebulon James Stinnett, had grown into a pleasant young man with a broad smile and round, open face. Zeb, one friend said, was "quiet and private; doesn't say much of anything."

Maybe that was one of the reasons why Bobbie Jo felt so close to Zeb: they were alike in so many ways.

After a small ceremony, which, it seemed, everyone in Skidmore attended, Bobbie Jo and Zeb rented that little place on West Elm, where they lived on the day Darlene Fischer/Lisa Montgomery walked into their lives. The white paint on the wood siding was flaking off; the roof, along with a few of the windows and doors, needed maintenance, but it was home. Zeb and Bobbie Jo were grateful for what God had given them. They had plans to buy their own place one day. They were young. Time was on their side.

"That was Bobbie's Jo's dream," a family member later told reporters, "to own her own home."

8

Through the bumpy backcountry roads of Skidmore, the Kawasaki Motors plant in Maryville, where Zeb and Bobbie Jo worked, was a good twenty-minute drive from their home on West Elm Street. On the morning of December 16, Zeb grabbed his lunch bucket, kissed Bobbie Jo good-bye on the way out the door, and headed off to work. Bobbie Jo was going to be home, as she had been the past few weeks, on maternity leave from Kawasaki. She had a lot to do. In a matter of weeks, she and Zeb would welcome a new addition to their family and begin making plans to purchase a home of their own and maybe even have another child.

Life was sweet.

A strong guy, physically and mentally, Zeb was a few inches taller than Bobbie Jo, who stood five feet six inches. Zeb had broad shoulders and radiated a country toughness that spoke of his roots in town. There was one photograph of Zeb standing next to Bobbie Jo at a dog show. Lisa Montgomery and her daughter Kayla were in the same photograph, standing to Zeb and Bobbie Jo's right side. Bobbie Jo was smiling, while Zeb held the ribbon she had won earlier with one of her prized rat terriers. With one arm around Bobbie and the other proudly displaying the purple ribbon, Zeb beamed with happiness.

Near the end of 2003, Bobbie Jo and Zeb's Happy Haven Farms breeding business took flight. Their main business was breeding rat terriers. "Our dogs are all Type A's . . . ," Bobbie Jo pointed out on her Web site. "We offer our puppies to GREAT homes only, as we'd rather keep 'em here, but realize we have to share."

By most standards, the business was small, which was what

Bobbie Jo liked. She and Zeb bred, on average, about one to two litters per year, but they had three litters between the summer of 2003 and late fall 2004. Bobbie Jo adored the small canines, especially her own terriers, Belle, Tipsy, and Fonzi; along with her Dalmatian, Maddy. Several photographs of her at various dog shows depict a young woman glowing with joy, showing her prized dogs, and just loving the life she and Zeb had built.

Near the end of March, beginning of April, Bobbie Jo officially announced she was pregnant with her first child. Within a few months, she and Zeb found out it was going to be a girl.

So Bobbie Jo picked a name.

Victoria Jo.

"Tori Jo," she told Zeb one day, "will be the child's nickname."

Zeb didn't like it all that much, but he wasn't about to argue with his wife, who could be, some said, rather strong-willed and stubborn, but only when it pertained to good things.

Thus, Tori Jo she would be.

Soon after Bobbie Jo found out she was pregnant, she registered at the local Maryville Wal-Mart for things any first-time mother might desire: "newborn onesies, pink and yellow blankets, pink burp clothes, and a diaper bag." She wanted common baby essentials that would help raise her daughter. What she could give the child more than any amount of money could buy was love—and she and Zeb, along with the Stinnett family and Bobbie Jo's mother, Becky Harper, were fully prepared to shower little Victoria Jo with all the love she could handle.

With a due date of January 19, 2005, Bobbie Jo was resigned to quit her job at Kawasaki near the end of her pregnancy and concentrate on readying the house for the baby and breeding rat terriers. Like millions of proud expecting parents, Zeb and Bobbie Jo were enjoying life's bliss in a trouble-free, uncomplicated way, just counting the days until their baby was born.

Life, indeed, should have gone on without a hitch.

9

By approximately 3:18 P.M., Becky Harper was getting worried about her daughter. She hadn't heard back from Bobbie Jo after their last conversation, which Harper believed was interrupted by a customer who wanted to purchase one of Bobbie Jo's rat terriers. A law enforcement official later said Bobbie Jo had even told Harper the person's name.

"Darlene Fischer."

Harper needed a ride to the garage to pick up her truck. But where was Bobbie Jo? What was taking her so long? Why wasn't she answering her phone?

Something was wrong.

According to law enforcement, at around the same time, Lisa Montgomery, posing as Darlene Fischer, was inside the house with Bobbie Jo. They were in the den, a room off to the left after you walked in, talking about several rat terriers Bobbie Jo had for sale. What wasn't clear later would be how Bobbie Jo reacted to meeting up with Lisa on that day, rather than with a woman named Darlene Fischer, whom she thought she had never met.

"It seems clear to me, but we don't know for certain," that same law enforcement official said, "that Lisa Montgomery likely knocked on the door and just introduced herself as herself, maybe playing like she was 'in the neighborhood.'"

If that were the case, Bobbie Jo would not have felt threatened in any way. She and Lisa had met and talked fairly regularly online. Bobbie Jo was under the impression Lisa was pregnant, too; and Lisa knew, of course, Bobbie Jo was expecting in a matter of weeks. Perhaps Lisa told Bobbie Jo she was just stopping by to say hello and wanted to swap stories as expectant mothers often do.

* * *

She was born Bobbie Jo Potter on December 4, 1981. That same year, Skidmore was on the verge of moral collapse. Not because the town's soybean or corn crop had dried up from the little bit of rain the region somehow endured, or the pig farmers had lost herds to disease. No. If that were the case, those problems could be dealt with agriculturally, or even governmentally, with funding and grants.

Instead, Skidmore's biggest problem was an event that would set an eerie precedent for some twenty years to come.

In 1981, a man had been running through Skidmore causing chaos and havoc. Ken Rex McElroy, a bull of a man with a beefy chest, tough jawline, and "I-don't-care-about-anybody-but-myself" attitude, had bullied his way through life in the same fashion an obnoxious senior in high school might torment a few chosen freshmen. The only difference was, McElroy beleaguered an entire town.

In fact, McElroy had terrorized not only Skidmore, but much of western Missouri for years. Locals had complained about his taking what he wanted, abusing the women in his life, drinking, fighting, shooting people, burning down houses, intimidating witnesses called to testify against him, and seemingly always finding a way to escape the mighty sword of the law, simply because people—judges and prosecutors included—feared his fury.

No one, it seemed, could catch McElroy committing a crime; thus he continually found a way to evade prosecution, having been arrested seventeen times without spending a night in jail.

On July 10, 1981, McElroy's violent run finally ended. Several townspeople, in an act of congregated and choreographed vigilantism, unloaded round after round of ammunition into his head and chest, killing him almost instantly, as he sat in his pickup truck alongside his wife, Trena, in downtown.

The brutal crime, immortalized in the bestselling book and movie *In Broad Daylight*, gave Skidmore a bit of unfortunate, violent notoriety that contradicted the true soul of the town.

McElroy pushed his luck. The breaking point for townsfolk came after he beat a reported twenty-two criminal counts in court, but was convicted of an assault for shooting a helpless, seventy-one-year-old town grocer whom he had intimidated and threatened for months.

Law enforcement had seen enough; the judge ultimately sentenced McElroy to two years in prison.

Shortly before he was murdered, Skidmore residents were astonished to learn that instead of going directly to prison, McElroy showed up in town hours after he was convicted. Apparently, he had been "freed on bail during a twenty-one-day appeal" process.

People were dazed. They couldn't believe it. After all he had done, everyone he had hurt, here was Ken McElroy, at last being sentenced, yet escaping justice *one more time*.

On the afternoon he was murdered, McElroy walked into the D&G Tavern downtown, as he had many times before, proudly displaying what was said to be "an assault weapon." After purchasing "a six-pack of beer, cigarettes" and a package of acid relievers, McElroy and his wife walked out the door and sat in his Silverado truck.

McElroy seemed to be patronizing an entire town by showing up after being sentenced. He was gloating, once again intimidating the people who had wanted him to pay for his crimes.

Locals who had heard McElroy was back in town gathered at the local Legion Hall a few blocks from the D&G.

Dan Estes, the local Nodaway County sheriff, was at the meeting, too, he later said on a radio program, trying to get a handle on what had become a mob mentality. But when he left, reports claimed, thirty or more angry residents, all armed, walked down to the D&G.

As the mob came around the back of the storefront, McElroy's wife, just getting into his truck, asked, "What are *they* doing?"

McElroy was at a loss for words.

"They got some guns," Trena screamed, looking around.

"Get in the truck," McElroy said, starting the vehicle and lighting a cigarette.

One shot rang out, hitting McElroy in the head. After that, another . . . this time hitting him in the chest . . . then another . . . and another.

As McElroy bled to death, his foot hit the accelerator of his truck and raced the engine.

Thirty-five to forty-five townspeople reportedly watched the murder take place and later refused to talk about it to anyone, including law enforcement. McElroy's wife, who was sitting next to him in the truck as he was shot to death, came out of it untouched.

One resident later called McElroy's killers heroes, comparing them to the inventors of penicillin.

The McElroy slaying was the first of a set of bizarre and unusually rare murders in Skidmore. In 2000, a local woman, Mary Gillenwater, was reportedly stomped to death by her boyfriend. Months later, a twenty-year-old, Branson Perry, vanished after leaving his house one afternoon. Law enforcement speculated Perry had been abducted by a local convicted child pornographer, but to date, the case remains unsolved.

Sixty-four-year-old Jo Ann Stinnett, Zeb and Bobbie Jo Stinnett's aunt, was Mary Gillenwater's grandmother. Branson Perry was her grandson. Such is life in small-town Skidmore.

"People will ask," Jo Ann told a reporter later, "'What's wrong with Skidmore?' But it's not Skidmore's fault. I love Skidmore."

10

Two key factors would emerge later regarding Lisa Montgomery's visit to Bobbie Jo's home under the subterfuge of buying one of her rat terrier puppies: one, Lisa had made a promise to herself she wasn't leaving Bobbie Jo's house without her baby; two, that Bobbie Jo wasn't going to stop her.

The blood–soaked wood-grain floors left behind in the den of Bobbie Jo and Zeb's house were an indication of the horror that took place in Skidmore that afternoon. The house Bobbie Jo and Zeb rented had a tiny living room off to the right side as soon as you walked in, which was directly across from their bedroom. If you walked toward the back of the house, there was a kitchen with a small dining room attached to it, which led into the den on the left. Bobbie Jo had fixed up this room—where, law enforcement later said, she and Lisa ended up—for her dogs. It had two black metal dog cages on the floor and an old dresser in the corner, where Bobbie groomed the dogs.

Bobbie Jo and Lisa must have talked for a time about rat terriers. They'd had several discussions online about the canines and here they were now face-to-face, brought together—albeit by a lie—because of the dogs.

Being eight months pregnant, Bobbie Jo was, of course, clearly showing. Photographs from the time prove she wore her extra weight well and had a lovely expectant-mother glow.

Bobbie Jo was under the impression that Lisa, too, was in the final stages of pregnancy. Lisa had told Bobbie Jo via e-mail and instant messages that she was carrying twins. Still, why wasn't Lisa showing? She wasn't overweight, nor was she trying to hide the fact that she wasn't pregnant. Wasn't she worried about what Bobbie Jo might say when they met in person?

Crime-scene photographs give clues as to what happened. In those photographs, blood is spread from one end of the room to the other; heel marks and palm prints were fused with several units of blood and smudged all over, as if a child had gone wild on the floor with red finger-paint, proving there was movement in the room *after* Bobbie Jo had been cut open. Moreover, authorities would later discover evidence on Lisa Montgomery's personal computer proving she had downloaded an Internet video of how to perform a Caesarean section.

"They struggled," said one official. "You can see, from the photographs, that Bobbie Jo didn't die immediately. Or you wouldn't have blood or blood clots spread all over the room like it was."

Because of the blood spread all over the floor, law enforcement believed there had been a violent struggle for life *and* death. Bobbie Jo fought for her child. That much was clear.

"What [happened] was that she [Lisa] took a quarter-inch rope and choked Bobbie Jo out with it."

The theory was that Lisa talked Bobbie Jo into bending down to open one of the dog cages on the floor, so she could pick up a terrier to show it to Lisa. The position made her vulnerable because she had to turn her back to Lisa while she was doing it.

"When Bobbie Jo bent over, Lisa came up from behind and choked her out. So she [Bobbie Jo] passes out, and Lisa starts cutting her open with a four-inch serrated paring knife she brought from her home."

Unlike the way it plays out in movies, choking a human being to death is not easy. It takes several minutes to cut off someone's oxygen enough to cause death. Yet, within a matter of seconds, the person being choked loses consciousness—as Bobbie Jo did. If the person doing the choking doesn't continue, the victim will regain consciousness at some point.

"After Bobbie Jo passed out, Lisa started cutting her open and . . . that's when Bobbie Jo came back to life."

Blood clots scattered around the floor in different areas of the room provide clues to a struggle that resulted *after* Bobbie Jo regained consciousness. While bleeding profusely from her abdomen, she fought for her and her child's lives.

"Well, the struggle was then back on. . . . Then Lisa managed to get Bobbie Jo choked out for a second time. By then, she had lost enough blood and was being choked to where she . . . well . . . she died."

During the fight for life and death, Bobbie Jo grabbed her assailant's hair and ended up with strands of it in both her hands. DNA testing later proved the hair to be Lisa Montgomery's.

Graphic doesn't even begin to describe the scene in Bobbie Jo's den when Becky Harper decided to walk over to the house and find out why Bobbie Jo wasn't answering her telephone.

11

Twenty-three-year-old Chris Law had lived a few houses away from the Stinnetts ever since they moved into the neighborhood. Law, though, had known Zeb, he told reporters later, "since we were in Head Start together."

On occasion, Zeb would pop over to the Laws', and the two men would work on cars together. Bobbie Jo would wander over sometimes, most likely just to be near Zeb, but Law said she rarely spoke and, at times, "hardly said a word at all."

On December 16, Law planned on visiting Bobbie Jo. Not to have coffee or chat about the latest gossip in town, but mainly to be a "good neighbor" and check up on his friend's pregnant wife.

"They were good-natured people," said Chris Law.

So, Chris Law was going to do what anybody else in town might have done under the same circumstances. Bobbie Jo had been to the hospital recently for several prenatal tests. As far as Law knew, she faced no major complications, but it wouldn't hurt to stop in and say hello on his way into Maryville to run a few errands.

"I observed a pinkish red two-door vehicle," Law told the FBI later, "in front of the Stinnett residence . . . possibly a Mazda, a Toyota, or a Hyundai."

Law was referring to Lisa Montgomery's car; she had been inside the house with Bobbie Jo at the time Law was considering stopping by.

When Law turned onto the corner of West Elm from North Orchard, he spied a "dirty" vehicle sitting in the Stinnett driveway and drove around the block in his truck, he said, "rethinking his decision" to pop in.

Well, she's got company, Law told himself, *and I won't bother her.*

"I never considered the idea that [Bobbie Jo] was in danger," Law said later on television. "Stuff like that just doesn't happen 'round here."

Moreover, the front door to the Stinnett house was wide open the entire time Law observed the red car in the driveway. It was winter. Although it was an unseasonably warm day, leaving the door open wasn't something Bobbie Jo likely would have done.

Then again, as Law explained it later, "If it had been a stranger, [Bobbie Jo] never would have let them in the house."

To some, Law appeared rough around the edges, with his gold earring, five o'clock shadow, grease under his fingernails, and mechanic hands as rough as sandpaper. He spoke with a Western drawl, like most in the neighborhood.

"[Lisa] was pretty much a part of Bobbie Jo's life, anyway," Law told a British television producer. "They went to dog shows together, swapped dog secrets, you know. I thought she was a friend."

Indeed, the visitor had to be someone Bobbie Jo knew and, perhaps, trusted. This led some to later speculate when Lisa showed up at the door, Bobbie Jo must have recognized her as Lisa Montgomery. The question became then: with her cover blown, did Lisa charge at Bobbie Jo and push the door open, forcing her way into the house? (Law reported the door being wide open when he drove by.)

Or did Bobbie Jo, recognizing her, invite her in?

12

Becky Harper started walking to her daughter's house some-time around 3:18 P.M., after she tried calling Bobbie Jo a few more times, but got no answer. Since Bobbie Jo had not shown up at Harper's place of work to pick her up, she decided to walk to West Elm Street and see what was going on.

A mother's instinct.

"I keep thinking," Harper later told a reporter, "I wish I had gone over there earlier."

When Harper arrived, Bobbie Jo's door was wide open. That was strange, since those unseasonably warm temperatures that had moved in during the early-afternoon hours had given way to the low thirties by late afternoon. There was also a slight southerly wind curling up around the fields south of town, kicking the mercury down a notch further.

Why was the door open?

"Bobbie?"

No answer.

"Bobbie," Harper said, walking in. "Honey, you here?"

The porch swing Bobbie Jo and Zeb had hanging from the ceiling of the overhead porch was rattling a bit in the wind. It was spooky. Bad karma was in the air. Something was obviously wrong.

At 3:26 P.M., Becky Harper entered the room in which the horri-bly bloodied body of her daughter lay. Bobbie Jo's arms were folded up over her chest; her face was covered with blood.

Although quite unnerved by what she was looking at, Harper

reacted immediately, reaching for her cell phone to call the Nodaway County Sheriff's Department in Maryville.

Speaking to the 911 dispatcher, Harper was frantic and struggled to find the right words. It couldn't be real. It had to be some sort prank, some inconsiderate joke that didn't make any sense.

"My baby is dead!" Harper screamed into the phone at 3:28 P.M., her voice raw with agony. "My baby . . . she's lying in a pool of blood."

"Ma'am, please tell us what happened," said dispatcher Lindsey Steins with as much composure as she could manage. "Please try to remain calm and give me an address."

Ben Espey, the county sheriff, was sitting in his office ten feet away when he heard the call come in. He walked toward Steins's desk, which was flanked by three computer screens, a switchboard, and several two-way radios. It was located in a dark area of the sheriff's department, in front of a line of jail cells. As Steins and dispatcher Melissa Wallace sat wearing headsets and typed on a keyboard, their work area resembled some sort of Bat Cave setting.

"It's my . . . my daughter . . . It appears as though her stomach is exposed."

Stomach exposed? thought Espey, looking at Steins.

As Steins and Wallace, who was now listening in, typed, Espey stood over their shoulders and read the computer screen, realizing there was a "major problem" in Skidmore.

"Hey," yelled Espey to one of his deputies.

"Yes, sir?"

"Radio my lieutenant investigator now and tell him to meet me in Skidmore ASAP. Give him the address."

Harper was delirious by this time. Bobbie Jo was sprawled on the floor, blood all over the room, a large pool of it underneath her lifeless body.

What is going on?

Even more disturbing to Harper was that Bobbie Jo's midsection was flat.

"It looks like her stomach exploded!" screamed Harper, in tears.

13

Within eleven minutes of the 911 call, Nodaway County sheriff Ben Espey arrived in Skidmore, one of his chief investigators not far behind. Espey was contemplating several different scenarios. "It looks like her stomach exploded" kept playing back in his mind. *What went on inside that house?*

"Nobody here could ever conceive of this taking place," said Espey. "It's inconceivable."

With sixteen towns in Nodaway County, housing some twenty-three thousand people in about five thousand households, the county seat is located in Maryville, a family-oriented town held together by strong bonds of community. Petit larcenies and drug-related felonies largely account for the majority of Nodaway County's criminal activities. In the twelve years Ben Espey had been sheriff, he responded to six murders, all of which he and his deputies, with help from other agencies, solved within a twenty-four-hour period.

Maryville and its surrounding counties are farming country, semiflat land amid rolling short hills spread out far and wide. People watch one another's backs and try to keep their communities as safe as they can. A crime such as the one just called into the Nodaway County Sheriff's Department on the afternoon of December 16 was beyond comprehension. As Sheriff Espey drove to Skidmore, he could see Christmas ornaments up all over the county. Inflatable Santa Clauses perched in front yards along the roadside, with plastic reindeer and tinsel dressed on pine trees throughout town greens. Churches were planning food drives and Secret Santa programs, midnight services and holiday celebrations. Houses were decked with colored lights and fake snow.

When Espey arrived at Bobbie Jo and Zeb's house, he ran into the den, where Becky Harper, crying desperately while pleading for help, was trying, she believed, to keep Bobbie Jo alive by administering CPR. One of Espey's 911 dispatchers, Melissa Wallace, had instructed Harper over the phone on how to do CPR properly.

"Does she have a pulse?" Melissa asked.

"I don't know."

"Is she breathing?"

"I don't know. I don't know."

"Well, I'm going to tell you how to do CPR. Have you ever done CPR?"

When Espey first looked at Bobbie Jo, he could tell "immediately," he said, it was too late. "I took a pulse and there was no life."

"Give me your cell phone," Espey told Harper. It was covered with Bobbie Jo's blood, dripping as Espey told his dispatcher, "I'm here. . . . I'll continue the CPR."

Despite the horror of the scene, Harper kept her composure and focused, she thought, on trying to keep Bobbie Jo alive.

"It was a pretty gruesome sight," Espey commented. One of the worst he had seen in his two decades of law enforcement experience.

Since Harper had started CPR, by law Espey had to continue.

"Step aside, ma'am," he said as calmly as he could after folding Harper's cell phone and throwing it out of the room. "Go get me a wet washcloth and bring it back."

Bobbie Jo's face was covered with blood, her mouth full of it. "I needed the cloth to wipe off all the blood."

"My daughter's eight months pregnant," Harper cried at one point.

Espey looked down. *Her stomach's flat. Pregnant?* Her words made no sense to him.

Within five minutes, medics came into the room and took over. As the medics responded, Espey began to think about what could have happened.

"She's eight months pregnant," Harper said again. "She's pregnant!"

For Espey, a seasoned cop who had thought he'd seen everything, what Harper was telling him sounded implausible. *Pregnant? What? Where is the child? There's no bulge in her stomach.*

As Espey began to assess the situation, a paramedic pulled him aside so Harper couldn't hear the exchange.

"The baby was cut out," the paramedic said softly. "The umbilical cord," he noted, "has been cut. Look," he added, pointing to Bobbie Jo, "there it is." He paused to allow the implications to sink in. Then he spelled them out. "The baby's gone, Sheriff."

Later, Espey said, "I would have never thought it possible."

Espey told two of his deputies, who had since arrived, to "seal off the house. Do *not* let anybody in." After photographs were taken, Bobbie Jo was placed on a body board and taken outside.

What happened here?

With his mind racing, neighbors and townsfolk congregating around the scene, Espey ran out of the house searching for one of his deputies.

"We gotta baby missing. We gotta try and find us a baby," he said.

14

Sheriff Ben Espey's reputation had come under fire recently, during what had turned into a heated reelection campaign for a chance at serving as Nodaway County's sheriff. During a debate in late September 2004, Espey, a proud Republican, spoke openly about his experience running the department. He had been in office almost twelve years, and during one election earlier in his career, he had run an unopposed campaign for the first time in sixty years of elections in the county.

The voters of Nodaway County adored Ben Espey. This last election, however, had turned into an old-fashioned Red-and-Blue fight for office with nastiness emerging from both sides. Still, with the race for office the closest in which he'd ever been involved, Espey didn't jump in and start playing politics. He hit the streets and lobbied for votes the same way he had every other election: "The community," he told voters, "should always come first.

"When you arrest somebody's spouse or kid," Espey said along the campaign trail, "some of the people aren't going to be happy with what you do."

Espey worried about the close contact between community members and deputies. One of the rules in his office had always been that his deputies were not allowed to drink in the local bars. "If you want to drink," Espey told them, "drink at home."

The grapevine was always a setback to living in a small town. Arresting someone you went to school with, or bowled with, or ran into every day at the general store or service station, didn't always sit well down at the Legion Hall, PTA, or neighborhood gin mill. But Espey was strict. It didn't matter who you were; if you broke the law, you were going to face the consequences. If his deputies were sitting there having drinks with people they might have to arrest at some point, it could lead to problems.

The sheriff's department needed to, Espey said, "do what was right" and "do it in a professional manner." He didn't think his opponent could achieve those tasks the way he could. It wasn't that his opponent was a bad person; Espey was just confident he could do a better job for the community because he had been in office so long and knew the people he served.

Throughout the campaign, "community first" became Espey's mantra. He had little patience for slackers and bureaucrats who wanted to milk the system. He was committed to giving the community the best law enforcement he could offer.

His opponent saw Espey's last few terms in office differently, and called for "new blood" in the position. During a debate, Rick Smail, who had made a few critical comments regarding Espey's ability to keep a tight grip on the department, claimed that Espey and his office did not respond to what Smail saw as "less serious calls" in a timely fashion, or sometimes not at all.

Standing at the podium, Espey hammered back by saying how hard it was to respond to *every* single call with only one full-time deputy on staff. Drastic measures called for drastic means, and Espey emphasized that he was fully prepared to lead the charge and meet the demands and needs of the community, regardless of what his opponent had to say about the way he commanded the ship—or, more to the point, how he handled 911 calls.

"Important calls must take precedence," Espey said.

After the debate, feeling he had fully defended himself and his position as sheriff, Espey said, "Rick's a good guy, but he doesn't really work the road and doesn't necessarily know how to control a budget. He's out of touch with making arrests, the booking process, and court work. I do these things all the time."

Rick Smail responded that it was time for a change in Nodaway County, and he was the man who could lead a much-needed revolution.

In the end, Espey won reelection. It was a long night and a close call (Espey won by fewer than twenty votes), but he was back in the department as sheriff, which was all that really mattered to him.

Now, a mere six weeks after the election, he was standing in Bobbie Jo Stinnett's den, staring at the remnants of her butchered body.

Who could do such a thing? Espey thought. Had it been a ritualistic murder? A Charles Manson–type slaying? Maybe a serial killer had passed through town and randomly chosen Bobbie Jo?

But the thought prompted by his investigative instinct was: *Could her husband have done it?*

The number one cause of death among pregnant women, most experts claim, is homicide. The most common perpetrator? Spouse or boyfriend. The recent deaths of Laci and Conner Peterson and Lori Hacking have helped put maternal homicide at the forefront of American crime news. But the truth is, for centuries, pregnant women have been targeted by their husbands.

"Send someone out to Kawasaki," Espey said to one of his deputies. "Check out the husband. See what he knows."

Could Zeb have committed such an unbearable horror? Would a man murder his wife and cut their child from her womb?

The idea seemed too horrible to consider. But regardless how surreal it seemed, while neighbors and townspeople gathered around the house, wondering why all the emergency vehicles and cruisers were lined up and down the street, it was Ben Espey's job to weigh all possibilities.

An even more awful thought crept into Espey's mind: *Could Bobbie Jo have done it to herself?* Was it possible Bobbie Jo had delivered the child herself in order to get rid of it? Good cops had to put themselves into every possible situation—getting to know both victim and perpetrator—to turn up leads when there were none to follow. It was a fact that sometimes young women delivered babies at home and disposed of the infants' bodies to cover up an unwanted pregnancy. Espey didn't know this family personally; he only knew what his twenty years of law enforcement experience had taught him: never assume anything.

As Bobbie Jo's body was being whisked away to the hospital, Espey and his deputies checked the entire house for bloodstains, trying to understand what had happened at the Stinnett home. "Go out and check all the garbage cans," said Espey.

In the end, they found nothing. But then, as it appeared they would have little to go on, a name that would later become synonymous with the murder of Bobbie Jo Stinnett surfaced. *Darlene Fischer*.

Before Becky Harper was taken away from the scene, Espey said later, she told him Bobbie Jo had "talked to someone named Darlene Fischer about coming over to the house to look at one of the dogs."

With that, Espey started calling teams of investigators in to help. His first objective was to find the baby, he said. Now at least they had a name to check out.

The Buchanan County (Missouri) Crime Scene Investigation (CSI) Unit was called in to go through the house and see what it could find. Part of its job would include logging on to Bobbie's computer and seeing what the machine yielded in the form of leads.

"You got to think of everything," said Espey, "because you don't know *anything*."

With the crime scene filling up with law enforcement, Espey did his best to lead the investigation. While cops did their jobs working in and around the house, Espey walked next door, to "the neighbor to the west," and started asking questions.

"A red car," the neighbor said. "There was a red car there. . . . It had a big H on the hood."

When they met up with Zeb and Bobbie Jo's neighbor Chris Law some time later, "he confirmed there was a red car there in Bobbie Jo's driveway," Espey said. But it was the neighbor next door who broke the "red car" lead, not Law.

Espey and his team had the following tips: a "red car" with an *H* on the hood, a "Darlene Fischer" name of unknown origin, and a premature newborn "hopefully still alive." Considering it was so early in the investigation—an hour hadn't even passed yet— Espey had quite a few leads.

Espey realized the first thing he had to do was find Bobbie Jo's missing child. No one knew what the child's kidnapper had in mind after cutting the baby from the mother's womb. For Espey, it felt personal. His daughter had just given birth to his second grandchild the week before. He knew what it was like to hold a

---

*Italics on first use of proper names and locations represents pseudonym or author's replacement.

newborn in his hands. He knew how special a time it should be for Becky Harper and Zeb Stinnett. With Bobbie Jo gone, finding the baby would be the only real victory he could give back to the family.

"I needed to find that baby," he said. "It was *very* personal to me—and, no matter who got in my way, I wasn't going to stop until I did."

15

Prosecutors believe that Lisa Montgomery left Skidmore with the child and traveled west out of town on Highway "DD," toward Hickory Creek and the Nodaway River. "The blacktop road," Ben Espey called it.

"She was heading out of town, going west," said Espey, "while we were heading into town, from the east."

They missed each other by fewer than thirty minutes.

Lisa probably chose Highway "DD" because it byspassed the more direct route of Highway 113 to Highway 71 toward St. Joseph and Kansas City. She must have realized urban authorities, outnumbering those in the outlying towns almost ten to one, would be looking for anyone—male or female—traveling with a newborn baby.

When Espey found out that the last vehicle to be seen at Bobbie Jo's was a red car, he radioed the lead out to every law enforcement agency, while his office in Maryville sent out a teletype. Shortly after the call went out, a Missouri State Highway Patrol (MSHP) cruiser engaged a red car in a high-speed pursuit on Highway 71 near Maryville.

"That pursuit," said Espey, "ended up back in toward us in Skidmore, so we joined the chase."

Espey wouldn't normally have left his post at a crime scene, but someone over the radio said, "Red car in pursuit on seventy-one, possibly connected to the death in Skidmore."

When Espey heard that, he took right off.

Fifteen to twenty minutes later, law enforcement ended up cornering a man in a red car on Route 29. He had nothing whatsoever to do with the crime. He was running from police because he had some overdue tickets and thought they were going to put him in jail.

Learning this, Espey headed back to the Stinnett home.

By now, the Buchanan County CSI team had logged on to Bobbie Jo's computer and figured out Darlene Fischer was, indeed, the last person to meet with Bobbie Jo, according to the e-mails they were able to retrieve. Based on one specific e-mail Darlene had sent to Bobbie Jo, authorities thought they knew where she lived: Fairfax, Missouri, one county over.

Espey and one of his deputies took off, lights flashing, sirens blaring, for Fairfax, to see if they could locate Darlene Fischer.

16

Heading south on Route 59 after leaving the blacktop road, Lisa Montgomery is believed to have hit Highway 29 and set a beeline for Topeka, Kansas. She had to be careful. It wouldn't take much to get pulled over: running a red light, speeding, weaving, maybe a broken turn signal on her vehicle she didn't even know of.

At some point during her trip, she pulled over on the side of the road, washed the baby, sealed her belly button with a pair of "clips" a hospital might use for the same purpose, and threw the bloodied towels and blankets into the trunk, where they sat next to the rope she allegedly used to strangle Bobbie Jo and the serrated paring knife she used to cut her open, law enforcement said.

Lisa admitted later that here, along the side of the road, she started to put her elaborate story of giving birth to the child into effect.

After cleaning up the child, she called Mike Wheatley, pastor of the First Church of God in downtown Melvern, Kansas, where Lisa's children had been going to church for the past four years.

"I just gave birth," she told Pastor Wheatley. She seemed excited.

"Congratulations, Lisa," answered Wheatley.

Lisa pulled out from the side of the road, Bobbie Jo's baby next to her in a carry-on car seat, and headed for Kansas.

17

While family members of Bobbie Jo Stinnett were contacted on the evening of December 16, doctors at St. Francis Hospital in Maryville pronounced the twenty-three-year-old wife and mother dead. The trauma had been too much. Her petite body couldn't take the punishment authorities claim Lisa Montgomery had unleashed in the act of violent fury that was, by now, being reported around the world.

Satellite trucks were pulling into Skidmore as Bobbie Jo lay on a gurney somewhere in St. Francis Hospital. All the major networks were sending reporters to the region: MSNBC, CNN, Fox News, even the British Broadcasting Company (BBC). Every major metropolitan newspaper across the country posted the story on their Web sites. The Christmas season was generally a slow news period. The murder of Bobbie Jo Stinnett was going to be a huge story. By nightfall, the world would hear of the horror in Skidmore. By the following morning, reporters would be swarming the area, looking to uncover anything they could about what had happened inside the small house at West Elm Street.

As word spread throughout town, Skidmore residents locked their doors and watched their backs, noting that until Bobbie Jo's killer was caught, things would never be the same. Most were obviously appalled such a crime could take place in their tight-knit, close community. And to think it happened right in the middle of the day.

"Things like that just don't happen 'roun he'a," said one local.

Reverend Harold Hamon, who had married Zeb and Bobbie Jo

about twenty months earlier, said he was likely "addressing Christmas cards" when the murder occurred. He remembered the time of day because a member of his congregation had called about the commotion going on up the road from his parish.

"Reverend," asked the worried neighbor, "I heard an ambulance down by the church. Was anyone near the church hurt?"

Hamon could see Bobbie Jo's house from the church rectory as he looked out the window. "Hold on," he said, staring down the street. "There's police cars down there. Don't know what's going on, though."

"It's almost unbelievable," Hamon recalled, "that right under your nose something terrible can be happening."

After talking it over with doctors, Sheriff Ben Espey was convinced there was a strong possibility Bobbie Jo's child was still alive. He had no doubt in his mind what he had to do next.

"That's the minute," Espey said, "I started pushing to get the Amber Alert issued." And that was where the problems and infighting among different law enforcement agencies began.

The base of the investigation had been moved from Skidmore to downtown Maryville. The Nodaway County Sheriff's Department on North Vine Street, just below the center of town, was a small station compared to bigger-city police departments. But Espey felt comfortable in the building. It was a second home to him. On the wall of its large basement was a long blackboard he could fill up with leads and ideas. By this means, he could sketch out the entire case and keep track of it, step by step.

Espey returned to the department and began a push to get the Amber Alert issued. *Find the baby, find the killer.* It seemed that simple. His emphasis was on finding the child first. After clearing Zeb Stinnett and informing him that his wife had been killed and his child kidnapped, Espey promised Zeb he would get his child back.

Getting an Amber Alert issued for an unborn child would be an unprecedented move, and Espey would run into harsh opposition in the coming hours regarding his desire to get it done, because an Amber Alert had never been issued for, as some were calling Bobbie Jo's child, "a fetus."

A major factor that made Ben Espey an asset to his community was his determination to get a job done when the powers to be, bound by bureaucracy, stood in his way. If Espey believed an Amber Alert was warranted, he was going get it—and no one was going to tell him he couldn't.

18

In the state of Missouri, Amber Alerts are issued by the Missouri State Highway Patrol when a child is said to be in danger. The MSHP relies on "detailed physical descriptions . . . such as the color, license plate, and type of vehicle to watch for," MSHP patrol spokesman Captain Chris Ricks told reporters. The reason the detail has to be as exact as possible is, Ricks added, "you're flooding your system with calls that don't mean anything."

If any vehicle even remotely matching the description became suspect, law enforcement had to chase down hundreds of leads that might never amount to anything. As of September 25, 2005, 377 children had been involved in 316 published Amber Alerts, issued in forty-two different states. It is a system that produces results when put into effect immediately.

How was the program initiated? In January 1996, nine-year old Amber Hagerman was riding her bicycle in a remote Arlington, Texas, neighborhood when a neighbor heard her scream. It was a terrifying cry for help, not as if Amber had fallen off her bicycle or was being chased by the neighborhood bully. There was no doubt she was scared and yelling for help.

When the neighbor ran toward Amber's voice, she saw a man pull the helpless child off her bike and toss her into his pickup truck.

Within seconds, the child was gone.

The neighbor ran back to her house and called 911 immediately. She provided a detailed description of the man who had abducted Amber, along with the vehicle he was driving.

It was enough to get law enforcement started, especially since the call had come in promptly after the abduction.

Police in Arlington, working with the FBI, canvassed the neighborhood and interviewed several other neighbors while a massive search got under way for the vehicle Amber had been abducted in and for the suspect, who had supposedly grabbed her.

Sadly, though, four days later, Amber's body was located in a ditch about five miles from her home. Her throat had been slashed.

Several concerned citizens, feeling angry and sick over Amber's death, thinking more could have been done to save her life, contacted a Dallas, Texas, radio station and changed the way law enforcement officials deal with child abductions today. One of the callers suggested local radio stations "repeat news bulletins about abducted children just like they do for severe weather warnings."

An early warning system was subsequently initiated by the Dallas-Fort Worth Association of Radio Managers, who teamed with local law enforcement agencies in northern Texas, developing an innovative system to help locate abducted children, or at least get word out of the abduction as fast as possible.

It was a brilliant idea, and general managers from several radio stations throughout the Dallas area signed up. Everyone agreed it was a public service that could save lives potentially, simply because time is an abducted child's worst enemy after being kidnapped.

Thus, by July 1997, about eighteen months after Amber's death, the Texas Amber Plan went into operation. Other states adopted the program in short order.

19

According to the Amber Alert Portal, a Web site dedicated to providing information about the Amber Alert plan, "once law enforcement has been notified about an abducted child, they must first determine if the case meets the Amber Alert Plan's criteria for activating an Amber Alert." Each law enforcement agency, "whether local, state, or regional, establishes its own Amber Alert Plan criteria."

Espey didn't have time for bureaucracy. He needed the alert issued right now, no questions asked.

"Let's find this child and fight about it later."

The first problem Espey faced came in the form of the National Center for Missing and Exploited Children, which suggests three criteria be met before an Amber Alert is activated: "Law enforcement confirms a child has been abducted; law enforcement believes the circumstances surrounding the abduction indicate that the child is in danger of serious bodily harm or death"; and, most important to the dilemma facing Ben Espey, "there is enough descriptive information about the child, abductor, and/or suspect's vehicle to believe an immediate broadcast alert will help."

In the Stinnett case, not much was known about Bobbie Jo's assailant. Espey was told no right away. An Amber Alert wouldn't work in this situation. Sorry. But it's not going to happen.

Espey didn't have time to deal with red tape. The sun had gone down. The child could be anywhere and Bobbie Jo's murderer was long gone. All he wanted was a chance.

"We can't issue an Amber Alert for a fetus," he was told over and over.

Meanwhile, Espey learned of a second major obstacle: could

the child have survived such a traumatic delivery by the hand of an untrained perpetrator, who had murdered her mother in the process? Doctors had said the child still might be alive, but looking at the crime scene, it seemed almost impossible. Espey had touched Bobbie Jo's cold body. He saw all the blood.

Prenatal care expert Elizabeth A. Chmura, who has worked in emergency room prenatal care for twenty years (but wasn't involved in the Stinnett case), later said, "With pregnant women who suffer an insult—such as strangulation—it is difficult to know exactly how long an infant in the womb can survive. But we know that, in some cases, it can be thirty minutes if the mom has some signs of life, which, from the evidence left behind, Bobbie Jo clearly did."

In general, if a pregnant woman dies before giving birth, the infant has approximately four minutes before hypoxia, "a pathological condition in which the body as a whole, or region of the body, is deprived of adequate oxygen supply," sets in, at which time death will likely occur for the child. Hypoxia is sometimes associated with high altitudes. If, say, an airplane's windows are blown out during flight at high elevations, passengers can die because there is not a sufficient amount of oxygen in the plane's cabin to sustain life.

As far as Ben Espey was concerned, as long as doctors were saying the child had even a "chance" of surviving the attack, he was going to do everything in his power to try to find her. Still, as time went by and the child wasn't evaluated by a doctor, her chances of survival dropped significantly. A newborn baby outside the womb, born prematurely under such unsanitary and violent conditions, was at risk of many things. Prenatal care expert Chmura noted, "Hypothermia (temperature dropping), blood and/or volume loss leading to anemia, respiratory distress, and, of course, infection" were chief among them.

These issues could cause big trouble for a newborn who was not maintained under sterile medical conditions in a hospital environment immediately after birth.

"Bobbie Jo's infant," Chmura explained, "was born about one month early, which makes for a great survival rate, since the lungs are fully developed toward this trimester. If she was kept warm and dry and stimulated to cry in order to get the fluid out of her lungs so she can, essentially, take that 'first breath,' and was given immediate nutrition, then she would be safe."

In addition, the umbilical cord, the end which would ultimately become the child's navel, needed to be clamped at the time of birth, or more trouble could arise.

Nobody in law enforcement knew for sure if Bobbie Jo's assailant had taken any of those precautions. They were assuming that whoever had taken the child was in a state of panic. Under those circumstances, anything could happen.

If the child was healthy and had survived the delivery without any lacerations or serious injuries, authorities believed Bobbie Jo's attacker had chosen to take the child at the perfect time, a factor that was likely a big part of the reason Bobbie was chosen as a victim in the first place.

"A lot of young pregnant women go into labor at thirty-seven to thirty-eight weeks," Chruma added. "Maybe Lisa Montgomery had a feeling she needed to wait until thirty-six weeks' gestation for a healthy baby, but not too long after, or Bobbie Jo would have gone to the hospital already. A little planning on her part, perhaps?"

After all the evidence was collected, there would be little doubt in the government's opinion that Lisa had planned on taking Bobbie Jo's child for at least one month prior to Bobbie Jo's murder. The very nature of the crime required premeditation and planning. How could Bobbie Jo's attacker know, for example, Zeb would be at work? And, how could she know no one else would be at Bobbie Jo's home when she arrived?

Ben Espey considered that whoever had gone to such great lengths to murder Bobbie Jo and cut her child from her womb had probably done a bit of research about how to keep the child alive. At least that's what he hoped as he faced a full night of searching.

20

Bobbie Jo Stinnett's killer had a thirty-minute jump on law enforcement, enough time to get away without anyone noticing. Driving to Melvern, Kansas, where she lived, couldn't have been a trip Lisa Montgomery had plotted out in advance. With a three-and-a-half-hour car ride ahead of her on a good day, without any traffic or car problems, she had to maintain the health of a baby, who had been born prematurely out of a hospital, as she drove.

By the time Ben Espey sent word out regarding what had happened, Lisa was not heading into Melvern, however. She was on her way to Topeka, Kansas, where, authorities say, she would put the second part of her plan in to effect.

Still a long trip, at two-and-a-half hours, Topeka was a town Lisa had chosen as part of her after-the-kidnapping plan because she would have to, at some point, explain to her husband, Kevin, that she'd given birth to their child. She couldn't just show up at home with her. He would wonder: *Why didn't you call from the hospital?*

She had to prepare a story explaining the birth. Kevin and two of her own children would play roles in the scenario she planned.

21

Beyond trying to cut through the red tape of getting an Amber Alert issued, Sheriff Ben Espey had several other problems as the critical hours after the murder ticked away. Most important, he had to rally several different law enforcement agencies and undertake the daunting task of knocking on doors in Skidmore, with the hope of gathering as much information as he could about the last minutes of Bobbie Jo's life.

While Espey was in the investigation room in the basement of the Nodaway County Sheriff's Department, filling his blackboard with information, a lead came in that seemed, at least on the surface, extremely promising. The first twenty-four to forty-eight hours of any investigation are vital to solving the case. With an infant born prematurely—and under the most inhumane circumstances imaginable— time becomes your biggest opponent. Espey hoped someone in the neighborhood had seen something, anything. The murderer was, likely, covered with blood—maybe the baby, too. There was also an indication the murderer had blond hair. Crime-scene technicians had uncovered several strands of blond hair from both of Bobbie Jo's hands.

Then a call came into the sheriff's department regarding a resident at a nearby nursing home who supposedly had been involved in selling black-market babies for $6,000 each. Espey sent two deputies to fetch the man. When they got him back to the department, however, they realized immediately that getting anything out of him was going to be almost impossible, or at least a long, tedious process that would eat up crucial hours they didn't have to spare.

"The guy was a deaf mute. I had to sit," explained Espey, "and write out all of my questions to him. We spent all night trying to get things out of him."

While that was happening, Espey had to brief the media, who were clamoring for a story. He stepped out from the basement of the department and held a short press conference in the back parking lot of the station.

"Someone was wanting a baby awful bad," Espey said. "The victim was killed no more than an hour before she was found. She may have struggled with her killer. . . . Blond hair was found in her hands."

Reporters shot questions at Espey in rapid-fire succession. He could give out only certain information. The investigation was ongoing. A killer was at large. A baby was missing. Compromising the investigation at such an early stage by giving out the *wrong* information was something Espey didn't want to do. "There were no visible signs of forced entry into the home," added Espey when pressed.

Reaffirming that the investigation was multipronged, Espey commended the many different law enforcement agencies helping out, "all over northwestern Missouri," including the St. Joseph Police Department (PD) nearby, which had sent in a CSI team. "They are very well-trained . . . and *very* good."

Espey made it clear Bobbie Jo's husband, Zeb, was no longer considered a suspect, because he had an alibi: he was working at Kawasaki Motors when the murder occurred and had several witnesses to confirm his whereabouts.

Eight FBI agents were sent to the region and became part of the task force. A murder committed in the course of a kidnapping was a federal crime, especially with a suspect possibly crossing state lines.

As Espey saw it, the FBI's presence early on was a godsend—specifically two agents who arrived hours after the murder.

Outside the department, on the street, Espey was still briefing reporters. "The doctors who examined Bobbie Jo gave us information indicating we probably would have a live child if we could find her. . . ."

As twilight turned the Missouri sky as black as the ocean floor, police in Atchison County, Missouri, radioed in a report of sighting a "red car." They were in pursuit of it.

Could it be?

But as cops tailed the car, they couldn't get a good bead on the driver. As they approached the car to get a closer look, the driver turned off the headlights and, racing along the back roads of northwestern Missouri, took a turn into the woods alongside the main road. Within minutes, it vanished.

A glimmer of hope for Bobbie Jo's family was gone as quickly as it came in. It would be the beginning of a long night of highs and lows for Ben Espey, as varying reports flooded the system.

"That red car in Atchison County," said Espey, "that wasn't our car. I knew it right away." He could feel it, he said.

Espey had his own hunch about the case he was about to follow through on—a gut feeling that, in the end, would help solve the case.

22

Police in Topeka had the description Espey sent out via teletype and were combing the region for a "red, dirty car with an *H* on the hood."

Lisa Montgomery worked her way through busy downtown Topeka, weaving in and out of traffic. By this point, anyone with a television set or radio knew what had happened in Skidmore. A woman with a newborn, a baby possibly bloodied and hurt, likely purplish in color, would stand out. Yet beyond escaping capture, Lisa soon had to face her husband and explain how she'd given birth to their child without letting him know she'd even gone into labor. Certainly he'd have questions.

While driving through a seedy section of town, filled with dingy bars, Laundromats, and check-cashing stores, Lisa drove past the Birth and Women's Center on SW Sixth Avenue and slowed her car. She saw the Birth and Women's Center sign written in white paint on the blue tarp overhanging the doorway. Directly across the street was a Long John Silver's fast-food restaurant.

Although Sixth Avenue was a busy thoroughfare, with people departing work and heading home, Long John Silver's appeared empty.

She could pull into the parking lot and, using her cellphone, call home.

23

As Ben Espey continued to push the MSHP to issue an Amber Alert, he was learning more about Bobbie Jo's murder. The ligature marks on her throat, doctors indicated, proved "she had been strangled from behind." Also, many of the postmortem tests conducted on Bobbie Jo's body pointed toward Espey's earlier assumption of her being ". . . dead at the house."

These corroborations were significant for several reasons. The fact that the Stinnett home had shown no signs of forced entry seemed to indicate that, although Bobbie Jo might not have known her killer, she trusted her enough to turn her back to her. In addition, it appeared that whoever had extracted the child knew what she was doing. The Cesarean section—if what was done could be called that—had to be carried out quickly, or the child could suffer permanent damage. With the results from the hospital, Espey knew for certain the baby, not Bobbie Jo, was the target of the attack.

Ben Espey hoped for helpful information from one other piece of evidence taken from the crime scene by St. Joseph PD CSI technicians: Bobbie Jo's computer. It was being examined as Espey continued to run the investigation from the basement of his office.

Today, more than any other time in law enforcement history, electronics—cell phones, iPods, laptops and personal computers—are among the first pieces of evidence collected at crime scenes. Most electrical devices contain information that can lead to arrests, and—as Ben Espey was about to learn—the Bobbie Jo Stinnett murder case would be no exception.

With two children of his own, two grandchildren, cousins, and kids around him his entire life, Sheriff Ben Espey was fighting ex-haustion, fatigue, fear of not finding the baby in time, and con-cerns about what might have happened to the child. But, as the evening hours wore on, the bureaucracy involved in issuing the Amber Alert ate at him most.

Finding Bobbie Jo's child was more than just a job for Espey. He was a family man. He raised horses and cattle, farmed hun-dreds of acres. But the most pleasurable part of his life, he ex-plained, was just being around his family, which included a new grandchild. His wife worked up the street from his office. On most days, they ate lunch together; took long walks, hand in hand, on his property; and rode horseback. ("The best friend I ever had," he recalled.) Espey felt lucky. Grateful. He had what Zeb Stinnett would never have. Yet he could give back to Zeb the one thing that might help the man get through the toughest days of his life ahead.

His infant daughter.

Each time he explained to the higher-ups why issuing the Amber Alert was probably one of the only chances they had of finding her alive, his pleas were met with a resounding no. Although many agreed with Espey's stance, no one, it seemed, wanted to stick his or her neck out to make it happen. There just wasn't enough information to send out the alert, Espey was told again and again. An Amber Alert could not be issued for a "fetus."

24

Kevin Montgomery arrived home from work at 5:15 P.M. He had already arranged to take off the following day, a Friday. "Kevin had taken that day off from work so he could go to the hospital with Lisa," a family member later confirmed. "Lisa had told him she was going to have her baby on that Thursday or Friday, so he put in for the day off." Kevin was becoming a bit unnerved by the entire situation. Too many times Lisa had taken him with her en route to a doctor's appointment, only to come up with an excuse along the way and send him back home. Every prenatal appointment Kevin and Lisa had planned on going to together failed to happen. Lisa would always instigate a fight so she could blow off the appointment at Kevin's expense. Kevin wasn't going to let that happen on Friday, he had said earlier in the week. He had gotten the day off and told Lisa there was no way she could stop him from going with her.

Kevin had short brown hair dusted with a tinge of gray, a thick goatee he kept well-groomed, and brown eyes. Kevin had been a self-proclaimed electrician his entire adult life, one source claimed. He and Lisa were married during the spring of 2000, about a year and a half after Lisa divorced Carl Boman for a second time. Kevin, too, had been divorced, and, like Lisa, had brought children from his first marriage into the new union. "Kevin was the type of guy whose mother, right up until the time he left high school," said someone who knew Lisa and Kevin for years, "still laid all his clothes out every morning."

The house Kevin and Lisa lived in on South Adams Road in Melvern, Kansas, was a modest farmhouse, big in structure and space, like many a Midwestern prairie home. Kevin and Lisa, many said, were attracted to the 1800s-era lifestyle made famous by the novels of Laura Ingalls Wilder. Mike Wheatley, Kevin and Lisa's pastor, said Kevin's parents had been members of the church for over thirty years. So Kevin had strong, firmly planted roots in the Christian community of Melvern. With fewer than 450 people in the town, everyone knew Kevin, and no one had a bad word to say about him.

When Kevin got home on the evening of December 16, he wasn't shocked to find Lisa was still out. Although she didn't leave the house much, she had explained to him the previous night that she was getting up early that day to go shopping in Topeka for baby clothes and a Christmas present for Kayla. Kevin thought the trip out of the house would do her some good.

Around 5:30 P.M., Lisa called. She was in the parking lot, she said, of the Long John Silver's restaurant in downtown Topeka. It just so happened the restaurant was across the street from the Birth and Women's Center on SW Sixth Avenue.

"My water broke and I went into labor and had the baby," Lisa said.

"What?"

"I delivered the baby. I'm on my way home right now."

"Where are you?"

"Long John Silver's in Topeka."

"I'm coming to get you," Kevin said.

"No, I'll drive home. I'm okay."

"No," Kevin said. "Me and the kids will come and get you. Don't go anywhere."

Lisa's fifteen-year-old son, *Ryan*, was home at the time with Kevin. Soon after Lisa called, Rebecca walked through the door.

"Damn it," Kevin said to the kids after hanging up.

"He was a bit mad," Ryan recalled, "that Mom had the baby."

Grabbing the two children, Kevin hopped into his pickup truck and hit the road en route to meet Lisa and his daughter in Topeka.

It was time to celebrate. After all the talk of Lisa's being pregnant and having one miscarriage after another, year after year, it seemed she had finally given birth to a child.

---

*Italics on first use of proper names and locations represents pseudonym or author's replacement.

25

Heading northbound on U.S. 75 from Melvern, Topeka was a forty-minute drive. The plan was for Rebecca and Ryan to drive Lisa's Toyota back to Melvern, while Lisa, Kevin, and the baby followed in Kevin's pickup. Kevin was excited. He was a father again. After so many complications and failed attempts at having a child over the past four years, here it was: time to hand out the cigars.

It's a girl!

When Kevin, Rebecca, and Ryan pulled into the parking lot of Long John Silver's, Lisa was sitting in her car, a baby in her arms.

"When we got up there, Mom was in the car with the baby," Ryan said later. "We had the truck. If I felt anything, it was happiness, but it wasn't very strong. Kevin was happy. Very happy."

Lisa got out and stepped toward Kevin's truck. "Get her things," Kevin said to one of the kids as he took Lisa by the arm. "You okay?" he asked her.

She moaned and put her hands around her stomach. "I'll be all right."

"Aren't you supposed to still be in the hospital?" Rebecca asked. Rebecca had taken parenting classes in school. She knew about the birthing process and the recovery time involved.

Lisa continued holding herself, acting as if she were in serious pain.

"Why aren't you still in bed, Mother?" Rebecca continued. Rebecca, like her younger sister Kayla, spoke fast: her words ran all together and came out quickly. Whether she was talking to her mother or anyone else, she was hard to follow at times. "My theory," she said later, "is that, because Mom was always reading a book or on the computer, growing up we had very little time to talk to her. You had to talk fast to get out what you wanted to say to her."

"They made me drink a bunch of apple juice," Lisa said as Kevin helped her get comfortable in the truck. "They made me go to the bathroom before I could leave."

When the truth was later known, it must have been doubly devastating for Kevin to accept. Years ago, Kevin and his first wife had lost a child, a girl, at birth. Some claimed Kevin had never recovered from the loss and that Lisa wanted to give him a girl to help ease his pain.

Ryan and Rebecca, however, were bewildered, to say the least. Could it be possible? Maybe their mom hadn't been lying about being pregnant, after all. The kids believed Lisa, but they always had misgivings. "My son had serious doubts," Carl Boman said later. "You have to believe Kevin *had* to have doubts himself."

One day, it seemed, Lisa was parading around Melvern, her stomach as flat as a fitness instructor's, telling everyone she was in her last trimester; and the next, she was sitting in her car at the Long John Silver's in downtown Topeka holding an infant she claimed she had just delivered.

Kevin and Lisa's two children pulled out of downtown Topeka on the evening of December 16, with Lisa and her new baby. According to Lisa's story, she had given birth to the child only hours ago. If that story were true, authorities later wondered, why was she in the parking lot of a fast-food restaurant waiting for a ride home? Why wasn't she at the hospital, which was just blocks away from Long John Silver's? Or, better yet, at the Birth and Women's Center, about fifty feet from the parking lot where Kevin and the kids met Lisa, the place where, she claimed, she'd given birth?

26

Although Lisa's second oldest daughter, *Alicia*, hadn't been there when Kevin and Lisa arrived home with Rebecca, Ryan, and the baby, one of the kids called her at work and shared the good news with her. Alicia wanted to rush home "to see the baby," but had to wait until the end of her shift. "She was all excited," a family member recalled. "Really looking forward to holding the baby and sharing in her mother's happiness."

When they got settled at home, Lisa dressed the child in a cute little white T-shirt with pink lettering: I'M THE LITTLE SISTER.

"It was very busy that night because Kevin was so proud and he wanted to tell his family," Ryan said later.

So while Lisa marveled at the child, with Rebecca and Ryan by her side, passing her around, playing with her, holding her, showing her the nursery she had spent weeks converting from an old bedroom, Kevin called family members with the good news: *It's a girl.*

Lisa then called her aunt. While she was brimming on the phone with excitement, describing the child's features ("How cute is she? Beautiful little girl, huh?"), Kevin's aunts, uncles, mother, and father showed up to share in the celebration.

Later on, Ryan called Kayla in Georgia. Like Kayla, Ryan was puzzled over the events of the past few hours.

"Kayla, how many people are in our family?" Ryan asked. His tone was stoic, as if he *knew* the answer, but wanted someone else to clarify it for him.

---

*Italics on first use of proper names and locations represents pseudonym or author's replacement.

"I don't know," Kayla said. She was even more mystified now than she had been throughout her mother's last failed pregnancy. "*What* are you talking about?"

"Well . . . we have a new addition, you know."

"What?"

After that brief conversation, Kayla questioned Alicia, who had just gotten home from work. Kayla believed Alicia would know more about the child than anyone else.

"What time was the baby born?" Kayla asked.

"I don't know."

"How much did she weigh?"

"Not sure."

"How long is she?"

Alicia didn't know. In fact, when Kayla asked the same set of questions later that night and the next day, Ryan and Rebecca didn't have any of the answers.

"Where was she born?"

"I have no idea."

"That, in and of itself," recalled Kayla, "gave me a bad feeling. I told Auntie M I thought it was weird that they couldn't answer any of my questions."

Lisa remained calm throughout the evening. When she complained about pains in her stomach from the delivery, family members gathered around and comforted her. Kevin was seriously concerned about his wife and the pain she was experiencing and did everything he could to comfort her.

"You okay, Lisa?"

"I'm fine," Lisa said. "I'm okay. Don't worry about me."

For the infant's first night, Lisa put her to sleep downstairs. "It was warmer than it was upstairs." The baby cried only once, Rebecca recalled; otherwise, mom and baby slept soundly through the entire night.

27

With everything else going on, Nodaway County sheriff Ben Espey was now contending with a public relations person from the FBI poking his nose into an investigation Espey believed he had well under control. The PR man's insistence on taking over and running the investigation turned Espey inside out.

Espey wasn't some hayseed local sheriff who could be pushed around; he was a consummate professional, soft-spoken and generally tranquil—the type of person who never showed his frustration or anger in a public setting. He acted on his instincts and moved forward despite opposition, doing, Espey noted, exactly what he thought Victoria Jo needed at the time.

By the middle of the night, the case was becoming overwhelming—not the investigative end of it (Espey could handle that), but his obligation to the press. Every hour, it seemed, Espey was sending out a news release.

Frustrated, he told a colleague, "If they won't issue an Amber Alert, I'll use the press in place of it."

Finding someone from the media wouldn't be difficult. Looking up the block from his office, Espey could see scores of satellite TV trucks camped in downtown Maryville, lighting up Main Street like a football stadium on game night. Espey had obtained the full cooperation of Sheldon Lyons, the MSHP's public relations official, who assured him the MSHP would do everything in its power to help him, especially where the press was concerned.

"That was a lot off of my shoulders," remembered Espey. "After I thought about it, I realized I needed the press to help me find the child."

There was still no Amber Alert. Its absence became the broken spoke in the wheel of justice during those crucial first hours. The sheriff continued to push for it, but was repeatedly told no.

The FBI's public relations agent from Washington, DC, soon explained to Espey and Lyons that they "weren't doing this right." His arrival included an incident with Espey's dispatcher. He had walked into the foyer of the sheriff's department, a four-by-eight-foot white tiled room, with vanilla-painted concrete blocks for walls, a door into the office and holding-cell area to the west, and a Plexiglas booth to the north, where the dispatcher spoke through a talkbox to anyone who entered.

Espey's dispatcher looked up as the FBI agent opened the door, took off his sunglasses and black leather gloves, and approached the window. "Can I help you?" she asked.

"I'm with the FBI. This is *my* case. I'm taking over," said the man, flashing his badge. Espey stepped out of his office.

Quite outspoken and dedicated to her boss, Espey's dispatcher looked at the G-man, bowed her head, and said contentiously, "Yeah, and I'm Daffy Duck."

Nevertheless, before long, the same PR man made his way into Espey's office and assumed part of the investigation, dictating who was in charge of what and whom, seeming to ignore Espey completely.

The bottom line for Espey was finding the child. A conflict with a member of the FBI held no interest for him. Espey wanted to find the missing child, and nothing else really mattered.

Espey finally told the intruder to get the hell out of his office as he slammed the door on his back. Then, he recalled, "I focused on finding the baby."

Espey realized that, in order to get the child back, he might have to allow the PR man into the investigation on some level. Perhaps he *could* help. Putting the well-being of the child first, Espey wasn't about to refuse more federal help. In truth, Espey was glad to have it—as long as the Federal agents didn't get in the way of what he was doing.

"But," Espey told another agent, who had since arrived, "you get rid of that little public relations guy, or I'll have him escorted out of the county." Espey meant what he said. He didn't speak often in anger. But when he did, his words commanded attention.

"This FBI guy," said another law enforcement official, "came in there and got in Ben's face. It was like he had just watched a movie, *Die Hard* or something, and was trying to be the quintessential FBI agent. The FBI is *not* like that."

"We got along real good after he left," explained Espey. "The guys that I worked with in the FBI, Kurt Lipanovich and Mickey Roberts, were just great. The best. I liked them a lot. The problem was that little press guy who wanted to come in and tell everybody what to do. He was probably told to do that from Washington, but I didn't want it. Not in my town."

Espey's problems with the FBI, however, wouldn't end there.

28

One of the most important investigative strategies Ben Espey initiated right away was to involve as many law enforcement agencies as possible, mainly the Missouri Major Case Squad, the MSHP, and a team of crime-scene investigators from the St. Joseph PD.

For Espey, though, every decision he made early on was based solely on the well-being of the child. The murder could be solved in due course—he was certain of that. But the baby could still be alive. She had to come first, whether anyone agreed with him or not.

With frustration building over seeing his Amber Alert requests repeatedly turned down, as it got later in the evening, Espey realized he was fighting the clock, now more than ever. He decided to turn to an old friend, Missouri congressman Sam Graves, who was nearing the end of his second term in office and planning a run for a third.

Espey had known Graves for twelve years. He'd even campaigned with him on the Republican ticket a few times, walking the streets together, waving in parades, knocking on doors, handing out buttons and bumper stickers. Graves came from a family rooted in law enforcement; his brother, Todd, had been a U.S. attorney for a number of years. Moreover, Sam supported local law enforcement and was considered an advocate of the sheriff's offices serving his constituency. A lifelong resident of Missouri's sixth Congressional District, he was popular among the people of Missouri because, some said, he "is one of them," having been a small businessman and a sixth-generation farmer himself. His congressional biography states that Graves, a father of three, "spent his life working to make Missouri a better place to live, work, and raise a family." Besides all that, Bobbie Jo's murder had hit home for Graves: he lived about thirty miles outside Skidmore. Bobbie Jo was like one of his own, Skidmore an adopted hometown.

If anyone could help, Espey knew, it was Sam Graves. Espey knew Graves was a caring human being with morals most public officials seldom displayed. Espey also knew Graves would understand how desperate the situation was. Here was a chance to save a baby. Graves knew how tight the community was and how getting the child back mattered not only to Zeb Stinnett, but to the township as a whole.

"We are fairly good friends," said Espey. "He became my contact person—the only one I could think of when all else failed."

As Espey struggled to come up with a way to convince the MSHP to issue the alert, he phoned Sam Graves at his home late that evening and asked him for help. Espey explained how he had been told repeatedly the case did not meet the criteria for an Amber Alert because authorities did not know the child's hair and eye color, or any other details. "I'm really aggravated, Sam. You have to pull some strings and get this thing done."

Amber Alert guidelines were set in stone, however. What could a congressman do to supersede national policies and procedures? The state of Missouri was still in the process of designing its own Amber Alert standards, thus forcing state officials to fall back on what had been accepted nationally.

"I'm not sure I can get anything done, Ben. The law is the law, you know."

"Fix the damn law," Espey said. He was desperate. Hospital officials were telling him the child was likely alive but could be in danger of suffering problems down the road if she wasn't found soon. Additionally, who knew what the child's kidnapper was doing to her?

"Give me two hours and I'll have it done," Graves said next, without hesitation.

"He really helped me," Espey recalled, "at a time when I needed it. Everyone helped, but Sam got things moving for us and got things done right away."

"I've known [Ben Espey] for a while," Graves said later in published reports, "and he was at the end of his rope." In another statement, Graves added, "We've got a problem with our system. Nobody really thought of this contingency."

Espey's chief argument throughout the night was that a newborn baby "looks different than *any* other child. In three or four or five days, well, you've got a baby. But a *newborn* baby, if I say that a baby was born within a few hours, anybody can look at a child and tell it's a newborn."

He couldn't understand why no one else, save for Sam Graves and the people inside his law enforcement circle, couldn't see it the same way.

29

A t around 12:45 A.M. on Friday, Ben Espey finally got his wish. Later, reflecting on that crucial time near midnight when word came down that the Amber Alert was going out, he said, "I was overwhelmed with the fact that we were going to be able to get this baby back."

It wasn't hard to figure out Sam Graves had pulled out some sort of trump card and used it.

"He could have easily claimed to have called a few people," Espey explained, "called me back and said, 'Look, I called some people and I couldn't get it done.' But Sam took an interest in it. Sam *made* it happen."

Early the next morning, an official Amber Alert went out to all law enforcement agencies in the immediate area: Iowa, Missouri, Kansas, New Mexico, Nebraska. Sent from the main office of the MSHP, the alert, in part, said police were searching for a suspect who may have blond hair and was possibly driving a red vehicle, "a two-door hatchback, possibly a 1980s or 1990s, Honda or Hyundai." It wasn't clear, the alert continued, if law enforcement was looking for a man or woman, but officials knew the child was female. If anyone spied a man, woman, or couple traveling with a newborn, he or she needed to call in immediately.

Time, of course, was of the utmost importance.

"I believe there is a live eight-month-old fetus out there and we need to find it," Espey told reporters early Friday morning.

No one had an idea then of the number of tips about to flood the system, and the work ahead. It was well after midnight, the sun close to coming up. Espey hadn't sat down or taken a break since finding Bobbie Jo's body. It would be a long morning, he knew, but with any luck, and some help from the public, Bobbie Jo's child would be returned to her family soon.

"It's very hard for me to accept this," Espey told reporters after issuing the alert. "Nobody here could ever perceive this taking place. To have a fetus taken out of a mother's womb and then an Amber Alert to try to find that child." He shook his head in disbelief. It was obvious the horrifying aspects of the crime and the missing child weighed on Espey. He had bags under his eyes: his skin looked gray and pasty; his lips dry and chalky, as though he were dehydrated.

"It's pretty tragic," continued Espey. "It's really tragic for the family to lose a twenty-three-year-old mother. The only light spot in this is the fact that the baby can be found alive." Espey's deep-set, Caribbean-blue eyes gave him almost a Hollywood veneer. Yet Espey had the faith and will of any spiritual leader that side of the Missouri River. Here was a grown man who welled up with tears at certain points when he spoke about the case to his colleagues and peers.

Later that morning, Espey indicated he believed "more than one person may be involved in the crime." Tips were coming in already. "I don't think one person could do it," he told reporters. "It took one person to choke Bobbie and one to cut her baby out."

As the sun dawned on a new day, he realized he hadn't slept in twenty-four hours. But he sensed that answers were about to come. Patience was the key now to saving Victoria Jo's life.

Wait it out. . . . Something will come in.

30

The water tower overlooking downtown Melvern stands at least one hundred feet tall watching over town like one of those four-legged Martian characters on the cover of HG Wells' classic *War of the Worlds*. It is a large steel tub, rusted, with faded black letting, positioned just east of Routes 74 and 31, which intersect at the center of town by the post office and one bank. The roads of Melvern are a mixture of fieldstone, crumbled tar, natural rock, and dirt. While driving along the road leading out of downtown, toward Kevin and Lisa's house to the west, you might see quail pop up out of the brush and scatter like minnows, or finch sail alongside the car like streamers. People look, nod, and go back to their business.

That Friday morning started out crisp and cold. Within hours, this Midwestern town would be exposed to the world as the gruesome details of Bobbie Jo's murder and the kidnapping of her child worked their way into the mainstream press. Reporters were showing up at Skidmore and Maryville, north of Melvern, interviewing neighbors and friends of Bobbie Jo's, trying to prod Ben Espey until he talked, keeping up on the investigation best they could, while sending live television feeds from across the street from Bobbie Jo's small house to points all over.

This was a major international news story now, hitting a nerve with people, reminding many that evil spared no one. If a horror of this magnitude could happen days before Christmas in a town of 342, anything was possible. Facts and evidence were, at best, sketchy, as speculation and rumor ran rampant. But the public reacted to the story with questions that defied answers: What type of person could do such a thing? Was there a human being alive who could butcher a young woman as innocent and pure as Bobbie Jo Stinnett and cut her child from her womb?

After they woke up and got settled a bit, Lisa and Kevin decided to take their new child around town and show her off.

Before she and Kevin left, Lisa took the child out of her crib and sat down in the living room cradling her. With two of her own children around her, getting ready for school, she took out one of her breasts and offered it to the baby. The child's eyes hadn't opened yet. A crusty film covering each eyelid needed to be washed off and treated. Lisa tried feeding the newborn for a while, but the baby wasn't interested in feeding at a milkless breast, or she didn't have an appetite.

31

In Georgia, Kayla Boman was at the house next door as usual, watching her neighbor's daughter before school. Realizing she needed to shake off whatever uncertainties she had about her mom and her new baby sister, she figured she'd log on to the Internet while her neighbor's daughter was getting ready for school and see if any of her siblings were online.

I need to get in touch with someone back home, she told herself.

Kayla's phone calls with her siblings the previous night weighed on her. She needed some sort of answer before leaving for school. Calling home to Melvern might shake off any negative thoughts she had about Mom and her new baby sister. Maybe just sharing in the excitement would help. Things were going to change. Overnight, she had the responsibility of another life in her bloodline, and she loved the feeling, she said, of finally being a big sister.

As soon as she logged on, she noticed Rebecca was online. "Call me," Kayla instant messaged Rebecca.

As she picked up the phone a moment later, she could hear the baby cooing in the background.

"She's so cute, Kayla," Rebecca said.

"I bet."

"You have to see her."

To Kayla, it was the "cutest thing," hearing her little sister cry and make baby sounds in the background as she and Rebecca spoke. The baby, she remembered, sounded content and happy waking up in a household showering her with the warmth of a family environment.

What Kayla didn't know then was that even though the child may have sounded "content," her health status was anything but. By now, she was having a hard time opening her eyes and hadn't been able to extend her eyelids all the way. Furthermore, several bruises on her face and legs were becoming more pronounced. Her arms wouldn't extend all the way, and her fingers were a whitish tinged hue of purple, clearly showing signs of circulation problems.

Was anyone noticing this?

Kayla surmised her mom must have made sure the baby was healthy, or she wouldn't have been able to take her home so quickly from the hospital.

"Send me some photos," Kayla asked Rebecca. She was thrilled and reenergized. She wanted to be back home, holding the child, like Rebecca, Ryan, and Alicia had done the night before. She yearned to be a part of what was happening.

"Sure," Rebecca said. "Hold on."

Within a few minutes, Rebecca took out her cell phone, snapped several photographs of the child, then e-mailed them.

Before they hung up, Rebecca put the phone closer to the child. Kayla could again hear her making sounds.

Then Lisa got on the phone.

"Hi, Mom," Kayla said. "Good morning." She was happy for her mother.

"Hello, Kayla. How are you?"

As Kayla sat at the computer waiting for the photographs to print out, she had one thought: *I'm finally a big sister.* She smiled. It made her feel important. She was happy her mom wouldn't be branded a liar, like her dad and her grandmother had been telling her for the past year or more. She'd had her baby. Maybe they could stop all the fighting now.

I'm going to take these photographs to school and brag to everyone I know about my new baby sister.

It was getting late. Kayla made sure her neighbor's daughter was ready for the bus and then walked next door to Auntie

Mary's. Mary was still in bed sleeping, but Kayla jumped up on her bed "real fast" and woke her up.

"Look," she said, holding up the photographs. "Isn't she pretty?"

Auntie Mary, just waking up, looked at the pictures with squinted eyes. "Yes, Kayla. She's pretty. Yes."

32

The child looked like a little Sunday-newspaper model all dressed up in her new outfit. Lisa was proud. She'd spent an hour, it seemed, picking the outfit out. This one here . . . it's perfect! She had tried to feed the child again, but Victoria Jo didn't want to nurse. So, Lisa dressed her in a pink Winnie-the-Pooh one-piece and got her ready for the day.

There had been some talk about a name, but it was official now. "We're calling her Abigail Marie." It was a name Lisa had hand-picked, she started telling everyone, from the Bible.

Lisa was never an ultrareligious woman, the sort that quoted verses and lived by the law of the church. According to many, her pretense of faith was just another falsehood she wanted people to believe, a part of the dream she was chasing.

"Lisa envied her cousin, who lived in *Arizona*," someone who knew her for most of her life said later, "and was trying—during that last year, 2004, when everything happened—to emulate her life."

Lisa's cousin was a devout Christian and lived every part of what she preached. She was a *real* Christian, not someone who pushed the Bible on others, knocked on doors, and preached "the Word" to strangers. But, as one of her relatives later put it, "[She] is perhaps over the top religiously, but she's a *really* good person. People respect her. She doesn't push her religion in your face; instead, she lives it."

She was also a woman who had eight kids and, as it turned out, was expecting her ninth.

*Italics on first use of proper names and locations represents pseudonym or author's replacement.

"[Lisa's cousin] was pregnant in December," that same relative added, "and due to have her baby in January."

Moreover, Lisa's cousin planned on naming her child Abigail (which she eventually did), and Lisa was well aware of it. As Lisa would later claim to several different people she spoke to while parading Bobbie Jo's baby around town that morning, she had chosen the name Abigail for "religious reasons," quoting the Bible as her source for the name. But like a lot of things in Lisa's life, it was another way for her to manipulate further the people in her life.

33

After the kids left for school, Kevin drove Lisa and the baby up the road to Pastor Mike Wheatley's parsonage across the street from the church. According to Wheatley, they arrived around 9:00 A.M.

From afar, the First Church of God looks like any other ranch-style home in the Maple Street neighborhood just west of downtown. Wheatley had known Lisa, Kevin, and Lisa's kids ever since Lisa and Kevin were married in 2000. Lisa and Kevin, according to one family member, weren't necessarily Christians in the sense they went to church every Sunday morning and read Bible passages before bed each night. In fact, "I wouldn't even consider them 'Sunday Christians.' It was Lisa's children who went to church every Sunday, not Lisa and Kevin."

Kevin's parents, who also lived in town, were dedicated members of the church and had been for decades. The Montgomery name, some insisted, was a staple in Melvern. Lisa had always seemed to carry herself in a different manner around town, as if she were constantly trying to live up to an image she believed the Montgomery family had of her.

"Lisa was quiet," Wheatley said later on television, while claiming to be the Montgomery family spokesperson. "I can tell you she was pretty much a person that would like to talk about herself a lot, and her children. If you wanted to talk about Lisa, she was mighty happy. But she was also a person who cared a lot about her children. And my wife and I decided she could have qualified as a pioneer woman, because she was quite capable of not having all the amenities that we have today and still surviving and teaching her kids how to do that. She was just a homebody.

She went to work, she went home, took care of her kids. She was kind of quiet most of the time."

When Lisa, Kevin, and the baby showed up that morning, Wheatley was pleasantly surprised, he later said, to see she'd had the child. Of course, he knew she'd given birth, according to one law enforcement official, because Lisa had called him the previous day and told him about it.

"Her husband," Wheatley added, "was obviously a very happy new father. He was just proud to be a dad. . . . [He] was absolutely grinning from ear to ear. He wasn't going to come out of the clouds for a very long time. He was a very proud papa."

Wheatley held the child for about fifteen minutes and then handed her to his wife, who spent the next forty-five minutes with the child. "I held the little baby," he said. "At the time, we thought her name was Abigail. . . ."

One could say Kathy Wheatley, the pastor's wife, and Lisa were friends. People in town had seen them together on occasion. They picked strawberries during the season and seemed to get along well. Others said, however, because the Montgomery name carried a certain social standing in the town, Lisa had an obligation to act a certain way while out in the community. Roaming around town with the pastor's wife was just one way for her to accomplish that task.

"She acted different when she was around those people," said one former acquaintance—"you know, the 'better than thou' people."

While the pastor and his wife played with the child, Lisa, at times stoic and passive, stood up at one point and talked in detail about the delivery and how her water had broken while she was "shopping in Topeka."

To those who were about to meet and hold Bobbie Jo's baby, life seemed to be coming together for Lisa and Kevin. Lisa had confided in Pastor Wheatley on several occasions about her desire to have a baby, as she had to others in town. She had told him about her supposed miscarriage a while back, and Wheatley, like any compassionate human being, had expressed sympathy for the loss. But none of that mattered now as Lisa and Kevin sat in the Wheatleys' home displaying a joy they had been looking forward to for so long. It didn't make any difference anymore that Lisa had lost so many children. It was time to rejoice and celebrate; their gift from God had finally arrived. Here she was bouncing on the pastor's lap, her mother and father looking on proudly with the delight only new parents could feel.

Darrel Schultz was another member of the First Church of God, who also happened to be Kevin's boss. The first time he heard about Lisa's latest pregnancy was back on December 10, just a week ago, when he ran into Lisa and Kevin at the local high-school basketball game. It was parent-senior night. Most in town had attended. In the Midwest, supporting high-school sports is as much a part of life as throwing bush apples at houses when you're a kid or raising cattle and goats.

Schultz viewed Lisa as a "pleasant person," he said later while sitting next to Wheatley on television. "When she talked about things—she . . . They, well, they (the Montgomerys) raised goats. And she talked about how they could take the wool from them and weave different things. And the kids learned to do that. They learned how to spin yarn and stuff."

Like most in town, Schultz saw this as good, wholesome family living, which allowed the family unit to become closer. Lisa and Kevin were just one more blended family making a go, a second chance at happiness.

When Darrel Schultz ran into Lisa back on December 10 during that basketball game, he hadn't noticed she was about to have a baby. A week later, when he saw her again and she had the child with her, like a lot of people, he began asking himself questions: *What's this? Where did this baby come from?*

"And that's why," he stated later, "of course, seeing her [at the basketball game] . . . and then seeing her a week later with a baby, why, we were just sort of *shocked* and *astonished*. I had no idea she was that close to delivery."

34

Ben Espey had a hard time finding much sympathy for the town of Melvern and the feelings many displayed later about being duped by Lisa Montgomery. In fact, Espey was disgusted with certain people involved in the case and what they later said.

"You ask Wheatley," suggested Espey, "how the heck he held that child and didn't realize there was an Amber Alert out for a newborn?"

To Wheatley's credit, at the time Lisa was at his home with Kevin and the child, he claimed he and his wife had not yet heard about the murder of Bobbie Jo Stinnett. It was a breaking news story on television and radio, but Wheatley was not one to make viewing cable-television news programs part of his daily routine. He had a church to run, people in town to counsel. The day's news events generally caught up to him, not the other way around. Beyond weather reports and the local news, he wasn't interested in the day's events outside his small world in Melvern, one could assume. When Lisa showed up with the child, he had no idea every law enforcement agency within a two-hundred-mile radius was on the lookout for a woman, man, or both, traveling with a newborn.

"Even when they were there that morning," recalled Wheatley, "I wasn't aware of any of this. As far as I knew, everything was just perfectly normal."

Questions did arise, however, between Wheatley and his wife after Lisa and Kevin left the house. Wheatley, for example, thought, *Why does she have a newborn baby out, showing it off so soon?*

Moreover, the child's appearance became an issue. Wheatley noticed it had "very long fingers," which he said neither Kevin nor Lisa had, and there were numerous bruises all over her face, both large and small, plus several visible scratches. A photograph from the previous night showed a beat-up child who had obviously gone through a turbulent delivery. Her fingers were, indeed, long and white, but also bony and bluish in color, as if she'd had problems with circulation.

"The term for bluish white extremities is acrocyanosis," a prenatal care specialist explained later. "This is very common in the newborn because of the folded fetal position of the infant in the uterus. The bending of the arms and legs constricts the arteries and limits blood supply to the hands and feet. This usually resolves [itself] in a couple of days."

Acrocyanosis would not be a major concern; however, that same expert commented, "lack of oxygen to the brain" could be. If Victoria Jo lost enough oxygen during the time it took to kill Bobbie Jo, brain damage in the child could occur later and show up in the form of cerebral palsy and/or learning disabilities, problems that may not be recognized for one to two years after birth.

"The major question is, how long did it take to get the infant out of the womb? It's hard to tell if an infant is truly affected until months later, when certain milestones are—or are not—met."

Above Victoria Jo's left eye, almost running along the path of her eyebrow, was an unmistakable one-inch-long wound, not too deep or wide, but consistent with a scratch left behind by the blade of a knife or an adult fingernail. Underneath that same eye was a more pronounced wound, a bit longer, yet similar in shape and scope. There was also a rather large bruise in the crack of the baby's cleft chin, and another on the right side of her face.

Taking a closer look, it would have been easy to tell the child did not resemble Kevin or Lisa in the slightest. Babies are babies, some might say. But Victoria Jo had a pudgy face and large nostrils, neither of which Kevin or Lisa could claim. All of Lisa's babies with Carl Boman had weighed fewer than five pounds. After eight months of gestation, Victoria Jo weighed in at eight pounds. Kevin himself had said "[Lisa] had little babies." Additionally, Victoria Jo's lips were plump and larger than a normal newborn's. Both Kevin and Lisa had thin lips.

These were features that generally showed up on babies during the first days after birth—features aunts and uncles visiting new mothers marveled at: "He's got your eyes . . . your nose . . . looks just like you did as a baby."

If anyone who saw the child that day had put a photograph of Bobbie Jo or Zeb up against Victoria Jo, the resemblance would have been unmistakable.

As the day moved forward, and Lisa and Kevin left Pastor Wheatley's, questions would emerge as they began showing up at other places around town. Why would this woman, who had supposedly just given birth to a baby the previous day, bring a newborn out in public so soon? Medically speaking, why didn't the child have a cone-shaped head, like most natural-birth newborns? Entering the birth canal, newborns develop a pointed skull as they pass through the mother's vagina and into the world. Called "molding," the condition generally resolves itself in a period of days and a healthy, normally shaped skull forms. Other signs of natural childbirth include a condition called "caput," which refers to a swelling on the top of the skull caused by fluid buildup during the birthing process. Caput, too, resolves itself within a few days after childbirth. One more common sign is cephalhematoma. Because of the "friction of the infant's head against the mother's pelvic bones," noted one pediatrician, "sometimes there is a blood collection on the outer surface of the skull." Generally, this condition is confined to one side of the child's head and can take anywhere from a few days to a few weeks to clear up.

But here was little Abigail Montgomery, with a perfectly round, perfectly formed skull. Sure, Lisa could have had a Cesarean section, but wouldn't she be all stitched up and nursing those wounds—and still be in the hospital?

Instead, Lisa was asking people to believe that, not even twenty-four hours after she delivered a child, she had been allowed to leave the clinic, take the baby home, and display her in public.

To say the least, her behavior was bizarre—yet no one, at this point, had made the correlation between an Amber Alert issued out of Maryville and a woman in Melvern who had claimed to be pregnant five times, but had lost each child, and was now showing off a newborn who looked nothing like her or her husband.

What struck Pastor Wheatley later on when he thought about it was the "little mark on her cheek." Wheatley noted how it "looked like she might have gouged herself. . . ." She also had a little "bruise on her hand," he added, "but other than that, she was absolutely beautiful. . . . It was hard to believe she was even a newborn."

35

Sheriff Ben Espey has a ruggedness born out of his broad shoulders, sun-soaked skin and meaty forearms, Midwestern accent and solid form, that is impossible to dismiss. He walks upright, with good posture, quiet and composed. As a lawman in a small town, Espey wears his holster and gun as if he were born with them. When he speaks, Espey pauses and then gives straightforward, to-the-point answers, which indicate how seriously he thinks about what he wants to say before uttering a single word. People say they feel safe around him.

While Lisa, Kevin, and the child made their way through Melvern, Amber Alert tips flooded the lines of MSHP's communications center, just as Espey had hoped and predicted.

Exactly what he needed.

Some citizens find it within themselves to make a 911 call, while others let it go. By early morning, Espey knew the crime had affected people in the region in the worst way, and public outcry would work to his advantage. Because of this, people stepped up and responded on a large scale.

After cops in Atchison County reported how they'd lost sight of a red vehicle the previous night, Espey received a tip regarding a woman in a nearby state who had arrived home with a newborn baby "that was not from a hospital."

Seemed promising. But as FBI agents, who were immediately dispatched to the home to investigate, found out, it proved fruitless, like a lot of anonymous tips.

Then word came in about "a baby sold [recently] on the black market" somewhere in the region where Victoria was kidnapped. Yet, any glimmer of hope diminished after authorities tracked down the basis of the tip. "I think that lead," Espey told reporters, "is possibly going to go up in smoke. The third party has misled us. We're not going to pursue that as hard as we are two or three of the other tips."

Law enforcement faced a new dilemma: was someone misleading police, calling in fake tips to throw off the scent? Espey didn't think so. Human error and enthusiasm, he felt, were leading to all the false leads and tips.

"I think people," he said, "get too eager when the Amber Alert goes out, and make a phone call, and make themselves very convinced that 'I overheard a person say this, and this is probably what happened.'"

In the basement of the Nodaway County Sheriff's Department, where Espey and his team were stationed, analyzing all the leads, and placing them on a blackboard, which ran the length of the wall, became a tedious task. Yet, each call, he said, was taken "*very* seriously.

"We charted each one," said Espey, "and each was assigned a different investigator."

By now, Espey had about eighteen investigators working the case.

"Everything completely snowballed," after the Amber Alert went out, he said. "We chased every single lead. Every lead was written down and checked. It was well organized."

Little did Espey or anyone in law enforcement know then of a quiet woman, wearing dark-rimmed glasses, living in a North Carolina suburb nearly one thousand miles from Skidmore, who would change the entire nature of the investigation, and, in one phone call, help break the case.

36

On any other day, the Stinnett home was just another white-washed house in a quiet town, on a quiet street, somewhere in Middle America. But over the past eighteen hours, this shoe box of wood and windows had turned into a revolving door of FBI agents, detectives, sheriffs, CSI technicians, and deputies. Neighbors in the immediate area were shell-shocked by the news of what had gone on inside Bobbie Jo's house. Had this horror really happened in their usually hushed and isolated community?

"Bobbie Jo bought some baby clothes from me in September," one neighbor told reporters that morning, "when I had a garage sale." The entire block had "witnessed evil," the same neighbor added, before wondering if she, or anyone else in town, would ever "feel safe again."

Many were at home when the murder occurred, going about their daily routines of folding laundry, cleaning the house, maybe working on a car in the driveway, or chopping firewood. It seemed surreal to think that something out of the most chilling horror novel had taken place in such a remote area—worse yet, at Christmastime, with the glow of holiday lights illuminating the skyline.

As one reporter put it during a live broadcast from across the street from Bobbie Jo's house, "People are puzzled. They're lost. They're confused.

"All sorts of emotions."

For some, the tragedy was more than they could put into words. The Devil had found Skidmore and wreaked havoc. The town would go on, certainly, but people stood shell-shocked Friday morning wondering when Bobbie Jo's killer would face justice and her child would be returned.

As sirens filled the air the previous afternoon, people in the neighborhood had assumed Bobbie Jo had gone into labor. Everyone in town knew Bobbie Jo was expecting a child. When you live among so few, news travels as fast as the prairie wind during tornado season. But now, amid the plastic yellow police tape closing off the Stinnett home and crime lab vans dotted along West Elm and Orchard, cops roaming through the streets asking uncomfortable questions, Skidmore's world had collapsed. Townspeople stood bewildered and breathless, holding rakes and shovels, gripping their children's hands. Some were crying, others shook their heads and hugged one another, wishing life could be the way it used to be before "it" happened, seriously wondering if things could ever be the same again.

Would Skidmore be able to redeem itself by returning Victoria Jo to Zeb? Could Victoria Jo be alive and well? Would she be returned home to give the entire town some sort of salvation from evil? Would God conquer?

As the morning dawned and the Amber Alert became topic number one in town, many held out hope someone would come forward. It hadn't been twenty-four hours since the crime, but a night had passed. "That child," said one man who had lived near Skidmore his entire life, "could be in Arizona, Nevada, or California by now. Who knows where she is?"

37

On the morning of December 17, Dyanne Siktar had been living in rural North Carolina for the past sixteen years. At fifty-three, having grown up in Michigan and, later, Florida, Dyanne was comfortable with the slow pace of life in the "small mountain town" of approximately thirty-six hundred in Macon County, North Carolina, she now called home. "Life here," said Dyanne, "is very relaxed. I live in an area where you never grow tired of the natural beauty. It is definitely not 'life in the fast lane,' which makes it very pleasant."

Part of her day was devoted to breeding rat terriers, a hobby she had turned into a growing business over the past fifteen years. With the rise of the Internet, Dyanne started selling the dogs online to buyers all over the world. During the past ten years, as the Internet grew into a planet of its own, she routinely visited an Internet message board, Annie's Rat Terrier Rest Area, a Web page, specifically, Ratter Chatter, where members met and talked about different aspects of breeding, selling, and caring for the playful pets. Bobbie Jo had made frequent posts on the site—as had Lisa Montgomery, both as herself and as Darlene Fischer—where everyone knew her as the lovable pregnant breeder from Missouri.

"Bobbie Jo was so pleasant and kind," said Dyanne.

Over the past few months, the message board, from Dyanne's point of view, had turned into more of a gossip site than anything productive in terms of rat terrier breeding and selling. Because of that, she said, she backed away from logging on and participating. The tone of the board, Dyanne felt, resembled that of a junior-high hallway in between classes, with people ruminating about life's little challenges and the attitudes of others, instead of supporting the business of rat terrier breeding and selling.

"Whispers, behind-the-back rumors, and cliques." For Dyanne, it just wasn't worth it anymore.

On the morning of December 17, Dyanne decided to log on to Ratter Chatter to see what was happening. She had no idea of Bobbie Jo's death. She was bored, she said, and felt like wasting some time chatting online before she had to go into town and run a few errands.

Part of Dyanne's makeup as a human being included "noticing things," she said. "I was always observant in a detailed way."

The first thing she noticed when she logged on to the site was that everyone was talking about Bobbie Jo's murder. All the Internet news sites were running wall-to-wall coverage, posting updates. It was impossible to log on to an Internet news group and not read something about Bobbie Jo's murder.

On the Ratter Chatter board that morning, all the usual complaining about mundane issues seemed to take a backseat as members shared their feelings about losing Bobbie Jo—"a friend"—in such a violent manner. Some had even turned into would-be cyber sleuths and had begun piecing together the final moments of her life.

Darlene Fischer, of course, became the focus right away; but almost everyone thought Darlene was a real person. Then another theory emerged as Ratter Chatter members began linking Lisa Montgomery to Bobbie Jo. Messages started to focus on the fact that Lisa had been discussing with Bobbie Jo over the past few months how she, like Bobbie Jo, was pregnant and expecting a baby around the same time.

Lisa had frequented several different message boards. Back on October 24, she posted a message, "Time is getting closer to baby time," and twenty-four hours later, "I haven't a single name in mind." In early December, she posted a note explaining how hard it had been for her to take photographs of her terriers and download them onto the board because "I cannot get down on the floor . . ."

Why?

". . . Due to being pregnant. . . ."

On Ratter Chatter Friday morning, when everyone was beginning to understand the connection between Bobbie Jo and Darlene Fischer, one blogger, after going back and rereading postings from the days and weeks prior, wrote, "Darlene Fischer was supposed to meet her [Bobbie Jo] on Thursday."

Was this the last time anyone had heard from Bobbie Jo?

Later, another member would bring a sense of reality to what had happened: "We just saw a murder plan in front of us. . . ."

Lisa, posing as Darlene Fischer, had even sent an instant message to one board member, explaining that she was due to have her baby the same day as Bobbie Jo.

"Now I'm just sick . . . ," the woman posted some time later, after learning the details of the crime.

As Dyanne Siktar sat at her computer and realized there might be a connection between Bobbie Jo's death and Darlene Fischer, instead of posting her feelings on the board, she acted. "I recognized her name immediately," Dyanne recalled, meaning Darlene Fischer. "When I did, my heart started racing."

Dyanne scrolled down the message board list to see if Bobbie Jo had posted any messages on the day she was murdered.

As far as Dyanne could tell, she hadn't.

Next, Dyanne learned Bobbie Jo had posted a message back on Wednesday December 15, the night before she was killed. In that message Bobbie Jo had given directions to her house in Skidmore to Darlene Fischer so Darlene could supposedly look at a few of Bobbie Jo's pups.

Staring at the post again, Dyanne found it odd that Darlene's e-mail address was Fischer4kids. It bothered her. *Fischer4kids?* In view of the details of the crime, the e-mail address seemed creepy.

"Fischer4kids," Dyanne kept repeating to herself. Something in the e-mail address struck her as "weird," she recalled. "And I didn't think about anything else at that moment except calling the FBI."

38

Pastor Mike Wheatley and his wife weren't the only people in Melvern to get a glimpse of the child Lisa and Kevin Montgomery were calling Abigail, on the morning of December 17. After Lisa and Kevin left Pastor Wheatley's, they drove to the Osage County Courthouse in nearby Lyndon, just outside Melvern. Authorities now believe that Lisa was on a mission to prove that she hadn't been lying about being pregnant, and this carefully staged visit to a friend of her mother's was designed specifically for that reason.

In Lisa's mind, some insisted later, presenting the child at the courthouse was a way for her to stuff her successful pregnancy in the faces of Judy Shaughnessy and her ex-husband, Carl Boman. They believed that Lisa knew all she had to do was bring the child into the courthouse, display it in front of a few people, and word would get back to Judy and Carl that she'd had the baby.

Apart from Lisa's kids and Kevin, no one in the family believed Lisa when she said she was pregnant. This trip to the courthouse, Carl Boman said, was Lisa's way of showing them she hadn't been lying. After all, here was the child. Who could question her now?

At about noon, Judy took a ride into downtown Lyndon with one of her daughters, Lisa's half sister, to run a few errands. Judy happened to run into her lawyer in the parking lot of the bank. "Congratulations, Judy," he said.

Judy had no idea what he was talking about.

"On being a grandma. Come on, Judy. You don't know?"

"What are you talking about?"

"Lisa had a baby and was at the courthouse earlier this morning."

Judy paused; then she said, "She either stole it or bought it." She shook her head and walked away.

"I knew she couldn't have kids and she had lied so much . . . ," Judy recalled. To her there was just no way the story held any truth. It had to have a reasonable explanation. Lisa certainly hadn't given birth to the child herself.

After they left the bank, Judy and her daughter drove to the courthouse so Judy could pay her taxes. "Again," Judy said, "another person told me Lisa had a baby girl."

Shortly after Judy got home, she e-mailed her ex-son-in-law, Carl Boman, and told him what had happened earlier.

"Just wondering," she asked Carl, "if she bought it. . . ."

Judy was beyond puzzled. She knew there had to be a rational explanation. Not once did she think Lisa had committed a criminal act; but still, what was going on? She had obviously gotten the child from somewhere.

At the end of her e-mail, Judy made an astute observation: "She'll make us out to be liars one way or another, Carl."

Shocked by the e-mail, Carl wrote back immediately. "Don't let this news bother you at all. We all know that she *was not* pregnant . . . and Kevin knew that, and so do the kids." Carl was baffled by the e-mail and could only draw one conclusion. "Listen, Judy, maybe she adopted the kid? Who knows?" Then came a bit of prophesy on Carl's part: "It might not even be her child, anyway, Judy. She is a *liar*, and we all know that, so it doesn't matter what she says or does. . . . We don't care if she's had a baby of her own, or has bought one from some place. What she does is only a sham and she is false. People will believe what they want to. Don't worry about her. Don't esteem what she says. . . . What she does can only hurt you if you let her bother you. She doesn't worry us at all anymore as we know the truth. . . ."

Carl had always viewed himself as a "Sunday Christian." God was a major part of his life, but he hadn't made church an everyday affair. Some (including Lisa) later called Carl a "fake Christian," but Carl was quick to admit he never claimed to be devout. If that was what people thought of him, who cared? He knew what he believed in his heart and how he presented himself in public.

Still, on that morning, God's word seemed to be infused in a lot of Carl's thoughts about the stresses Lisa had brought into his life recently.

Carl ended the e-mail to Judy with: "We know God, who is the Truth. Let Lisa go and wait for the reaping to start as we *all* reap what we sow in the end. We love you guys and look forward to seeing you over the holiday season. . . . Truth will always win out in the end."

Neither Carl nor Judy had any idea just how close they were to the truth. If there were two people who knew Lisa's history better than most, it was Judy and Carl. They knew she had lied about being pregnant and had tubal ligation surgery in 1990. There was no way the child could be hers—no matter what she was telling people.

Judy wrote back to Carl later that night and observed that Lisa's life, and her many claims of being pregnant, "just continues one thing after another." She then questioned her own feelings for Lisa, saying she really didn't feel "anything" anymore, which made her consider how "heartless" she was for, basically, deserting her own daughter. "All mothers," she continued, "should love their children. . . ." Yet, there was too much baggage between them. It had all built up over the past few years. No one, Judy said later, could reach Lisa anymore. She was in her own world, as if something in her had just snapped.

"I love my daughter and always have, still to this day," recalled Judy. "A mother's love is always there, no matter what. You might not like what your children do or the things they say, but the emotion of your heart tells of the love. I also can hate the things they do and I know that everyone makes mistakes. . . . Unlike a lot of people, I have had to endure a lot of things in my life with my children. We've survived. My love for Lisa will remain in my heart and will always have a place."

From Lyndon, Lisa and Kevin drove to the Whistle Stop Café, on Southwest Main Street, in downtown Melvern. Lisa and Kevin knew many of the people who hung around the café, either personally or by common acquaintance. The Whistle Stop wasn't a place Lisa frequented, but people recognized her. It was pushing noon now. The Whistle Stop seemed like the perfect place to have a bit of lunch and, naturally, show off the newborn, before heading home to give the child a well-deserved nap after another attempt at breast-feeding.

39

On the day following Bobbie Jo's murder, the search for Victoria Jo continued throughout the morning and into early afternoon. In the span of just two minutes, Sheriff Ben Espey pointed out later, the case took a remarkable turn because of two important telephone calls. One of the calls came from Dyanne Siktar in North Carolina.

Throughout her life, Dyanne had been a bit of a whistle-blower. As a young woman, she worked for a large food corporation in Florida. One day, she noticed what she called "shady business" going on at the New York City division of the company in charge of shipping products overseas. "The invoices," recalled Dyanne, "were being typed up under an assumed company name with the same typewriter that the people who worked for [my company] on the same pier used to type up their expense report vouchers."

Dyanne believed the company being billed for services was fictitious: the brainchild and cash cow of someone in the company she worked for. The typewriter made certain letters and numbers almost identically for both companies, which had given it away.

Dyanne called authorities and reported what she had observed. "They sent the auditor up there," Dyanne said, "and he got rear-ended on his way to the pier." It was like a scene from a Hollywood movie, *Silkwood, Norma Rae*.

In the end, "a couple of heads rolled." It was apparent the company had ties to the mob and was skimming money off the books. Dyanne stated, "I didn't think about it—I just called someone and believed I was doing the right thing."

When Dyanne realized she had potential information that

might help find Bobbie Jo's child and killer, she called information and asked for the number of an FBI office in Missouri.

"Which office would you like, ma'am?" the dispatcher asked.

Dyanne said, "I don't care. . . . I don't care."

Time now seemed crucial. As minutes went by, Dyanne became more anxious.

"Any office will do, ma'am. *Please,*" she said during a long pause in the conversation.

The number Dyanne was given turned out to be the FBI's Resident Agency Office in St. Joseph, Missouri. ("Just a lucky break!") Special Agent (SA) Kurt Lipanovich took the call. (Another lucky break.) Lipanovich had been working the case all night long. Ben Espey later praised Lipanovich for his efforts. "Kurt was terrific. A professional all the way."

An agent for fifteen years, Lipanovich handled jobs including "investigating violations of federal criminal law in the seventeen northwest counties of Missouri," which included Skidmore, in Nodaway County.

When Dyanne Siktar got Lipanovich on the phone, she said, "I think I know who was in contact with the victim of that murder case in Skidmore."

Although the Amber Alert had generated scores of tips, nothing had really panned out for Espey and the FBI. They had the name Darlene Fischer an hour or so into the investigation, after one of Espey's men had pulled it from Bobbie Jo's computer, but they had no idea how—or even if—the name was connected to the case, or where Darlene Fischer lived.

Dyanne Siktar was now connecting the two.

Lipanovich was floored by what he was hearing. Here was a "tipster," which this case desperately needed, possibly handing over the murderer.

"The agent, Kurt Lipanovich," recalled Dyanne, "got really excited when I told him what I knew."

"I'll call you right back," said Lipanovich after Dyanne explained how she had logged on to the Ratter Chatter Web site and made the connection between Darlene Fischer and Bobbie Jo.

Moments later, Lipanovich called Dyanne back and asked if she had any more information about the Web site, specifically an

IP (Internet protocol) address. With it, the FBI could find out whose computer the e-mails and instant messages written to Bobbie Jo had been generated from.

"I have to go," Lipanovich said after Dyanne gave him as much information as she could, "but I will call you back when I can."

Meanwhile, in Maryville, Ben Espey was hunkered down in the war room of the Nodaway County Sheriff's Department, going through every lead coming in, assigning different officers their jobs. With his wrinkled shirt and five o'clock shadow now grown out, Espey was feeling the effects of not having slept in some time. Yet, the adrenaline rush of maybe finding Victoria Jo was pumping energy into him. Surprisingly, he felt wide-awake.

At nearly the same time Dyanne Siktar called the FBI, a woman in Georgia (thought to be Auntie Mary) called in a second tip after seeing the Amber Alert and adding it to what she already knew about Lisa Montgomery's newborn. "She said she knew a woman named Lisa Montgomery, who lived in Melvern, Kansas, had been showing off a 'newborn' child earlier that morning, but suspected the she was never pregnant."

With Dyanne Siktar and the woman in Georgia calling in tips within minutes of each other, the only problem became putting the two tips together: one had been phoned into the FBI, the other into the Amber Alert hotline.

Ben Espey never stopped communicating with Zeb Stinnett. Throughout the night, he had given Zeb as many details as he could regarding how the investigation was unfolding, without giving him false hope or "insider" information he didn't need to know. Now, with these two new leads, Espey was more confident he was going to be able to fulfill a promise he'd already made of getting Victoria Jo back to Zeb.

Espey had set Bobbie Jo's family up with a press spokesperson he knew could field questions and keep media away from the family. Dan Madden, a "super guy," Espey noted, recently had been appointed director of communications for the Conception Abbey Development Office, in Conception, Missouri, seventeen miles from Maryville on Route 136. The Conception Abbey was many things to the community of West Missouri. According to its statement, the Conception Abbey was there to "praise God and become more Christ-like through a common life as given in the Rule of St. Benedict."

There was a bit of history between Espey and the Conception Abbey. Back on June 10, 2002, a gunman—a former postal worker— entered the abbey and went on an "eight-minute rampage," wounding Father Kenneth and Father Norbert and murdering Father Philip Schuster and Brother Damian Larson before taking his own life. Espey, along with one MSHP trooper and two of his deputies, were the first officers to respond to the scene. Their actions helped save Father Norbert's and Father Kenneth's lives.

On December 17, Dan Madden showed up at Espey's office and offered himself to the Stinnett situation, saying he had seen the news and decided to make himself available to help in any way he could. Espey knew Madden could be an asset to the Stinnett family and Becky Harper, who were being hounded by the media.

After introducing Madden to Zeb and Becky Harper, Espey walked over to Zeb. He didn't know what to say. Leads were coming in. The investigation had taken a promising turn. But who knew what would come of it all? The last thing Espey wanted to do was make a promise he couldn't keep. But still, he felt something. Espey couldn't explain it. He just knew Victoria Jo was okay and they were going to find her soon.

Turning, looking at Zeb, he introduced Dan Madden and then said, "I won't sleep until I find your baby, Zeb."

40

L ocated in the center of town, across the street from the park, the Whistle Stop Café, with its Native American storefront design of red-and-white-brick diamond shapes over a canopy of asphalt shingles, served up ham and eggs, steaks, coffee, beer, meat loaf and potatoes. With a soda machine standing guard out front the Whistle Stop had always been one of those hometown diners many residents in Melvern made a routine part of their day.

Kathy Sage owned the Whistle Stop and worked hard to serve home-cooked meals to the tough men who worked with their hands (and there were plenty of these rugged men in Melvern), "sunup to sundown." Because the café had a television set on most of the day and night, patrons had seen reports of the murder in Skidmore and the abduction of Bobbie Jo's child.

Inside the Whistle Stop, men sat at booths and on stools, wearing farmer jeans and John Deere caps, killing time and swapping stories. To owner Kathy Sage and those who hung around the Whistle Stop on that Friday, exactly one week before Christmas, it was just another mundane day in the heartland. Talk centered on the murder in Skidmore, but also on politics, religion, the economy, and sports, just as it did in thousands of communities throughout the Midwest. Crop prices were down, inflation rising through the roof. Heating oil was going to be more expensive as the winter progressed.

The Whistle Stop door creaked as Lisa and Kevin walked into the diner. Victoria Jo was sitting comfortably in a portable car seat Lisa was toting her around in, not making much noise.

A few customers turned and looked as Kevin and Lisa entered. "Hey," someone said, with a nod and two-finger salute.

Sitting down at a booth, Kevin and Lisa reportedly ordered eggs, bacon, and hash browns, while the baby sat in her seat on the floor nearby. A few customers walked over to the table and marveled at the child. *How cute. . . . She's beautiful. . . . How old?*

Lisa smiled. "Pick her up if you like. Go ahead."

While Lisa and Kevin ate, a patron took the baby around the restaurant and showed her to some of the other customers.

As the child was passed around the restaurant, Kathy Sage walked over to Lisa and Kevin's table and asked Lisa how old the baby was. She thought the infant looked awfully young to be out and about.

"Yeah, she's only a day old," Lisa said. She seemed excited.

"We didn't know you were expecting, Lisa," said one woman.

"Most people didn't," said Lisa.

Listening to this made Sage, who recalled the story later to reporters, "irate." She was disturbed because Lisa and Kevin had shown up with the child to begin with. "You don't bring a newborn out in public."

The child was, by Lisa's own account, a day old, and she and Kevin were passing her around the restaurant like some sort of family photograph, while filling their faces as if it were just any other ordinary day.

"You hear about this stuff happening in Los Angeles or New York City," Kathy Sage stated after she learned the truth. "But not here. Not home."

41

With Dyanne Siktar's tip, Ben Espey and the FBI now had a tangible piece of the puzzle they could work with. Dyanne had provided SA Lipanovich with the IP address from Darlene Fischer's computer. Essentially, the FBI had a computer fingerprint, which could lead them to the home address where the electronic messages between Darlene and Bobbie Jo had originated. Having it was not only a break in the investigation, but a possible lifesaver for Victoria Jo.

FBI SA Mickey Roberts, who had arrived in Maryville and begun working the case with Espey, was running down leads he had obtained from field agents in Missouri and Kansas before Dyanne Siktar came forward with her tip. Since Dyanne had called into the FBI, several other Ratter Chatter members had also phoned in information. Hearing the same thing from several different sources, the FBI knew, meant the information carried a considerable amount of weight. For Mickey Roberts, though, all he had at this point was what Ben Espey had given him, along with what those FBI field agents were reporting: a woman who was eight months pregnant with a female "fetus" had been "strangled in her home, her abdomen . . . cut open and the fetus removed. The victim . . . found with blond hair clenched in her hands; the victim does not have blond hair."

After SA Lipanovich became involved, he was briefed by Ben Espey about the case. According to an affidavit prepared later by the FBI, Espey told Lipanovich everything his office knew as it came in. Dave Merrill, a MSHP trooper, had processed the crime scene and found the computer in which Bobbie Jo "had been active on the Internet in connection with her dog-breeding business."

This was an important find now because Dyanne had come forward with information that Bobbie Jo was, right up until those final hours before her death, communicating online with someone by the name of Darlene Fischer. Everything, it seemed, was beginning to fall together. This was how cases got solved. Dyanne's phone call, on top of the Amber Alert tip supposedly called in by Auntie Mary, had opened up an entire new vein of the investigation.

But where did Lisa Montgomery fit into it all? As the morning of December 17 turned into afternoon, she was still a part of the puzzle law enforcement hadn't put together.

The new tips provided hope, a shot in the arm that these tired lawmen needed to keep them focused. Most everyone involved in the case had been awake now well over twenty-four hours. Where was the child? Time was an issue now more than ever. If the child was still alive, was she being fed properly? Cared for? Had she been injured during her violent delivery? What would happen when they finally located the child and her abductor? Would there be some sort of showdown?

42

Throughout the early-morning hours of December 17, several law enforcement agencies worked in unison to find Darlene Fischer. Based on Darlene's final e-mail to Bobbie Jo (and Bobbie Jo's response), law enforcement agents were convinced she was the last person to have seen Bobbie Jo alive. Becky Harper had even told Ben Espey not long after he arrived at the crime scene "someone named Darlene Fischer" had made plans with Bobbie Jo to look at a few puppies. Even if Darlene Fischer wasn't responsible for the crime, there was a good chance she could help the investigation move in the right direction.

But where was she?

After the MSHP's Dave Merrill processed the crime scene in Skidmore, it was handed over to the evidence response team from the St. Joseph (Missouri) Police Department for further study. Detective Curt Howard, a forensic computer examiner, spent some time with Bobbie Jo's computer and found several interesting items that, coupled with the information Dyanne Siktar had recently given to SA Lipanovich, began telling a story of Bobbie Jo's final moments.

Among the things Detective Howard found were message board chats from several people who had been communicating with Bobbie Jo. One Hotmail user, Jason Dawson, a fellow rat terrier breeder from the same Ratter Chatter site, had spoken to Bobbie Jo online through her Happy Haven Farms Internet account.

It was an important discovery, but the identity of the actual person behind Fischer4kids at Hotmail was still unknown. What was obvious, though, according to the information Howard uncovered, was that Darlene Fischer had been interested in looking at a few of Bobbie Jo's dogs, which confirmed Becky Harper's lead. Darlene claimed she lived in Fairfax, Missouri, and it was established she had, at some point, asked Bobbie Jo for directions to her house in Skidmore, which Bobbie Jo provided.

For thirty-three-year-old Jeff Owen, a forensic examiner with the Kansas City Regional Computer Forensic Laboratory (RCFL) and an MSHP trooper, at present assigned to the Division of Drug and Crime Control (Criminal Investigations Division), the Christmas season wasn't about eggnog, tinsel, and parties. Jeff had been going through a rough time of late. He and his wife of many years were in the process of a divorce and Jeff was missing his kids, ages one and three, something bad. To make matters worse, Jeff's stepsister, with whom he had grown up, had been murdered a few years back during the Christmas holiday season. One of the only highlights of Jeff's day lately was waking up and going to work, where he could lose himself and focus on helping people.

"It was comforting for me to have a simple, small role in helping solve this horrible, heinous crime," recalled Jeff. "It was tremendously gratifying to me as a person and cop."

MSHP colleague Dave Merrill had called Jeff the previous night and briefed him about Bobbie Jo's computer ("They had really hit a brick wall . . .")—but Jeff had his kids; he couldn't just drop everything, as he had been accustomed to doing while married, and run right in. ("I'm a single father. What could I do?")

But first thing the following morning, he drove to the lab, preparing to lose himself in Bobbie Jo's computer and see what he could find.

After Jeff checked in, he spoke to Detective Howard, who explained the chats Bobbie Jo had with Darlene Fischer and Bobbie Jo's online activity.

"We have her computer here," said Howard.

"Thanks. I'll be up as soon as I can to get it," said Jeff.

When he returned, Jeff sat in the lab and started going through Bobbie Jo's computer. Almost immediately, he realized Darlene Fischer didn't live in Fairfax, Missouri, as she had told Bobbie Jo and, for the most part, law enforcement still believed. The IP address she had been using, Jeff could tell by looking through the cached files Bobbie Jo unknowingly left behind, had originated in Kansas somewhere.

"We believed," remembered Jeff, "as a group, Fairfax was not accurate. . . . We assumed it was a pseudonym and fake address, but at that point, had no idea where it was from."

At his disposal, Jeff had specialized software allowing him to peer inside Bobbie Jo's computer for deleted files, and files Bobbie Jo didn't even realize she had on her hard drive, without damaging the computer or overwriting files.

Figuring Darlene Fischer was likely a ruse, Jeff dug further and found out Bobbie Jo had been online for much of the day she was murdered—shopping on eBay, browsing for Christmas presents on other sites, looking at items for the baby and the house—but there was a break in her activity shortly before Becky Harper dialed 911.

"She was extremely active," said Owen to a colleague, looking through Bobbie Jo's history online. "But there's a period here where she disappears from the computer and never returns."

"That's probably where our suspect entered the scene."

As the morning progressed, another important element of Jeff's work included "imaging" each file he viewed. If a suspect was caught and the case went to trial, the prosecution would need evidence. In a sense, Jeff was investigating the case in real time, but also preserving evidence as he went along, copying the files he was looking at.

At some point that afternoon, SA Kurt Lipanovich called. Kurt and Jeff had known each other for years and worked on several big cases together. A large man at about six feet two inches, two hundred pounds, Lipanovich was in excellent physical shape, more muscle than flab. Being a member of the FBI's SWAT team, Lipanovich had a larger-than-life presence about him; he looked like a tough cop. Yet, he had no trouble sharing his rather "dry sense of humor" with fellow agents and lawmen, and then, quite quickly, falling into seriousness when the situation called for it.

"Jeff, we got this tip from some woman in North Carolina," said Lipanovich over the phone.

"What is it?"

"Some sort of message board: Annie's Rat Terrier Rest Area."

"Great."

"Can you check it out?"

"Of course."

"When you go through her browser history," Lipanovich added, "see if Darlene Fischer visited that site, too."

"Got it."

Within an hour after Jeff found those pages where Bobbie Jo and Darlene were logged on to Annie's Rat Terrier Rest Area and communicating with each other, he had all of their online discussions staring him in the face.

Even better: on every post, at the bottom of the screen, was the IP address of each user.

As soon as he had the IP address Bobbie Jo had been communicating with, Jeff ran a check under the Patriot Act on public available databases and—lo and behold—came up with a server, as well as the company maintaining it.

"I have that information, Kurt," said Jeff after calling Lipanovich back. There was enthusiasm in his voice. It was the first major breakthrough in the case. They were onto something big; both could sense the momentum.

Even so, the computer forensic work was still somewhat of a side show to the traditional gumshoe investigation Ben Espey and his crew were doggedly pursuing. The St. Joseph PD had recovered the e-mail addresses from the chats between Bobbie Jo and Darlene Fischer the previous night, but the follow up with Microsoft, according to Jeff, had not been done to secure IP information. So, in effect, "the digital evidence was known," but the additional steps needed to find out who Darlene Fischer was had not yet been done.

Known as the Heart of America Regional Computer Forensic Laboratory in Kansas City (HARCFL), the lab Jeff Owen worked out of "accepts requests for computer forensics services from any law enforcement [agency]" within its service area, which comprises counties encompassing the entire state of Kansas and two-thirds of Western Missouri. The HARCFL also takes on cases from local police departments and the FBI. The goal of the RCFL (which has labs all across America) is to be a "one-stop, full-service forensics laboratory devoted entirely to the examination of digital evidence in support of criminal investigations."

It's a simple concept. The lab, a "one-stop shop" devoted to computer forensic work, can get a lot more done in a day than other agencies involved in different aspects of a case. Much of the RCFL's time is dedicated, "but not limited, to terrorism, child pornography, crimes of violence, theft or destruction of intellectual property, Internet crimes, and fraud."

One of HARCFL's most recent accomplishments was the work the lab did in a serial killer case of high notoriety, which went unsolved for decades: the arrest of Dennis Rader, who admitted to being the BTK killer. Five computer forensic examiners from HARCFL traveled to Wichita, Kansas, where they "assisted the Computer Unit of the Wichita, Kansas, Police Department by imaging numerous computers using the most advanced forensics equipment available." As a result, they were able to obtain digital evidence that, "when analyzed, was instrumental in the investigation and ongoing prosecution" of Rader.

These men and women spend hours doing tedious computer work. But for RCFL examiners like Jeff Owen, their work is a vocation that can solve an otherwise impenetrable case.

"It's very rewarding," said Jeff. "What's great is, everyone here works for a different agency, but we work whatever case needs [to be] done. It is one of the rare examples of true cooperation in law enforcement."

A father of three and dedicated husband, James Domres had been involved in computer forensics for the New York State Attorney General since before the Internet became a staple in millions of American households. Domres, a member of the Western New York RCFL Executive Board since its inception, had been an asset in cases ranging from prosecuting members of al-Qaeda to an undercover operation exposing date rape drug sales over the Internet. His accomplishments have resulted in over one hundred arrests, capped off by an international investigation of forged identities, which led to the arrest of a man who had counterfeited hundreds of driver's licenses, including one with a photograph of Khalid Sheikh Mohammed, a major al-Qaeda operative and suspected national terrorist.

In the field of law enforcement computer work, James Domres, Jeff Owen, and their colleagues all over the world are considered masters of their craft. It takes tremendous discipline to solve a crime by sitting in an office searching through the bowels of a box of plastic, wires, and circuit boards. But most agents love it.

It would be safe to say James Domres is one of a handful of individuals in the United States who know more about the underlining operational procedures of the RCFL than most.

The RCFL, Domres said, had been one of the best tools to come around in decades, aiding in several different types of investigations. He noted that computer crimes weren't necessarily the only ones the RCFL could help local and federal law enforcement agencies with. Blackberries, iPods, and cell phones also leave strands of digital "DNA" evidence everywhere they go.

"You see, before RCFL came about," said Domres, "you had investigators doing both: forensics and computer investigations. We saw the need, to have labs where people did nothing but computer forensics—something that could support local agencies."

For Bobbie Jo Stinnett's newborn child, possibly still alive, and her husband, who had lost a wife but still hoped he would be united with his daughter, the work Jeff Owen was doing was perhaps the most important job anyone had been given in the investigation thus far. It was up to the RCFL now to find out who Darlene Fischer was—and the residential address from which she had logged on to her computer.

Jeff Owen traced Darlene Fischer's IP address back to Qwest Communications. He phoned SA Lipanovich with the news. "I got it for you, Kurt."

"You do? What is it?"

With the phone cradled between his shoulder and ear, Jeff read the IP address straight from the Internet message board, which he had logged on to "live" on one computer at his workstation. He swung around in his chair and checked it with the IP on Bobbie Jo's computer, which he had sitting on another desk. "It's a company out of Virginia, Qwest Communications."

"That's great!"

"Here, let me give you their number. This is what you need to tell them. . . ." Jeff explained what Lipanovich needed to say once he got Qwest on the phone.

"Great work, Jeff!" Lipanovich roared.

"Kurt, you must understand," said Jeff before they hung up, "what we have is the cyber equivalent to a return address on a letter from the *suspect*. The Internet service provider should be able to pinpoint exactly what address it went to—where the suspect lives."

43

Special Agent Lipanovich called Qwest and spoke to Melissa Erwin, a senior security specialist.

"Yes," Erwin explained to Lipanovich, "that IP address is assigned to us. Let me see what I can do to find out where it originates."

Qwest, an Internet Service Provider (ISP), had nothing to do with Darlene Fischer, other than providing her, like millions of other computer users, with access to an Internet server.

"Thanks," said Lipanovich. "Make it quick, though. We're fighting against time here."

Soon, Erwin called Lipanovich back. As luck would have it, he had Jeff Owen on another line. "Jeff, hold on, that's Qwest calling back."

Erwin said she needed more information.

Lipanovich asked Jeff, "Can you verify exactly when Stinnett and Darlene Fischer chatted?"

"Yup, hold on." Jeff gave Lipanovich the actual times.

"We're going to get an actual physical address, Jeff," said Lipanovich.

"I told you."

"Based on the usage of that IP address," Erwin said a minute later, "on December 15, 2004, I was able to determine through a reverse domain name system search that the server being used was located in Topeka, Kansas."

Topeka made sense. It was in the region where Bobbie Jo had been murdered. "There's more," added Erwin. "By reviewing our Internet connection logs, I was able to determine that the IP address used on December 15, 2004, between those times we discussed, was assigned to 'kelimont at Earthlink dot net.'"

Furthermore, it was a dial-up connection, as opposed to a cable modem, making it easy to trace.

"Go on," said Lipanovich. Everything was at last coming together.

Erwin said, "I even did a reverse Internet search for the phone number and found that the number is being billed to a guy by the name of Kevin Montgomery. He lives on Adams Road in Melvern, Kansas."

And there it was: *Kevin Montgomery. Melvern, Kansas.*

While Jeff Owen continued to gather evidence on Bobbie Jo's computer, SA Lipanovich had a solid lead from Qwest Communications: a name and address of a male who was apparently the last person to communicate with Bobbie Jo online.

Within a few hours after receiving the lead, Lipanovich found out Kevin Montgomery had three kids of his own. He had been married to thirty-six-year-old Lisa Montgomery for four years. Recently they had been celebrating because Lisa was in the last trimester of her pregnancy, and she and Kevin were preparing for the arrival of a new baby. That Kelimont e-mail address had been set up by Lisa, using an acronym: "Ke" stood for Kevin; "li" for Lisa; whereas "mont" referred to their last name, Montgomery.

Lipanovich now had a name and, even better, an address in Melvern, Kansas.

44

Sitting at his desk, Sheriff Ben Espey was preparing to brief the press when he heard about the latest break.

SA Kurt Lipanovich had been working closely with Espey throughout the morning and into the afternoon. Espey liked Lipanovich, respected his work ethic and resolve to find the child. Now, with a team of federal agents heading to Melvern to find out if Kevin Montgomery had anything to do with the case, it seemed the situation was out of Lipanovich's and Espey's hands.

Espey had a gut feeling going into the early afternoon they would locate the child in Melvern. The tipster from Georgia, who had called in Lisa Montgomery's name, had solidified the connection, at least for him. Coupled with what he had heard from the FBI, Espey knew where the child was—there was no doubt about it.

"The baby was in Melvern, Kansas," Espey said later. "As soon as I realized that, I sent my own men there to get her, whether the FBI would welcome them or not. It was about the child for me. My men were going to Melvern with one purpose: finding Victoria Jo. And the FBI wasn't going to do anything to stop them from doing their jobs."

The race was on.

45

FBI agents converged on Melvern and set up a surveillance around Lisa and Kevin Montgomery's home during the afternoon of December 17.

As it happened, two additional agents headed to the west end of town on an entirely separate mission.

With fewer than one hundred students enrolled during any given year, Melvern's Marais des Cygnes Valley (High) School would be considered a foreign educational environment to most kids from larger cities and towns across America. In contrast to the overflowing classrooms more common elsewhere, ten students per classroom might be considered a lot in towns like Melvern and Skidmore.

"School was very personal," commented one former Marais des Cygnes Valley student. "If something happened on one end of the hall, it would be at the other end of the hall within five minutes. Everyone knew *everything* about everyone. And there was a *lot* of one-on-one time between teachers and students. Come to think of it, the teachers probably even knew our middle names."

Lisa's children loved the intimacy of growing up in small-town America. Having an education system in place considered by many to be first-rate, and extremely personal, was an added bonus.

During the latter part of the morning, Ryan, Alicia, and Rebecca were going about the daily routine at Marais des Cygnes Valley as if it were just another school day. The only difference in their lives was that they had a new baby sister at home waiting for them when they got out of class.

Two FBI agents showed up at Kevin Montgomery's parents' house across town to discuss the best possible way to pull the kids out of class without making a scene. The FBI explained to Mr. and Mrs. Montgomery that they needed to question the children about Lisa and Kevin.

"It involves a kidnapping."

Undoubtedly shocked by this, Kevin's mother agreed to pick the kids up at school and bring them back to the house.

"Great," said one agent, "just don't tell them what's going on."

Burrowed in the brush behind the barn in back of the farmhouse and around the cornfields corralling the land near Lisa and Kevin's house, several FBI agents were looking for any sign of a red car or newborn baby.

As of early afternoon, no one seemed to be home.

From his office in Maryville, Espey heard the FBI was planning on staking out the house for twenty-four hours, in order to watch Lisa and Kevin's movements. The FBI wasn't sure if they were dealing with a "drug house," or if Kevin and Lisa were operating some sort of black-market baby factory, Espey explained.

When Espey confirmed how the FBI was handling the situation, he called in Randy Strong and Don Fritz, two investigators—"the best in the state"—with Missouri's Initial Response Team. Randy Strong worked for Maryville Public Safety as one of its chief investigators. A man with an intense dedication to law enforcement, Strong understood that Espey's main concern was for the child.

"Get in a car and get to Melvern as fast as you can," Espey told Strong and Fritz. He was frustrated over the FBI's desire not to move in right away and get the child to a hospital.

"Sure, Sheriff," said Strong. "We're on our way."

"Just get into that house and get that baby. Drive through anybody that gets in your way."

Based on a piece of "solid" information Espey had uncovered himself, he believed the FBI was planning not to let any of his men go near the Melvern house, where they suspected Lisa and Kevin and the baby were going to show up anytime.

Espey was firm in his conviction. "Drive onto that property. Knock on the front door. Walk in. And get that child."

At twelve by twelve feet, Espey's office inside the Nodaway County Sheriff's Department was as cramped as a jail cell. Espey didn't use a computer. He had a few awards and commendations tacked to the cinder block concrete walls around him, but spent as little time as possible inside the confining room. His job, he maintained, was out in the field. He usually showed up at the office by 8:00 and was on the road by 9:00 A.M. He had no use for sitting behind a desk, pushing a pencil, staring at police reports and rap sheets. His heart was in working the streets. The FBI wasn't going to walk into Espey's county and take control at the last minute. He had made promises to Bobbie Jo's family and told Zeb he'd bring his child back home. Regardless of the fallout later on, no one was going to stop him from attempting to make good on those promises.

Would Strong and Fritz make it to Melvern in time? Espey had overheard an agent working out of his office tell another field agent that they were taking over the investigation now that they had solid information as to the whereabouts of the person responsible for sending the last e-mail to Bobbie Jo.

"We're not going to rush this deal," Espey heard the agent say over the radio. "We're going to do the stakeout. And we're going to sit on it for a day or two."

This comment, specifically, upset Espey, who had been told repeatedly by doctors he had to get the child to a hospital as soon as possible after locating her.

"I represent the community in northern Missouri," said Espey. "That's why it was so upsetting to me."

Espey faced one other major problem: the Kansas FBI regional office called to tell him he didn't have jurisdiction in Melvern, Kansas.

"That's right, I don't," Espey told himself. "But it's my case."

He hung up the phone.

Espey radioed Randy Strong and Don Fritz as they headed down Highway 71 toward Kansas, reaffirming his position: "You drive through whatever barricade you have to in order to get that child back. Don't worry about the FBI. I'll handle them."

46

A quick background check told the FBI neither Kevin nor Lisa had any prior arrests or convictions. Both were clean, as far as the law was concerned. Maybe there wouldn't be any resistance. Perhaps it would all go smoothly.

Still, why would a married couple with seven kids of their own between them murder a young expecting mother and cut her child from her womb? If, in fact, Kevin and Lisa were responsible, something was wrong with the entire scenario. As much as all the evidence seemed to point to them, there was a missing link. How did Kevin Montgomery fit into the picture? Had he helped Lisa? A few tips Ben Espey received the previous night made him consider the child might have been taken for resale on the black market. Detectives were still working on one of those leads. Were more people involved? Had Lisa and Kevin gone off to sell the child?

The Melvern house Kevin and Lisa called home was a two-story white farmhouse set back from a gravel road about fifty yards. Surrounded by hundreds of acres of farmland, a muddy driveway led up to the door the family used on the side of the house. Another door faced the road, but nobody entered through it. Down the street, the closest neighbor was a good half-mile away. Lisa's goats were out back. Her dogs were barking.

The setting seemed perfect from the FBI's standpoint. It was rural. Very few civilians were around. The G-men found plenty of places for agents to hide with no chance of Kevin or Lisa spotting any of them.

The house had five bedrooms, one master bathroom, a living room, and a dining room and kitchen, where everyone congregated during the evening. In the large cellar downstairs, Lisa kept the canned goods she demanded the kids jar up every fall. From the outside, it looked like a house filled with good wholesome family farm living. But the atmosphere inside on most nights, at least according to one of the children, wasn't as relaxed as it might have appeared.

"When my mom was home, she was normally on the computer. She was kind of quiet, but when she was mad, she would yell and make everyone's day miserable. Sometimes, though, she was in a really good mood. Like when we were canning, or doing something with the garden, or the animals, or stuff like that. But when she got mad, I always tried to avoid her (which was hard sometimes). She would threaten to leave Kevin, or she would get all mad at us for one thing or another (like if we were supposed to be cleaning and we didn't, or we ate dinner an hour ago and the dishes still weren't done). I remember sometimes it would be like nine or ten o'clock at night when we finished eating dinner, and we would have to stay up to do the dishes no matter how tired we were."

Now there were scores of FBI agents camped out around the house, with binoculars and high-tech gadgets, waiting for Lisa and Kevin to arrive—and two rather committed investigators from Ben Espey's county racing toward town, preparing to drive through the FBI's surveillance and find out for themselves if Lisa and Kevin had Bobbie Jo's child.

47

Kevin Montgomery's mother walked into the office of Marais des Cygnes Valley (High) School and explained to the principal that Lisa's three children had to be taken out of class.

"It's an emergency. We need to get them home right away."

All three kids were summoned to the office. They had no idea what was going on.

"You need to get your stuff," Kevin's mother said, "and come home with me now. Something's happened. Hurry."

Rebecca had driven her own car to school. She told Mrs. Montgomery she'd drive her brother and sister to their grandparents' house and meet her there.

Back at the house ten minutes later, the FBI separated the children and began asking questions.

"When we got home," one of the children said, "at first we thought [the FBI] were lawyers."

Must have been the way they were dressed.

Throughout the entire time the children were questioned, the reason why never came up. The kids were forced to wonder what was going on as the FBI shot one question after another at them, yet failed to explain the reason why they were probing into what had been, up until that point, a rather ordinary life in the middle of nowhere.

"You can't tell anybody about this," said one agent to Rebecca. Largely, the questioning was framed around what Kevin had been doing over the past twenty-four hours. Why wasn't the man at work? Why had he taken the day off? Where was he now? Then, "Tell me about the baby. Did the child have any scratches on her? Do you have any pictures of her?"

"I don't know," answered Rebecca, overwhelmed by being put on the spot.

"Did your mom and Kevin have any problems?"

"Normal marital things, I guess. I don't know. I don't know."

The FBI wasn't being pushy, the kids later agreed. ("They were very nice. They weren't mean or anything. They just wanted answers.")

After Rebecca was questioned, Ryan was pulled into the same room and Rebecca was asked to leave.

"Are your mom and Kevin happy?" asked one of the agents.

"Yeah, I guess."

"How was the atmosphere at the house most of the time?"

"Fine."

"What was your mom like the past few weeks?"

Ryan was "clueless," he said, as to what was going on. Where Rebecca began questioning things in her mind, Ryan still didn't have any idea what to think. He had spent last night with his new baby sister. He was happy for Mom and Kevin. What was the problem?

"Everything was okay last night?" pressed an agent.

"Okay, let's . . . ," Ryan said, and then hesitated. He had a question of his own he needed to ask. "Is this about my mom and Kevin splitting up?"

The agents looked at each other. They had to feel sorry for the kid. Here he was thinking the FBI had pulled him out of school to tell him his mother and stepfather were separating.

"Listen," one of the agents said, "your mom is one of two suspects in a kidnapping case we're working on."

Ryan was stunned. His heart raced. ("I was one of the first to see the baby, and I thought it was ours.")

Both Ryan and Rebecca agreed that talking bad about Kevin just wouldn't be right. Kevin had his hang-ups, but he "wasn't a bad person." He was quiet and reserved, sure, but he never raised his voice or hand to Lisa or the kids. And he supported them, unlike Lisa, in nearly everything they did. ("Kevin was at every single one of the games I cheered for," recalled Rebecca. "My mom never came.")

"He was," Kayla Boman added at a later date, "a really nice guy, and a great stepfather." In no way, she added, was he mean.

And, while he "occasionally drank a beer," he was "definitely *not* a drinker."

Kayla said the one thing about Kevin all the kids stood behind was that, "he loved my mom with all his heart . . . and would do—and still will—anything for us. He loves us almost as much as he loves his three boys."

Most of the reservations the children, especially Kayla, had were centered around Lisa, particularly her frequent statements to people around town that she was pregnant. During the past few weeks, however, Lisa's claims of being pregnant started falling apart. Although she had moved to Georgia weeks ago, Kayla still kept tabs on things back home. Like any kid her age, she made instant messaging and e-mail part of her daily life. Lisa wasn't calling her or writing, so Kayla kept up to date with everyone by phone and the Internet.

"Did I have questions?" Kayla asked herself later. "Yes. Did I doubt at times that my mom was pregnant? Yes!"

"It all seemed a little weird to me, but I guess it was 'cause I had a 'bad feeling,' which normally I do when something bad happens, or something is wrong . . . like a gut feeling, I guess you could say."

From the FBI's perspective, it was beginning to look more like Kevin was involved on some level. How could he *not* be? His phone line had been used to communicate with Bobbie Jo. The feds even had an e-mail in their possession fully explaining how "Darlene Fischer" had made plans to meet with Bobbie Jo. Anyone, at this point, could be Darlene Fischer: Kevin, Lisa, even one of the kids.

When the two agents finished questioning the kids, they left the Montgomery house without mentioning a word of their next move. If the kids were confused before they were questioned, now they had no idea what was going on. Like most kids, they weren't newshounds; they had no idea that a young woman had been murdered in Skidmore and a massive search was under way for a child someone had cut from her womb. Why so many questions about the previous day? Mom had given birth yesterday.

What could the simple birth of a child have to do with anything of a criminal nature?

48

During Friday afternoon, December 17, while the kids were at the Montgomery house talking with the FBI, SA Mike Miller, watching from a foxhole somewhere around Kevin and Lisa's Adams Road house, spotted a "dirty red Toyota Corolla, bearing a Kansas license plate . . . pull up in front of the residence."

It was the infamous "red car" every law enforcement agency in the Midwest had been looking for, only there was no *H* on the hood, contrary to what a witness had told Ben Espey the previous day.

After Lisa and Kevin got out of the car, Lisa walked around to the back of the vehicle and took the child out of her car seat.

The FBI agents didn't move. They watched as Lisa and Kevin took their time entering the house through the side porch door, where an old refrigerator and washing machine sat rusting on top of rain-soaked, rotting pine planks.

Within minutes, Lisa and Kevin were inside the house with the child.

Soon after, Randy Strong and Don Fritz arrived on the scene, pulled into the driveway, and parked in back of Kevin's pickup. They met no opposition from the FBI agents, who were still in position around the property, likely wondering what was going on.

Fritz called Espey from his cell phone: "We're here, Ben. As soon as we know something, we'll call you back. We're shutting down our cell phones now."

"Good luck . . . let me know as soon as you do."

"All right. Here we go."

Meanwhile, Espey heard a rumor that the press had figured

out what was unfolding in Melvern. A few helicopters were hovering over Lisa and Kevin's house, filming and circling it.

When he confirmed the report, Espey's concern for the child grew.

"Someone had already killed the mother of the child—we knew that," said Espey. "What if they came out of the house and saw the helicopters? There was a real good chance, I believed, they could dispose of the baby."

Randy Strong jumped out of the car first and walked up to the door. Composed and collected, he knocked.

Kevin answered. "Yeah?"

"I'm a special investigator from Missouri," said Strong. "My partner is with me. Can we come in?"

"Sure," Kevin answered, opening the door. He seemed a bit frazzled but completely forthcoming and cooperative.

As Fritz and Strong walked in, they spied Lisa sitting in the living room holding the baby; she was watching television. Oddly enough, the Amber Alert, Strong noticed, was scrolling across the bottom of the television screen as he walked up to Lisa and asked her to hand the child to him.

"Why? What's going on?" Lisa wanted to know.

As that happened, the FBI started coming out of hiding and pulling into the driveway.

Randy Strong took the child from Lisa and ran outside with her, handing her off to an agent, saying, "Take the child to the hospital—*now*."

"It all worked out," Espey said, "because we went out of our jurisdiction and took control."

Immediately Lisa and Kevin were separated.

"Kevin Montgomery advised," FBI SA Craig Arnold wrote in his report, "that yesterday, December 16, 2004, he arrived home from work at about five-fifteen P.M."

"She called me and told me she went into labor and delivered a baby," a thunderstruck Kevin Montgomery explained to two FBI agents asking him questions. "What's going on?"

"Where?"

"Well, in Topeka. So me and the kids, we, we . . . got into my pickup truck and drove to Long John Silver's, where she said she was."

"What happened then?"

"We picked her up and drove back home. What's this? What's happening?"

Uncertainty had settled upon Kevin. *The FBI?* Nothing was making sense.

As Lisa stood in the living room, a startled look on her face, Randy Strong walked over to her. It wasn't hard to put two and two together: Lisa had streaks of blond in her hair, there was a "dirty red car" in the driveway, and she'd had in her possession a baby who was, as far as anyone could tell, a day, maybe two days old. How many other suspects did they have, or sightings for that matter, matching up so perfectly? Strong asked her about the baby.

"I've been pregnant and delivered the child yesterday," stated Lisa.

She certainly didn't look like she'd just given birth. Where was the extra weight? Could she produce any records from the hospital? Maybe an identity bracelet most hospitals put on mother and child?

"Where?" asked one agent.

"At the Birth and Women's Center in Topeka. What's the problem here? I don't understand. . . ."

As Lisa continued, Strong asked her more detailed questions. It was the beginning of what would amount to a four-hour interrogation by Strong, who, Espey said, "is one of the best interrogators the state of Missouri has."

Regardless of what Lisa and Kevin were saying, most everyone involved in the arrest had a quick moment of triumph.

"I wasn't there physically," one FBI agent said later on television, "but the agents and police officers who were there told me they were absolutely ecstatic. All you had in this case was the fact that you had a dead woman; you had the idea that this person, the suspect, had blond hair and was driving a red car. And that's all you had."

Espey heard about it immediately. "I was thrilled, but more than anything worried about the child's welfare and getting her to a hospital. I knew with Randy on the case that he would break the suspect. I wanted that child to be evaluated immediately so she could be united with Zeb."

As Strong kept questioning Lisa, it didn't take long before she cracked. After one FBI agent read Lisa her constitutional right to remain silent, she started crying.

"Is there something you want to tell us, Mrs. Montgomery?" asked Strong. He looked down and saw "numerous cuts on her fingers." Later, it would be confirmed that the presence of Bobbie Jo's DNA was found underneath Lisa's fingernails on her left hand.

With that, FBI SA Craig Arnold wrote later, "Lisa Montgomery . . . confessed to having strangled Stinnett and removing the fetus . . . [and] further admitted the baby she had was Stinnett's. . . . ."

But it was Strong, Espey insisted, who had taken Lisa's full confession.

"I lied to my husband about giving birth to a child," Lisa said at one point.

"Where did you go after you left Skidmore?" Strong asked after Lisa admitted strangling Bobbie Jo and cutting the child from her womb.

"I . . . I drove west," Lisa said. "Yeah, west. And I stopped. I stopped about seven miles out of Skidmore and pulled over and cleaned up the baby."

"Take it easy," Strong advised. "It's okay."

"I clipped her belly button, you know . . . and then I . . . I . . ." Lisa broke down again.

Strong sensed how uncomfortable it was for her to make the admission. "Take your time, Lisa. No hurry here."

"Well, I . . . I put all of the dirty blankets in the trunk with the rest of the stuff."

Next to the blankets, Strong would soon find the bloody rope Lisa allegedly used to strangle Bobbie Jo. DNA from the blood and hair attached to the rope would be a match to Bobbie Jo. The knife Strong found in the trunk next to the rope had dried blood on one side of it, which would later be proven to contain a mixture of Bobbie Jo and Victoria Jo's DNA. The handle of the knife was even more damaging—it held a blend of "genetic information" from Bobbie Jo, Victoria Jo and Lisa.

"Okay," Strong said, "Continue."

"Then I called Pastor Wheatley from my cell phone and told him I had the baby."

"How long was that after you left Skidmore?"

"I don't know, maybe ten minutes. Yes, about ten minutes."

There it was: Lisa had been found out. She was never pregnant. She had lied to her children, mother, sisters, husband, and Bobbie Jo Stinnett.

If what authorities (and Lisa herself) said was true, Lisa had handpicked Bobbie Jo, waged a carefully thought-out campaign to kidnap her child, and hadn't allowed murder to prevent her from carrying out the diabolical plan—all because she didn't want people to think she wasn't pregnant.

The announcement of Lisa's arrest and the return of Victoria "Tori" Jo to her father would send a shot of hope throughout the heartland. But as Lisa began spending her first few days in lockup, having time to contemplate the events of the past few months, she would begin to change her story and to remove herself from the situation as if she hadn't even been present when the crime occurred. In the next month, she would take it one step further by telling a member of her family, "No, I didn't do it. Someone handed me the baby. . . . I don't remember being there."

49

Good news travels fast. Within hours after Lisa's arrest, as she and Kevin were taken into custody, the airwaves lit up with "breaking news reports." As Victoria Jo was rushed to the Stormont-Vail Regional Health Center in Topeka and news outlets converged on Melvern, Alicia and Rebecca sat at Kevin's parents' house trading stories about why the FBI had taken them out of class to be questioned. They still had no idea what was going on.

While the kids were sitting on the couch, the local news channel aired an alert on the bottom of the screen: "Kansas woman in custody, suspected in the murder of Missouri woman and the kidnapping of her fetus."

Alicia and Rebecca looked at each other: *No way. It can't be.* While watching the report, Alicia, especially, had a "sickly feeling that she will never forget," a family member said later.

That report still wasn't enough to convince them, however. They asked Mrs. Montgomery what was going on.

She wouldn't tell them.

A second report flashed across the screen thirty minutes later: "Tests have confirmed: the baby found in Melvern is Bobbie Jo Stinnett's."

The previous night replayed in their minds: Mom trying to breast-feed the child, dressing her up in that "I'm the little sister" T-shirt, cooing with her, calling her Abigail Marie, Kevin's parents and his aunts and uncles.

It was all a show.

At this point, people had more questions than answers. How was the baby doing? Victoria Jo hadn't been all that vivacious over the past twenty-four hours. She hadn't cried much the previous night. She wasn't moving her hands and legs as a newborn should. Would she survive such an ordeal? Had she suffered any brain damage during delivery? And the biggest question: What kind of monster had committed such a horrific act of violence?

As pieces of the story surfaced, people waited and wondered. Perhaps no one waited with more anticipation than Zeb Stinnett, who would have the opportunity inside the next hour to see his daughter for the first time.

It was comforting to most to think the one man who had lost and suffered the most would be able to carry on his slain wife's legacy. By her own admission, Lisa Montgomery had, in effect, taken half of Zeb's life from him. But that bond between parent and child, which Lisa herself seemingly craved so badly, was a part of the Stinnett family she could never separate.

II

A SORT OF HOMECOMING

50

"See, now do you believe me? *Now* do you want to go live with your dad?" Lisa asked. It was well into the evening on the night she had presented her new baby to the family. Lisa picked up Abigail and handed her to Ryan, who had been asking lately about going to live with his father, Carl Boman. "He's the liar, Ryan. Not me!" Lisa continued, apparently relishing having given birth, thus proving Carl wrong.

Carl Boman believes that everything Lisa did up to the point when she was arrested had been planned around her having a child that never actually existed. Kevin, Lisa's unsuspecting husband, bought the entire scenario from day one: nine months of feigned morning sickness and nausea, no doctor visits, shopping for baby clothes, crib, nursery, and a made-up due date, December 13. Not that Kevin had been fooled because of what many later presumed was an overwhelming naïveté on his part. Lisa had done a good job of deceiving him. All those supposed "prenatal care" appointments; Lisa worked hard at getting out of them.

"I'm going to be sick, Kevin, turn around," she said one day. They were driving toward one of her medical appointments. Kevin stopped the car and brought her back home. Once inside, Boman says, she picked up the phone and made a bogus phone call to a fake doctor's office and canceled the appointment. Another time, he believes, she started an argument halfway there and again demanded Kevin turn the truck around and return home. When they arrived, she told him to get out. "I'll drive myself," she said, and took off.

Pastor Mike Wheatley knew the Montgomery family well. He had counseled Lisa. The last time they spoke was in October.

Wheatley was concerned about Lisa, he said in press reports later. Not about her state of mind. But because, according to her, she was pregnant, had lost one of her twins, and was scheduled to give birth to the other child somewhere around December 13. She was worried about the second twin—if she would make it.

"I wasn't aware of anything [unusual]," Wheatley said. "As far as I knew, everything was just perfectly normal."

Despite what many of Lisa's siblings, her mother, and Carl Boman were telling him, Kevin and many Melvernians were under the impression Lisa had been pregnant with twins and had lost one. But it wasn't the first time Lisa had claimed to be pregnant. There had been at least four other instances where she had made the claim but had never produced a child.

"I had gone to doctor's appointments with Lisa when she was pregnant with our children," Carl Boman recalled. "I saw sonograms, medical charts. . . . I was in the birthing room when Lisa had each child. I paid the doctor's bills!" Carl had a fairly decent relationship with Kevin, but at times argued with him over how the children were being treated. One day, he asked Kevin about Lisa's supposed pregnancy. Carl had heard for the past four years about Lisa's being pregnant and was taken aback by the notion of her seemingly fooling Kevin so easily. There was one time when Lisa told Carl she was pregnant, "but the baby was absorbed into her uterus. . . . I 'lost it, Carl.'" But Carl never bought into any of it.

Was there a man alive who could be deceived so effortlessly? Carl often wondered about Kevin. Apparently, Lisa had found him.

"How could you not do any of that?" Carl asked, referring to Kevin not going with Lisa to any medical appointments. "How could you believe her when everyone else is telling you different?"

Carl said Kevin just stared at him with the gaze of a man who perhaps knew something was wrong but didn't want to admit or confront it. Or maybe he just couldn't see it for himself. Carl wasn't the only one telling Kevin about Lisa's lies. Lisa's mother, Judy Shaughnessy, and her sisters, *Tonya* and *Farina*, had been telling Kevin for years that Lisa was lying about being pregnant and that it had become an obsession with her to give birth again.

Judy and her new husband, Danny Shaughnessy, took a ride

*Italics on first use of proper names and locations represents pseudonym or author's replacement.

into town one afternoon to discuss the situation with Judy's lawyer.

"Can we have her committed?" Judy asked.

"What's going on?"

"She's lying all the time about being pregnant," Judy explained. "I think she believes herself." They were tired of listening to Lisa and her stories, Judy continued. Things were escalating, bordering on getting out of hand. "I'm worried she might do something."

"You can't commit Lisa, unfortunately, until she hurts herself or somebody else," Judy recalled her lawyer advising.

When Carl asked Kevin about all the missed prenatal appointments, reminding him how many people were saying Lisa was lying, Kevin said, "Well, Lisa told me. And I *believe* her."

Carl shook his head and walked away.

Many claimed Lisa had no trouble convincing Kevin of anything she wanted. While they were dating, she had told him she was pregnant and needed an abortion (a procedure she always had professed to regard with absolute disgust, both on moral and religious grounds).

"From what I understood," a family member said, "Kevin gave her the money for the abortion." The story was unearthed in a letter Lisa had written to Kevin while he was courting her. Early in the relationship, it appeared she was already spinning her lies and manipulation. "The letter was about her having another child and she thought it was dead, but found out it was alive—and also said something about her having twins. I think she was misleading Kevin to believe she had twins when she had the supposed abortion."

"This is what Lisa did: she manipulated people," said Carl Boman, who was married to Lisa twice over a thirteen-year period. Carl met Lisa when she was sixteen. She was his stepsister then. "My kids would tell me what was going on with Lisa and Kevin because they were there; they lived in the house."

At about six feet, in remarkably good shape, Carl Boman had a deep voice that suggested a career in radio, a low baritone, like an opera singer. At times, he fumbled with his words, digging deep to find the right phrases to explain his view of things.

For years, Carl had been telling the children Lisa wasn't pregnant. Still, they believed she was, simply because Lisa kept drilling it into them. The fact that they lived with Lisa gave her more time to control the situation. Well aware Carl had been steering them in the opposite direction, Lisa made it a point to work hard at convincing the children Carl was "the bad guy," he said, for denying her the right to be pregnant and share that excitement with the kids. By handing Ryan the child and saying, "Now do you want to go live with your dad?" Lisa was, Carl insisted, insinuating, *I'm no liar. Your dad is the one who lies. Here's my baby, here's my proof.*

Eight months pregnant, Bobbie Jo Stinnett was found murdered in her Skidmore, Missouri, home. *(Courtesy of Nodaway-Holt High School Yearbook)*

Nodaway-Holt High, in Graham, Missouri, where Bobbie Jo and husband Zeb Stinnett attended school.

The Skidmore Christian Church, about one hundred yards away from the murder scene, where Bobbie Jo and Zeb were married.

State Highway 113, the road Lisa Montgomery took into Skidmore.

The road that Lisa Montgomery took out of Skidmore as Sheriff Ben Espey raced toward the murder scene from the opposite direction.

The Kawasaki Motors plant in Maryville, Missouri, where Bobbie Jo's husband, Zeb Stinnett, worked.

The Nodaway County Sheriff's Department, in Maryville, Missouri, investigated Bobbie Jo's murder.

Sheriff Ben Espey was responsible for getting the first Amber Alert in history issued for a newborn child.

Long John Silver's in Topeka, Kansas, where Lisa Montgomery met her husband and children and first presented Bobbie Jo's child as her own.

The Birth and Women's Center where Lisa Montgomery claimed she gave birth.

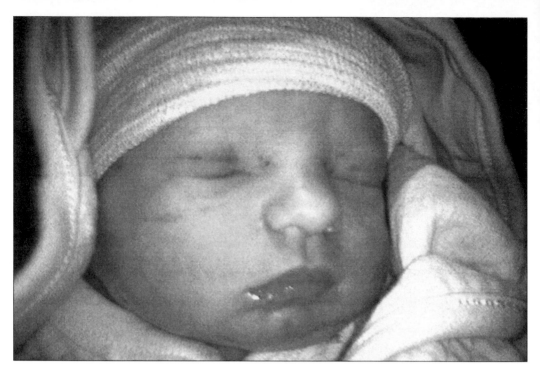

This photograph of Bobbie Jo's child was taken on the day she was kidnapped. She sustained scratches and bruises during the violent, premature delivery.

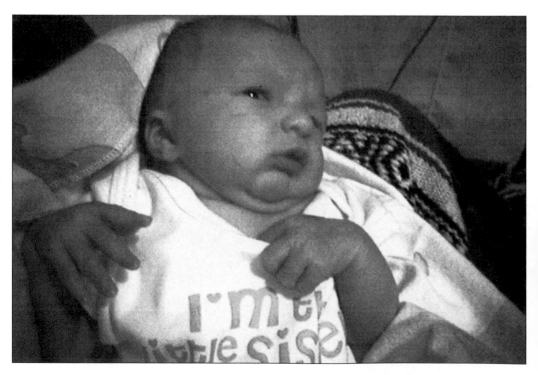

Lisa Montgomery dressed the baby in an "I'm the little sister" T-shirt.

North Carolina dog breeder Dyanne Siktar's call to the FBI helped lead authorities to Lisa Montgomery. *(Courtesy of April Siktar)*

Kevin Montgomery told police he had no idea his wife was faking her pregnancy and believed that Bobbie Jo's child was his daughter.

Four-year-old
Lisa in 1973.
(Courtesy of Judy Shaughnessy)

A year later, Lisa enters kindergarten.
(Courtesy of Judy Shaughnessy)

Lisa at ten years old.
(Courtesy of Judy Shaughnessy)

By her freshman year, Lisa was a popular teen, stunningly beautiful, scoring high grades. *(Courtesy of Judy Shaughnessy)*

Lisa and her mom, Judy Shaughnessy, during what were described as happier times. *(Courtesy of Judy Shaughnessy)*

A smiling Lisa at her high school graduation in 1986.
(Courtesy of Judy Shaughnessy)

In this photograph of Lisa in 1988, when she was six months pregnant with her second child, it was easy to tell that she gained weight and *looked* pregnant.
(Courtesy of Judy Shaughnessy)

This photograph was taken approximately four weeks before Lisa was charged with murdering Bobbie Jo and kidnapping her baby. At the time, she claimed to be eight months pregnant.

Lisa Montgomery was arrested in this farm house she and Kevin rented in Melvern, Kansas.

Downtown Melvern.

The Whistle Stop Café in downtown Melvern, where Lisa and Kevin showed off "their" child.

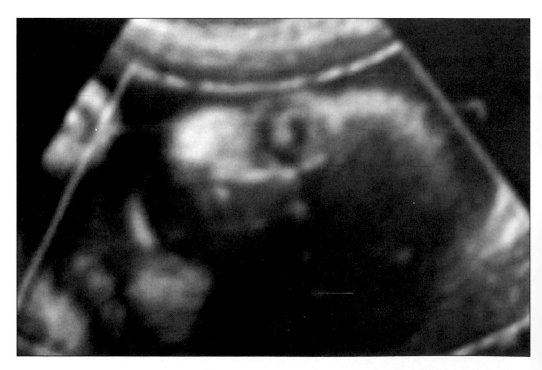

Lisa Montgomery downloaded this ultrasound photograph from the Internet and used it to persuade family members that she was expecting.

Lisa at sixteen years old, when she first met her stepbrother—and future husband—Carl Boman.

Lisa and Carl Boman, in August 1986, after they were married the first time. (Courtesy of Judy Shaughnessy)

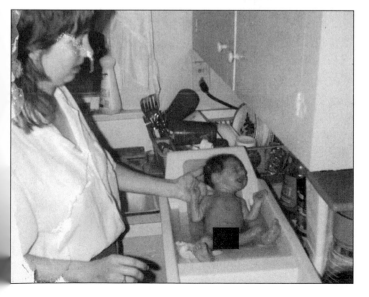

Lisa in 1989, after having her third child with Carl Boman.

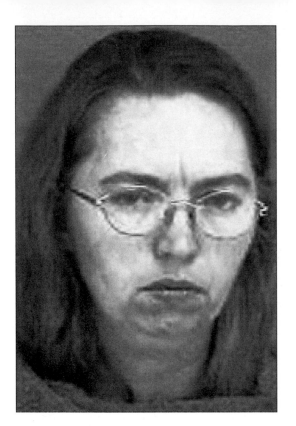

This mugshot of Lisa Montgomery was taken after two of Sheriff Ben Espey's deputies took a four-hour confession from her. (Courtesy of the Nodaway County Sheriff's Department)

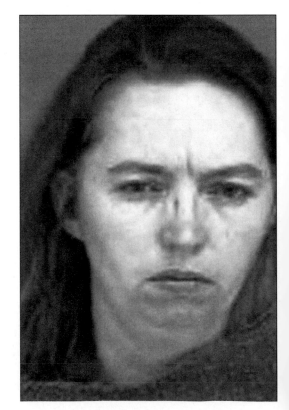

A second mugshot was taken of Lisa not wearing her glasses. (Courtesy of the Nodaway County Sheriff's Department)

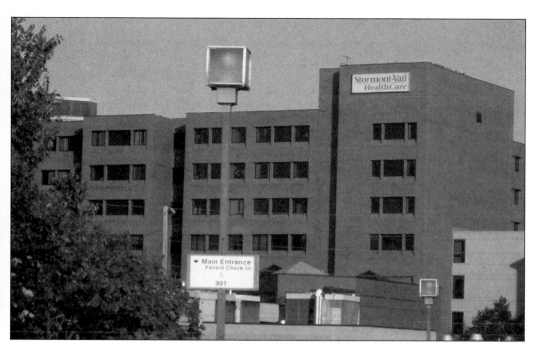

Sheriff Ben Espey's deputies rushed Bobbie Jo's child from Melvern to the Stormont-Vail Health Center in Topeka.

Carl Boman with his daughter, Kayla, in October, 2005.

This sign marks the cemetery on the outskirts of Skidmore, Missouri, where Bobbie Jo Stinnett is buried.

On Bobbie Jo's gravestone, her family paid tribute to the wonderful person she was: "Beloved wife and mother of Victoria."

51

The sinking feeling Kayla Boman had regarding the new baby was washed away by one simple conversation she had with her sister Rebecca and Mom before she left for school. The photographs of the baby that Rebecca had e-mailed helped. Now Kayla was in school, photographs in hand, bragging to fellow students about how beautiful the child was. "I'm *finally* a big sister," she said to more than one classmate.

Kayla liked living in Georgia with Auntie Mary. She and her mother had been moving away from each other emotionally at the time she left Kansas. If you ask Kayla, she'd say her mother rarely paid much attention to her or her siblings; everything Lisa did, at least during the final year Kayla was in Kansas, revolved around her own selfish needs.

Lisa "loved the children," but the "newness" of them being babies always wore off, Carl said, by the end of the first year. Her interest in them continued to diminish in their formative years and teens.

"This is why," Kayla added, "I think it's crazy now that my mom wanted another child so badly—especially after having four of us she pretty much ignored."

Nonetheless, as she went about her day on Friday in school, Kayla couldn't have been happier for her mother.

"Can you believe it—she's my sister."

The photographs proved it. Mom had finally given birth.

Lisa Montgomery and Carl Boman's children had always been well-behaved, closely controlled kids. Despite the emotional ride Carl and Lisa put the children on during their years of marriage and divorce, the children, for the most part, had managed to deal with their lives in a healthy way, staying focused on the future.

Rebecca, the oldest, was admired by the others. According to Carl Boman, not only had Rebecca cultivated a more mature relationship with her mom, but the other children always turned to her for advice, even comfort. Certain characteristics of the children's personalities were framed around the way Lisa raised them. For instance, no matter whom they were speaking to, the children talked in rushed sentences, lacking any structure or continuity, as if they were jockeying for position with an invisible opponent. At times, Lisa would ignore the children to the point where they had to tussle with one another for attention. When Lisa decided to turn from her computer screen (or lift her head up from whatever book she was reading) and focus on what the children were saying, they struggled to keep her attention by speaking quickly. This, Boman said, was Lisa: selfish, unsupportive, nefarious, and abusive. Two of the children said when they were younger, she would whip them with a long stick.

For Kayla Boman, moving to Georgia was like being rescued from a sinking ship; only she didn't realize it until later on, when she was able to look at the situation and put it all together. Certain parts of her mom's personality became clear to Kayla after she stepped back from the family and had time to look at the way she had been treated for the past ten years. Not that Carl Boman was the father of the year; but his shortcomings had been in the form of abandonment. What Carl *didn't* do was the problem, not what he did. Kayla now realized the life she'd had with her mom, although she loved her, was not the kind of life a child deserved.

52

Kayla was kicking stones and staring at her watch. Waiting. Wondering. *Where is he? Why is he so late?*

She stood outside the front door of her school, unsure of why her ride home was late. The woman Kayla lived with in Georgia had a son, seventeen years old then. *Robert* attended the same high school. Generally, Robert would meet Kayla out front and drive her home. But not today. For some reason, he was running awfully late.

Where is he?

Kayla didn't know it, but Robert had taken the day off.

Auntie Mary's next-door neighbor *Julie Harrison* routinely left for work at three or four in the morning and wanted someone to be in the house when her daughter woke up at 5:30 A.M. Kayla would stay over at times, wake the child up, and make sure she got ready for school in time. It soon dawned on Kayla while she stood outside waiting for Robert that Julie was likely home and could possibly pick her up.

"Robert didn't show up today. . . . I need a ride home," Kayla said when she got Julie on the phone.

"Sure, honey. I'll be right there."

As Kayla sat on the curb waiting, Auntie Mary was back at home deciding how to tell Kayla what had happened. Thus far, Kayla had no idea what was going on back in Melvern; that her mom had been arrested for killing a young woman and stealing her baby. Within the next hour, Kayla's life was going to be

---

*Italics on first use of proper names and locations represents pseudonym or author's replacement.

flipped on its side. The authorities' allegations would be doubly disturbing to her because her mom had not only supposedly committed murder—but Bobbie Jo Stinnett was someone Kayla had looked up to and valued as a friend.

"By the way," Julie said as she and Kayla headed home, "my computer isn't working right today for some reason. I have to get it fixed." Julie knew Kayla liked to stop by the house and use the computer before she went home to Mary's.

"Okay," Kayla said.

By December, Kayla had gotten used to life in Georgia. She liked living amid different surroundings and began to see the life she left behind from a different perspective. First and foremost, she understood, even at fourteen years old, how much her mother had lied to her throughout the years, neglected her, and failed to parent her in a way she needed. Not that Kayla didn't miss her mother and siblings, she did. But living in Georgia had cleared her mind. She was focused now on training and showing rat terriers.

When they arrived at Julie's, Kayla noticed her dogs were already outside next door at Auntie Mary's. One less chore she had to do.

She walked into Julie's with the thought of doing some laundry. Kayla kept clothes at both Julie's and Mary's. She had a room at Julie's, too.

While sorting her dirty clothes—"jeans, whites, lights, darks," it was like a song she sang to herself to pass the time while separating the items—Kayla heard the front door open. Julie had gone into another room by then and was busy doing household chores herself.

It was Auntie Mary. Kayla poked her head around the corner and watched Mary walk into the house. *That's odd*, she thought, *Auntie's still wearing her nightgown*. Her face was reddish, flushed, as if she had been running.

53

Ben Espey sat at his desk and looked over his notes. A pool of reporters outside the sheriff's department braved the cold temperatures, waiting for Espey to emerge with an update. It was Espey's job, he knew, to keep the media at bay as much as he could. As news spread about the arrest of Lisa Montgomery, it was impossible for Espey to think he could ignore the mass gathering.

By early evening, word of Lisa's arrest had hit the international wires and airwaves. WOMB-SNATCH KILLER, one headline in an Australian newspaper read. WOMB-THEFT BABY HOME, echoed a South African headline. From Japan to Russia to England, and all across the United States, the arrest of Lisa Montgomery and what she had reportedly done to Bobbie Jo Stinnett struck a nerve with people. Here was a young, twenty-three-year-old victim brutally murdered in Small Town, USA, pregnant, newly married, her baby ripped from her womb as if part of some satanic ritual. For some, the girl next door and the American Dream were destroyed in one night.

As gruesome as the story appeared to be, it was news, nonetheless. It meant ratings. During what was normally a slow news period, most Americans would celebrate Christmas exchanging some sort of opinion about the most merciless murder the Midwest had seen in years. The only cause for celebration was that Victoria Jo had been found alive and would be returned to her father and Bobbie Jo's family.

Espey walked slowly from the basement room he had turned into investigation ground zero and opened the door. He had tears in his eyes before he uttered a word.

"We're confident we have the little girl that was taken from Skidmore," Espey told reporters while standing in the back parking lot of the sheriff's department. "We have canceled the Amber Alert." Later, Espey recalled the moment he emerged from the basement and addressed the press for the first time since finding Victoria Jo: "It was one of the happiest moments of my life, just to say that we had found that baby alive. I could hardly get the words out of my mouth."

FBI SA Rick Thorton then took a step toward the microphones, further spreading the joy that anyone who had been involved in the investigation surely felt. Unfortunately, most child abductions didn't turn out this way. It was time to spread the good news.

"The father of the child will be reunited [*sic*] with the baby," Thorton said. It was obvious he, too, was holding back emotion.

In handling any story that tugs at the heartstrings, reporters generally have the professionalism to stay objective. Such discipline is part of their credo. But this story, in all of its horror, seemed to expose a vein of emotion many reporters couldn't keep buried. Many news agencies focused on the prospect of a happy ending. Having Victoria Jo in the arms of her father was, in spite of Bobbie Jo's death, a small victory.

As word spread, residents of Melvern, especially those who knew Kevin and Lisa, began to look at the last twenty-four hours in an entirely different light. Suddenly, everything Lisa and Kevin had done seemed suspect.

54

As soon as he heard about Lisa's arrest, Darrel Schultz called Pastor Mike Wheatley. It was about ten minutes before the evening news came on. Darrel was Kevin's boss and a member of the First Church of God in Melvern.

"Do you know anything about this?" Schultz asked. "Were you in the middle of it all?"

"Of course not, Darrel," the pastor explained.

Lisa's arrest had caused people in Melvern to look for explanations. How could she fool us like that? Was Kevin in on her plan, too?

"Actually, what makes this whole thing so difficult," Wheatley told reporters, "is that she had everybody pretty snowed. I mean, as far as we knew, everything was just absolutely normal about Lisa. She was just doing her working and going home, and back and forth. There wasn't any sign at all of any difference in her."

Wheatley pointed out that the people of Melvern, beyond Kevin and the kids, didn't see Lisa every day. No one could really know a person without living with her; and even then, who really knew the person they slept next to every night?

"I mean, the last time I saw her," added Wheatley, "was in October when she came by the house and appeared to be pregnant. So, that was the only time I'd seen her since, before the day she came by with the baby."

Lisa may have appeared to be "normal" to her small circle of friends and townspeople she saw occasionally, but those closest to her, especially Carl Boman, had seen signs of a person struggling with a perception of reality for a long time.

"Lisa was the type of person who could pick up anything,"

said Carl, "and was capable of doing it. She was smart. She was amazing that way, with certain things. When it came to artsy type of things, lace and doilies, she could do it. But she could also lie to your face and make you believe what she wanted you to."

Indeed, Lisa had no trouble convincing people she was a respectable member of the community, having been involved in the local 4-H club and other community-oriented programs. But that was one of Carl's points: Lisa showed the veneer of a normal person, so she could pull the strings behind the scenes more convincingly.

The impression Lisa had given to neighbors regarding how she lived, Carl added, and the actuality of the situation were "two totally different things." She lied, Carl went on to say, to Wheatley and everyone else in town, not just about being pregnant.

"Her whole life was a deception."

In 1998, shortly after Carl and Lisa divorced for the second "and last" time, Lisa took two of the children and moved from New Mexico to Topeka, while Carl took the other two and moved to Bartlesville, Oklahoma. Lisa ended up moving in with her mom and immediately, Carl insisted, started making up stories about him.

"She turned into someone totally different than who she truly was, and projected this 'new' person on the community there in Topeka. She told people all sorts of stories about me."

As Carl told the press at the time, Lisa cheated on him no fewer than six times throughout both marriages, he said. "But it was probably a lot more." When she arrived in Kansas, right around the time she met Kevin, she played a "whole different role there, like she had just come out of an abusive marriage."

It was all part of an elaborate plan, Carl maintained. Lisa worked hard to take the focus off herself and put it on someone else so she could play the role of victim, culling as much sympathy as she could from people. Her secrets would be better hidden that way.

Some of the rumors Lisa spread about Carl when she got into town began trickling back to him.

"In a way, now it's funny. It doesn't even anger me because it is all so far-fetched. There's people there in Kansas who hated me but would not have even known me if they saw me on the street."

Carl believed Lisa could influence people into thinking whatever she wanted, as she did after meeting Kevin and moving to Melvern. Soon she had many in the town believing she was repeatedly pregnant and regularly losing her babies. The pattern, according to Carl, was a continuation of what she had been doing to him for years.

"Lisa, what the hell are you doing, telling people all these lies about me?" Carl asked one day after hearing a story about himself.

"Oh, please, Carl," she said. "I never said any of that."

That kind of denial would get to Carl the most. He'd talk to Lisa and, at times, he was sure she didn't even listen to him, blowing off his questions as though he had never asked them.

"She never confronted anything."

Furthermore, whenever Carl would hear she was pregnant and call her on it, Lisa would say, simply, "Whatever, Carl."

"Avoidance, even to the point of hanging up on me," he said.

Whereas Lisa had people from all across the Midwest bad-mouthing her, claiming she lied at dog shows regarding the pedigree of her dogs, not many—outside the family—had a bad word to say about Carl Boman. He had a solid reputation of being a hardworking man, a "Sunday Christian," and a person who liked to keep to himself without interference from outsiders. To have to defend himself tore Carl apart as time went on and Lisa's stories became more bizarre.

55

Kayla Boman was throwing dirty clothes into a laundry basket when Mary walked into the room and approached her. Mary moved slowly, her head bowed. It was obvious she had been struggling with something upsetting.

"Hi, Auntie," Kayla said, turning, looking at her.

Mary didn't say anything at first. Just then, Julie, also showing signs of being distraught, walked up from behind.

"Auntie?"

"We need to talk, Kayla," Mary said.

Realizing something was wrong, Kayla stepped closer and stared at Mary. She could see Mary's eyes were swollen and blood-shot. Clearly, she had been crying.

"Hold on, hold on," Kayla said, perhaps nervously ignoring what was to come because she knew in some way it was going to be bad news, "let me just get this load of laundry into the washer and get it started."

Kayla immediately considered something had happened to her little sister. The karma in the room was heavy; she could sense negative energy. In those photographs Rebecca had sent her earlier that morning, the baby didn't look right, Kayla had thought all day long. Although she had spent a better part of her day bragging to fellow students and showing off the photographs, the more she thought about the situation and studied them, the more she understood something was wrong. She was sure Mary was coming to tell her the baby had died.

"The baby?" Kayla asked.

"No."

Kayla put her laundry basket down and sat on the floor. Julie came over and sat next to her. Mary sat on the bed. The pain on their faces was immeasurable, Kayla remembered.

"Kayla," Mary said in nearly a whisper. She was holding a Kleenex, crumbling it in her hands, stopping every so often to stare at it. "I have to tell you something. I'm not going to sugarcoat it or anything." Mary felt Kayla was old enough and smart enough to accept the truth. It was better she heard it from someone she loved rather than the newspapers or on television, which were running wild with the story.

Kayla dropped her head. She didn't know what was coming, she admitted later, but had a feeling it was something "very bad."

Oh, my gosh, there's something wrong with Abigail. No. No. No.

"Your little sister," Mary said, her voice slow, comforting, cracking, *"isn't* your sister." ("Talk about confused," Kayla recalled. "The whole time my mother was 'pregnant,' I had my doubts, and I always talked to Auntie M about it.")

Mary had most of the afternoon to figure out how to break the news, but hesitated for a moment before continuing, "Bobbie Jo's dead, Kayla."

"What?" Kayla said. She began crying. *Bobbie Jo's dead? Bobbie Jo can't be dead.*

"Your mom murdered her and cut Bobbie Jo open and took her baby."

Julie crept up closer to Kayla and put her arm around her shoulder; Kayla fell into her chest and sobbed. Bobbie Jo was Kayla's friend. Kayla had gotten close to Bobbie Jo since they met back in Abilene in April, at the same dog show where Lisa had first met her.

Kayla got up off the floor and walked next door. She didn't want to believe it. She turned on the television and saw the news story featuring Lisa's mug shot and talking about the charges pending against her.

That's my mother? My mother did this?

"Turn off the television," Mary said. "You don't need to see that."

Jumping off the couch, Kayla walked back to Julie's, logged on to the computer, and started deleting all of her e-mails. Reporters had already located her e-mail address and were sending questions.

Soon after, she retreated to her room at Mary's. After closing the door behind her, she sat on the floor with her back to her bed and thought about everything.

Bobbie Jo's dead? Bobbie Jo? She still couldn't believe it.

Mary's son, Robert, knocked on the door.

"Come in."

"Hey . . . ," Kayla said, looking up at him, then back down at the floor.

"Hey. You want to go to Adventure Land? I'll take you."

It seemed odd to Kayla. Robert had never wanted to take her anywhere before.

Kayla jumped up. "You know, at least it's better than being here with nothing to do but think. Yeah, sure. Let's go."

56

When Judy Shaughnessy heard the news, she called Kevin's parents' house in Melvern to see if she could help out in any way and also check on the welfare of her grandchildren. She was concerned about how the kids were reacting to Lisa's arrest.

She got no answer. The kids and the Montgomery family were there, but the phone would not stop ringing as reporters, friends, and family kept calling.

Judy tried again and left another message.

Thirty minutes went by.

Nothing.

What is going on? Does anybody care about my concern for the children?

"When I found out about Lisa," Judy recalled, "I called the Montgomery house. They did not return my call. They didn't even contact Carl. My heart goes out to the Stinnett family, and I still grieve for them, as I also grieve for my daughter. I love Lisa, but, unfortunately, our relationship was over some time ago."

Any hope of a relationship between Judy and Lisa was severely damaged in late 2003. Lisa's nephew had been taken by the Department of Social and Rehabilitation Services (SRS) in Kansas. A custody fight had been ongoing between Judy and the state of Kansas. Lisa's half sisters were also involved. The child's mother and Judy's son had signed over parental rights to Judy and her new husband, Danny. Her son had been arrested on a drug offense and was headed to prison. He wanted the child taken care of in his absence. Who better to do that than the child's grandmother?

Near the end of the custody battle, Lisa got involved. At first, no one could understand why she stuck her nose into it. But the answers would surface as Lisa began to get caught, once again, in several lies.

Judy wanted to give her grandchild a "normal" life in a family environment, she said. Judy and Danny owned forty acres in Lyndon, where they had been living a *Green Acres* lifestyle of farming for the past four years. Both had been married before and believed they finally had found the right partner.

"Danny and I bought this farm," Judy said, "to be in the country and live in peace and harmony, have visits from the kids and grandchildren. But we never thought we would have to do the things we have done."

They raised pigs, sheep, milk goats, cows, geese, chickens, turkeys, dogs, and cats. "We also have bees. . . . We do our own butchering. We have a big strawberry patch, and I usually have a big garden and I do a lot of canning."

A yearning, recalled Judy, to "live like our ancestors" drew her and Danny to their life style. Lisa tried to project the same image of "living off the land," but those who knew her claimed she was more interested in making people *think* that was how she lived rather than actually doing it.

Because of the problems Judy and Lisa had between them as mother and daughter, Judy hadn't seen her grandchildren on Lisa's side much. But she felt she could raise her son's child and maybe break a cycle of dysfunction, which had been so much a part of their lives for years. Yet, as Judy prepared to do battle with the state over her son's child, Lisa stepped in.

Judy had been taking care of the child while her son and his girlfriend stayed on her farm. Things were fine. But in Judy's opinion, it was after Lisa got her brother "all worked up" one night that he took the child and his girlfriend and ran off to Oklahoma without warning.

According to Judy, Lisa had been going over to the house while Judy and Danny weren't home and telling her brother "things."

When Judy heard her son had left town, she took off for Oklahoma to search for him. As she put it, Judy knew "the baby didn't have a chance in that drug life of [his]."

After going to some of the usual places her son hung out, Judy couldn't find him. So, she instead turned her son and his girl-friend in to the state—who did find them.

About six months later, her son, his girlfriend, and their child returned to Kansas and ended up staying with one of Lisa's sisters. Judy claimed that one night Lisa stopped by and again interfered in the situation. So, "he got mad and took off again with his girlfriend and the baby." They were on foot this time, walking down the street toward the house where Lisa lived with Kevin.

Soon after, the state stepped in and took the child into custody. Lisa was so wrapped up with having the child stay at her house, Judy said, she had gone out and purchased a playpen, crib, and other infant essentials. Carl and two of Lisa's children later backed this up.

"It was like the war was on now because I upset her apple cart," Judy said.

Judy didn't give up her fight, however, over the custody of her grandson. By this time, the state had placed the child in foster care after Judy's son was sentenced and sent to prison. As Judy saw it, the child didn't belong in foster care. Why allow the child to get attached to a foster family—or the other way around—when he had a home with members of his own family?

Eventually the dispute was put before a family court judge. Lisa became involved again and favored, shockingly, the foster family. If she couldn't get the child herself, it seemed she felt, Judy wasn't going to get him, either. Essentially, Lisa was going against her mother, brother, and sisters, walking into court and claiming the child was better off in foster care.

During one of the court hearings, Lisa was questioned under oath about all the times she had claimed to be pregnant. If Lisa wanted to sit on the stand, Judy felt, and try to stop her from getting custody of her grandchild, she should have to undergo a personal analysis of her own. Whatever she had done in the past would now become part of the record.

"During that hearing," Judy recalled, "Lisa said she had a baby and she gave [the infant] to science in Manhattan, Kansas. I can't remember which pregnancy she was talking about, but she also said she was pregnant with twins and one had died earlier."

Lisa had committed perjury.

"Lisa actually wanted Judy's grandson," Carl Boman agreed. He remembered the situation vividly because he, too, had found himself in the middle of it all. "A lot of nastiness between them all came out. Lisa had her eye on that baby—and not for reasons of wanting him in a safe environment or out of foster care.

"She wanted that child as her own."

When Lisa lied on the stand in court, her false testimony not only gave Judy grounds for proving how unstable she was, but it allowed Carl the opportunity to use the same ammunition in his forthcoming custody fight with Lisa, which was set for mid-January 2005. It was one more piece of evidence to prove Lisa had lied routinely throughout the years about being pregnant. By Judy's count, at least five times between 2000 and 2004.

"I tried to tell them and tell them," Judy said, meaning Kevin and his parents and people in Melvern, "but nobody listened."

Several of Lisa's family members claimed that around the same time she became involved in her nephew's custody fight, Lisa also developed an obsession over wanting to give Kevin a female child.

"I really think Lisa wanted a child to make Kevin happy, preferably a girl," Judy said. "So if it makes sense, I think she wanted *my* grandchild just to make me mad and cause problems—but she also wanted a girl for Kevin."

Kevin had three sons from a previous marriage. He and his then-wife had a stillborn daughter years ago.

"Kevin always wanted a daughter," someone in the family said. "His only daughter died."

Lisa knew how much the loss had wounded Kevin's soul. Part of her position was that she wanted to lessen his pain by granting him another child, preferably a daughter.

Carl Boman described a claim made by Lisa that she was "impregnated by her stepfather" years ago, and had wanted to keep the child. Lisa didn't believe in abortion, Carl added, even under such inherently immoral circumstances.

But again, it went back to the question: was Lisa actually pregnant?

"No," Judy insisted, "Lisa did not get pregnant by her stepfather. I took her to the doctor to make sure."

By the time the custody fight was over and Judy was awarded

custody of her grandson, "All of Lisa's lies were catching up with her," Judy concluded. Speaking of Lisa's mindset and her admission of killing Bobbie Jo and kidnapping her child, Judy said, "I think the desperation got to her."

She believed Lisa needed a newborn so she could prove to everyone she wasn't a liar, which was why she paraded the child around town: to shove it in the faces of those who had questioned her.

"Even if she only had one day to show this child off and bask in that glory of being redeemed," Carl Boman commented, "I believe, in some way, it was all well worth it for Lisa. She was right and everyone else was wrong, if only for a few hours."

57

"The baby is fine," U.S. attorney Todd Graves said the first time he addressed the media. "The baby is doing great."

A clean-cut man of thirty-nine years, with a shock of tar-black hair he kept parted on one side, Todd Graves was raised on a family farm near Tarkio, Missouri. Married for the past fourteen years, Graves had fathered four children and later moved with his wife, Tracy, to a family farm of 270 acres north of Kansas City. The land had been in the Graves family for over one hundred years.

In 1988, Graves received his undergraduate degree in agricultural economics, with a minor in political science, from the University of Missouri-Columbia. He was graduated summa cum laude. Three years later, he received a law degree and a master's in public administration from the University of Virginia.

Graves's path toward the U.S. Attorney's Office in the Western District of Missouri, where he would eventually end up, was a textbook academic ride built on a foundation of hard work. Becoming a U.S. attorney is an appointed position, made by the president of the United States. If Graves wanted the job, the top dog himself would have to put him there. His work ethic and moral fiber certainly proved he was deserving.

From 1992 to 1994, Graves worked as the Platte County prosecuting attorney, one of the youngest ever to fill the position. Before that, he had a private practice. In 1991, he took on a job as an assistant attorney general for the state of Missouri. Through that, he served as a staff assistant on the Governor's Commission on Crime. Anyone who knew Todd Graves had no doubt that any criminals to come through West Missouri and break federal law would be met with the stiff arm of "Lady Justice." In 2002, Graves met U.S. Attorney General John Ashcroft in Kansas City while Ashcroft was on a three-city junket through the state he grew up in. During the tour, Attorney General Ashcroft talked about cyber crime and terrorism. At a Kansas City news conference, Graves said the "heartland had witnessed an explosion" of Internet-driven child exploitation and pornography in recent years, and he was going to do everything in his power to try and stop it.

"I believe the Kansas City region will become the model in fighting the growing wave of crime against children," Graves said, standing proudly. He was preparing the city for its recent inception of the RCFL, which later would become a major part of the investigation into the Bobbie Jo Stinnett murder case.

"Our children will be safer because of these efforts."

The recovery of Victoria Jo two years after Graves made that speech certainly validated his promise; but there was more to Todd Graves than going after the latest criminal element. On top of his core belief of going after child predators, Graves was often applauded for his stern stance on prosecuting any type of corruption inside the system he valued and worked so hard to keep clean. He wasn't one to pass up a chance to go after anyone, including colleagues who broke the law. It hadn't mattered to Graves what job you held inside the government, where you were born, or who your daddy was. If you decided to break federal laws in his jurisdiction, consider yourself his enemy.

In late 2000, President George Bush noticed the work Todd Graves was doing in Missouri and nominated him for the state's top federal law enforcement job in the Western District. That was on July 30, 2001. Then, six days after the United States experienced its worst act of terrorism on domestic soil, as the Twin Towers in New York and the Pentagon in Virginia smoldered, and more than three thousand people were considered missing and presumed dead, Graves held up his right hand and took the oath of office. He was confirmed approximately one month later, in October 2001.

With a staff of 119 in downtown Kansas City, where Graves's office overlooks East Ninth Street in the Charles Evans Whittaker Courthouse building, the office Graves manages oversees more than half of Missouri's 114 counties. Among them is Nodaway County, where Lisa Montgomery had admitted strangling Bobbie

Jo Stinnett and snatching her fetus from her womb. Because Lisa allegedly had taken the baby over a state line into Kansas, she had committed a violation. of the federal law, thus making the case, which was already building against her, Todd Graves's job to prosecute. The actual charge Lisa would face was severe: kidnapping resulting in death, a crime punishable by the death penalty or a mandatory life sentence and a $250,000 fine.

If she was found guilty, Lisa Montgomery's life would be over. Her children would never see her again as a free woman. Contact among them would be through a three-inch-thick section of Plexiglas, their voices resonating over an intercom phone monitored by prison officials.

On the night Victoria Jo was found, the press hounded Graves's office. Ben Espey fielded hundreds of calls from all over the world. Espey continued working the microphones, trying to relate any detail he could without damaging the case being built against Lisa. In the end, Espey had done his job and fulfilled a promise he had made to Zeb. As Espey saw it, the legal case was out of his hands. The feds could have their way and take all the glory for all he cared. The baby was back home.

"That was all I ever wanted."

After commenting on the status of Victoria Jo, Todd Graves had little to add.

Espey, who was going on two days without as much as a catnap, made himself available all evening. He announced the baby's name for the first time in public and told the press she had been united with Zeb at Stormont-Vail Regional Health Center in Topeka.

Announcing the name of the hospital sent a herd of press racing to the parking lot of Stormont, hoping to get that first exclusive interview with anyone close to the Stinnett family, or better, a photograph of the baby the entire world was eager to see.

Lisa, meanwhile, continued to spin one lie after another. Espey and Graves shared with reporters some of what she had been telling investigators while in custody.

"She had a miscarriage at some point this year," Espey said, "and lost a twin." He didn't mention where the information had come from, but it wasn't difficult to ascertain Lisa was starting to talk. Nor did Espey know she was lying.

Espey took it one step further when he told one reporter that Lisa "was six months along when the child was lost."

Reporters, curious to learn anything they could about Lisa and her state of mind, asked Espey about a possible motive.

"I think she was probably going to take it because she had lost one through a miscarriage. . . ." Additionally, Espey said that "the attacker worked deftly and probably had some medical knowledge."

Many of the reporters wanted details regarding Victoria Jo's health. Lisa was no doctor, and she had not taken the child to see one. Considering the violent delivery, how was the child faring?

"We have no indications that the child was hurt in any way," Espey confirmed. "The child's probably going to be okay."

Smiling, Espey took off his sheriff's cap and wiped his brow, taking a long breath. What a day and night it had been.

One reporter asked about the details of the crime.

"More than likely, our victim has been strangled. . . . Evidence would show the baby was probably wrapped up and taken home."

Some of the evidence included bloody sheets and blankets found inside the trunk of Lisa's car, one insider noted later, along with "other items" leading authorities to believe Lisa had worked alone.

Espey wanted to stress that without the Amber Alert, the child would not have been found.

"We may have not ever recovered this little baby if the Amber Alert system was not put into place," he said. "I'm overwhelmed."

As reporters continued to launch questions, the exhausted sheriff kept speaking from his heart.

"The FBI, there were seven or eight FBI agents that came in, tremendously helped us. Because some of the computer stuff was a little bit out of our control, they knew about it, and they were able to dig right into that and get things going. And Randy Strong, he started from hour one and stayed with us through the whole thing. Most everybody here's been up continuous. And we've run leads all night long. And we continued to run leads. When this Amber Alert came out, that's the greatest thing that's ever happened to law enforcement and to *our* children. We took an anonymous tip that came from several states away from here"—the Dyanne Siktar IP address of Darlene Fischer and Auntie Mary's phone call—"[that gave] us some information that led us to Kansas . . . and we may have not ever got that. We may have not ever recovered this little baby—if the Amber Alert system was *not* put into play."

After stepping back from the assortment of microphones in front of him, collecting himself, Espey added one final thought: "And so with that, we're happy. We're *very* happy."

Sergeant Sheldon Lyons, a spokesman for the MSHP, thanked everyone who had helped work on the case. "This is a great day for law enforcement in Northwest Missouri," Sergeant Lyons said.

To Ben Espey's chagrin, FBI SA Jeff Lanza, who had stood in the background as Espey laid out the details, took a step forward. "Just also want to say thank you to the sheriff's department," said Lanza, "for the fine work they did, and the Missouri Highway Patrol, of course."

Rick Thorton, a colleague of Lanza's, stepped forward next. Building on what Lanza, Espey, and the MSHP had said already, Thorn echoed their sentiments and reiterated the belief that the investigation was a "collaborative effort.

"This is how it's supposed to work. Where we all come together. We bring our own unique strengths to the investigative arena, and at the end of the day, in this case, it was a good outcome for us, the best outcome we could hope for."

Reporters had a barrage of questions, beginning with, "If not for the Amber Alert, would this baby have been possibly in danger?"

"The baby was certainly in danger throughout . . . ," Lanza said.

"Father and baby are together right now?"

"That's my understanding," someone said.

"Is it a man and woman in custody?" one reporter shouted from the back.

"We're not going to comment on anything of that nature at this point now," Lanza said.

"But no arrests so far?"

"That's correct. Thank you very much."

58

Annie's rat terrier message board, Ratter Chatter, was brimming with emotion on the night of December 17. Rat terrier breeders and fellow terrier owners were saddened at the thought that one of their own had been brutally murdered. Even more affecting was the government's allegation that Bobbie Jo had been murdered by a fellow breeder.

After hearing Lisa had been taken into custody, one woman wrote, "I cannot believe how sorrowful I am. . . . I don't know what's worse: the horrible crime, or the possibility that it might be Lisa."

Another member said, "I am sitting here in shock. . . . I am absolutely horrified."

In Topeka, at the hospital, Zeb Stinnett, still in mourning over the loss of his wife, had pulled himself together enough to release a statement after he and members of his immediate family had seen Victoria Jo for the first time.

"She is a miracle," Zeb said through the statement. "I want to thank my family, friends, Amber Alert, and law enforcement officials for their support during this time."

On Bobbie Jo's Web site, someone summed up the day's events poignantly: "Thank God the precious baby girl was found alive and well. Bobbie Jo will live on through her daughter."

The clergyman who had married Bobbie Jo and Zeb, Reverend Harold Hamon, who was said to be preparing to officiate Bobbie Jo's funeral service after her body was released from the coroner's office, put it all into simple terms by saying the town of Skidmore was "stunned by everything" and would never be the same. "The only one who can figure this out is God," Hamon continued when reporters caught up with him. "You can't explain it. You can't understand it. The funeral is going to be a tough one."

The focus for most reporters soon shifted to the Stormont-Vail Regional Health Center in Topeka, specifically its neonatal care unit, one of the few facilities of its kind in West Missouri. Every newspaper editor and television producer wanted the first photograph of Victoria Jo. Just a simple shot of the little "miracle child" with her father was headline news.

That first photograph wasn't going to appear any time soon, however. Security around the hospital was tight, especially near the neonatal unit, with extra security personnel visible immediately upon entering the parking lot. The hospital put Carol Wheeler, its acting spokesperson, in charge of juggling hundreds of requests from the media.

Every major American television network and newspaper, Wheeler said, called the hospital for an update on the child's condition. The BBC and several British newspapers were also making inquiries. By late evening, Wheeler said, the hospital had fielded some "three hundred media phone calls and other requests." Producers from the *Today Show*, the *Early Show* and *Good Morning America* were calling, as were dozens of local television and radio stations.

"Everyone except Oprah," Wheeler added, "called at some point."

Doctors were "somewhat surprised" at Victoria Jo's condition. "She really is a miracle," Wheeler reiterated. The hospital's early assessment found no sign Victoria Jo had suffered any long-term injuries or was in any immediate medical harm. In fact, despite her traumatic delivery and being born one month premature, not to mention the extraordinary life she apparently had led over the past twenty-four hours, the child was in superb physical health. She would have to stay in the neonatal unit for an undetermined number of days, but with any luck, Zeb would be able to take her home by the middle of the following week.

Lisa Montgomery was being held in Kansas at the Wyandotte County Jail and was expected to make her first appearance in federal court on Monday, December 20, 2004.

There was still some question regarding whether authorities

would be pressing charges against Lisa in Missouri or in Kansas, but since Todd Graves had made it a point to involve his U.S. Attorney's Office, most believed Lisa would be extradited soon to Missouri.

Late that night, Ben Espey told reporters he and other law enforcement officials were having serious reservations about Lisa's story of being pregnant.

"She told people she was pregnant and had a miscarriage and lost one of the twins," Espey said, "[but] we're thinking she never was pregnant." He raised his eyebrows as he spoke, hinting that he knew more. Then he said he couldn't take any additional questions but would have more information the following morning.

59

As the night progressed, the story of Bobbie Jo Stinnett's murder and the recovery of her stolen child took on gargantuan proportions as talking heads hosted experts in every crime field imaginable on air, trying to understand the nature of the murder, how it could have happened in the heartland of America, and who was this woman who allegedly had committed such an unthinkable crime. Not even an undersea earthquake of biblical proportions, which would occurr in the coming days, was enough to reduce coverage of the Lisa Montgomery story. Because of the size of the quake, reverberations on the surface of the water generated a tsunami that killed a reported 150,000 people, making it one of the deadliest disasters in history.

As reporters and television talk-show hosts looked for any background information they could dredge up on Lisa Montgomery, other similar stories, which hadn't generated the same amount of attention or press coverage, surfaced.

Bobbie Jo's murder was not the first case of maternal homicide in the Midwest. Moreover, a yearlong study by the *Washington Post* concluded that over the past fourteen years—1990 to 2004— some "1,367 pregnant women and new mothers" had been killed. Although the "phenomenon . . . is as consequential as it is poorly understood," wrote *Post* staff reporter Donna St. George, it is also "largely invisible."

The most noticeable difference between the victims in other maternal homicide cases and Bobbie Jo Stinnett was that most of the other women hardly fit the "girl next door" image that Bobbie Jo had. In many of the stories published about the other cases— stories few and far between—the victims were rarely mentioned.

The general buzz of the reports centered on the alleged murderers. In contrast, with Bobbie Jo's story, the focus always had been on her young life being cut short, her unborn child, the small town she grew up in, and the people in town who spoke of her as the crown jewel of the community.

Cable television talk-show hosts and journalists—Anderson Cooper, Dan Abrams, Larry King, Greta Van Susteren, Rita Cosby, Catherine Crier—were running daily coverage of Bobbie Jo's story, reporting every development as it became known. The print media were even more varied, running the gamut from tabloid magazines to every major newspaper in the country and all over the world. Reporters were flying into Kansas City and heading northwest toward Skidmore and south toward Melvern, looking to answer the question everyone seemed to be scratching their heads over: why would a woman—a mother herself—allegedly commit such an inconceivable act of violence against another woman? Lisa Montgomery had not one criminal count against her before December 17, 2004. What was it in her background, in her life, that led her down such a path? How did she turn out the way she did? What truly motivated her?

The answers, of course, were in Lisa's past, leading right up until the day Bobbie Jo was murdered. Although the press hadn't caught up to him yet, there was one man who knew Lisa better than anyone, someone who, indeed, held all of her secrets.

60

Carl Boman was at his sister's house in Bartlesville, Oklahoma, a four-hour drive south on Route 75 from Melvern, when he heard his ex-wife had been arrested and was likely going to be charged with murdering a woman and kidnapping her unborn child. Carl's current wife, Vanessa, called him with the news.

"Hurry up and get home," said Vanessa in a rush of words.

A heavyset woman, with curly brown hair and a pronounced British accent, Vanessa grew up in England and, she said, "had always wanted to live in the United States. I was offered the chance by a Mennonite Church [in the states] to come over and work as a teacher's aide for some kids who were out of control." After arriving in the States around 2000, and meeting Carl Boman under "rather bad circumstances, in the middle of the night, on my way home from the airport in Phoenix, Arizona," Vanessa said she has "lived to regret the choice to be with Carl, as it has been so very painful for me. . . ."

In the fairy tale of her life with Carl's children, Vanessa quickly became the Wicked Witch. She was at odds, it seemed, with Lisa and the kids all the time.

When she called Carl and told him what Lisa allegedly had done, she was frantic and "very upset," recalled Carl.

"Are you kidding?" said Carl.

"Tonya called me," said Vanessa. "I cannot believe this, Carl." Tonya had been watching television and saw a live feed from a local station, which showed helicopters flying over Lisa and Kevin's house in Melvern. She recognized it right away and put it all together.

According to Vanessa, she collapsed on the floor after seeing Lisa's picture "on the computer" and again when they started showing photographs of Bobbie Jo on television. She had a daughter from a previous marriage around the same age as Bobbie Jo and was "sick" over how Carl's kids were going to be affected by what was being reported.

"Pull yourself together," said Carl when Vanessa broke down on the phone.

"I can't help it. . . ."

Later, Vanessa said: "He was mad at me. I was so hurt by this and was very shocked that he was uncaring to me. I cried all the time . . . and couldn't imagine how [Bobbie Jo's] mother must have felt to have found her dying that way and with no baby there, either . . . Carl had told me that he hoped he would push Lisa over the edge, to get the kids, but neither of us thought anything like this would happen."

At first, Carl had mixed feelings. "It seemed so damn surreal," he recalled. "I just hopped in my truck and fled home."

Over the years, Carl had metamorphosed from a lanky U.S. Navy brat into a solid, outdoorsy, blue-collar man's man, who had his mind set on fighting his ex-wife in court for custody of two of their children. Before he even knew what Lisa had been accused of, Carl had made plans to drag her into family court and, among other things, prove Lisa had been lying about being pregnant all those times over the past four years. Although he hadn't been treating the children as a father should during the past four years, Carl could make up for his shortcomings now by doing the right thing. Yet, no matter what he did, Lisa made the situation unbearable, he claimed, causing a negative impact on his relationship with the kids.

Carl was remarried now. He was building a life in Oklahoma, and wanted the children to be part of it. He wasn't afraid to defend himself against anything Lisa threw at him. The children, he urged, suffered the most from her lies. Lisa never cared that when she hurt him by spreading lies, she was placing a burden on the children, too; or when she talked about the children's father, her criticism was a reflection on them.

"Lisa cared about herself," said Carl. "And nobody else. I

haven't done everything I should by my children, but I was willing to accept my faults, look ahead, and rebuild their lives for them. Lisa could never do that."

Carl later remembered little of the ride home from his sister's house, which took about fifteen minutes. Vanessa had the television on when Carl walked in. CNN, MSNBC, and all the local affiliates were running moment-by-moment coverage.

It was just after 6:00 P.M.

Throwing his keys on the kitchen counter, Carl sat down on the couch and stared at the television. The first thing he saw was Lisa's booking photo.

At one time, I loved this woman. She's the mother of my four kids.

Carl had no idea then how involved the children were—that three of them had held the stolen child in their arms and played with her as if she were, as Lisa had told them, their new sister.

"Where are my kids?" Carl said, standing up, nervously running a hand through his hair, massaging the back of his neck.

Had Lisa taken one of the kids with her when she committed the murder? Were they in custody, too?

After watching the television coverage, allowing the news to settle on him, Carl got on the phone and called the Nodaway County Sheriff's Department and local FBI.

Neither would tell him anything.

He put in a call to Kevin's parents. Perhaps they knew what was going on. Or at least where the kids were.

No one answered the phone. One would have to assume the Montgomerys were still being bombarded by media requests.

When he realized he wasn't going to get much information from anyone else, Carl called Rebecca on her cell phone, hoping she would pick it up when she saw his number appear on caller ID.

"Rebecca," Carl asked when she answered, "where are you guys? Is everything okay?"

"We're at the Montgomerys', Dad."

"Are you *okay*?"

"Dad," Rebecca said, fighting back an overflow of emotion, "I can't believe it."

"It's going to be okay, honey."

"I can't believe it," she said again. ("Probably four or five more times," recalled Carl.)

"Where is everyone else?"

"We're all here, Dad."

Carl had filed for custody of Alicia and Ryan days before. He had a court date with Lisa scheduled for the first part of January. Rebecca was turning eighteen on January 11. Because of her age, Carl left it up to Rebecca where she wanted to live. With Kayla in Georgia, he had the sense "she didn't want to hurt her mom by moving in with me. Her mom was, at one time long before all this happened, her best friend." Kayla, who had turned fourteen over the summer, was going to be able to decide for herself whom she wanted to live with. Alicia, who had turned sixteen on July 7, and Ryan, who turned fifteen in October, had declared their loyalty to Carl and told Lisa they wanted to live with him.

Pacing in the kitchen, shaking his head, trying to figure out his next move, Carl wondered if calling his lawyer was the next logical step. "Should I call James?" he asked Vanessa.

"It won't hurt."

After several tries, Carl heard back from his lawyer's receptionist. "He's out of town. He won't be available until tomorrow morning."

"Great! Just great. . . ."

Carl wanted his children back. Right now. He couldn't wait until tomorrow.

Still, he didn't want to ride into Melvern like a cowboy and demand the children leave with him; he wanted to take action legally. The kids were safe at the Montgomerys'. Carl knew the family well. He trusted and respected them. It was late. Melvern was four hours away.

"Should I go?" he asked Vanessa.

61

Kevin Montgomery was released from custody late Friday night. He was not charged with the murder of Bobbie Jo or the kidnapping of her child. As far-fetched as it seemed, Lisa had apparently fooled her husband into accepting she was pregnant and had delivered a child in Topeka. Naive didn't even begin to express what people were thinking of Kevin.

"There's something missing," one Melvern convenience store owner said when reporters interviewed him. His comment seemed to summarize the town's immediate reaction.

Authorities must have believed what Kevin had told them, because as the sun rose on Saturday morning, December 18, Kevin was at his parents' house in Melvern, waking up to what would be one of the most peculiar days of his life.

For Carl and his children, the question of whether Kevin played a role in Lisa's alleged crimes was never an issue. The kids liked Kevin, appreciated him, and spoke highly of his good nature. They knew how Lisa had treated him, which somewhat explained how she could have convinced him she was pregnant all those times.

"Rude and bossy," said one of the kids, describing Lisa's attitude toward Kevin. "Always arguing with him over his ex-wife and his boys. . . . I sometimes wondered if she really loved him. She would always throw things in his face, especially when it had to deal with his ex-wife, their kids, or child support."

"Kevin was always very supportive of us," said another child.

When asked whether Kevin had questions about his wife's pregnancies, another family member said, "I would sometimes wonder. But I certainly wasn't going to question [her], because when I started to talk about 'the babies,' she would have to always 'go do something else.' She avoided talking about it. So I would never ask Kevin about it, either."

Lisa told all of her children she was expecting twins, and they had no reason not to believe her. Kayla, however, learned about the twins before anyone else.

Before she moved to Georgia, Kayla was upstairs in the house one afternoon while Lisa was online with a friend, explaining how their ram had bred with their goat. At one point, as Kayla looked over Lisa's shoulder, she watched her type "something about Kevin 'not having to jump any fences to get to her,'" making the correlation between the animals' breeding habits and how open Lisa was to Kevin's advances.

Kayla was confused. At fourteen, she was sharp, but her mom talked about some things that didn't make sense to her. Kayla decided to ask Lisa about the online chat.

"Are you talking about what I think you are talking about?"

"Were you reading my conversation?"

"Are you, Mom?"

"What—a baby?"

"Yeah!"

Lisa nodded.

Kayla took it as a yes.

Kayla could not think of a time when her mother told her she had lost one of the twins. Lisa e-mailed Auntie Mary about it, however, cautioning her not to tell Kayla. But Kayla read the e-mail, which confirmed her suspicions. Lisa would not be happy until the remaining baby was in her arms, the e-mail said in part.

"That just makes me *really* mad thinking about it now," said Kayla, reflecting on the situation.

Lisa frequently communicated with other dog breeders online. When Kayla got bored, as she often did, she'd log on to Lisa's account and check her e-mails. "Just to see what she talked about with other people." Kayla knew she was being nosy. "But, as she wasn't honest with me very much, I wanted to find out more about what she told other people."

There were hints. Mary once said, "Your mom 'lost' one of the 'twins.'" Lisa would refer sometimes to a "baby" instead of "babies." Then, one day, Kayla saw "she" instead of "they" in one of Lisa's e-mails.

"But at that point I was feeling even worse about it all, so I didn't know what to believe."

To make matters even more confusing, in 2002, Kayla and one of her sisters found a letter addressed to Kansas State University, written by Lisa. At the time, Kayla was looking for any sign her mother was not the liar some were claiming her to be. She wanted to believe in her mom—celebrate the fact that she *was* pregnant. She wanted to give her mom the benefit of the doubt.

The letter said "something about the baby"—the child Lisa claimed was stillborn that year—"being donated to Kansas State University for study, but that [the baby] had to be returned in a year."

After reading it, Kayla put it in the bottom of her dresser in back of some socks, underwear, and pajamas.

"Nobody should have known I had it there, which is why I was *so* confused when it came up missing later on. Kinda odd to me."

As Kayla woke on Saturday morning, the weight of not only losing her friend, but learning that her own mother could be responsible, hit her hard. A guttural cry turned into the numbness of emotional pain, making her entire body weak. Even though it was a Saturday, she had to go to school for a half-day of make-up finals.

When she arrived, a friend who had no idea what had happened, but had seen Kayla the previous day showing off photographs and bragging about Abigail, came up to her and casually asked, "So, what are you getting your little sister for Christmas?"

"Nothing," she shot back without explaining.

"Well, that's mean," he said.

Kayla stared at her friend. *If you only knew the half of it.*

62

Carl Boman wasn't even out of bed on Saturday morning when his mind started racing. The anxiety of what had happened was all-encompassing. He was trying to analyze everything Lisa had said to him over the past few weeks to see if she had given some sort of sign of what was to come.

Should I have known?

Carl viewed Lisa as an unfit parent, unstable, a bad influence on the kids. In the months leading up to Bobbie Jo's murder, her behavior had gone from strange to outright bizarre. Carl had spent a considerable amount of time the past year working out the details of Lisa's life so he could use her actions against her and get his kids out of her custody. Just five days before she had been arrested, on December 12, Carl had his lawyer, James Campbell, file papers in court seeking legal custody of Ryan and Alicia.

"She was lazy," said Carl. "When she lived with Kevin, my kids did everything around the house: clothes, cleaning, yard work. She watched television, surfed the Internet, and just lounged around all the time. Add to that the lying about being pregnant, and I was tired of her poisoning the minds of my children. It had to stop."

"I do know the children believed their mother," Judy added later, speaking of Lisa's convincing argument that she was pregnant, "and they believed her every time she told them."

Just about everyone outside the immediate family agreed Lisa was emotionally abusive toward the children and constantly filled their heads with so many different versions of the truth they couldn't possibly have any idea what to believe anymore.

Lisa was a thirty-six-year-old mother of four grown children on the day she was arrested. Medically, she'd given up the chances of being a mother again back in 1990, when she was only twenty-two. Did she really think it was possible for her to have another child?

Lisa's cousin in Arizona had eight children, four of them reportedly born after the woman had had her tubes reconnected. But the procedure was expensive and performed only in certain states. Had Lisa somehow raised the money and had the procedure done?

"That would be impossible," said Carl. "Not only because she was penniless, but Lisa had her tubes burned, not tied."

One day, Carl confronted Kevin, who was standing outside his parents' home. Carl asked Kevin for the second or third time since Lisa's arrest, "How could you not know Lisa was never pregnant?"

"Well, she has small babies," replied Kevin. Indeed, all of Lisa and Carl's children were under five pounds. Kayla was under three, born prematurely. Kevin was correct about that.

"Yeah, so . . . ? Your point?" Carl wanted to know.

"She *looked* pregnant!" insisted Kevin.

"No, she didn't. Listen, Kevin, you can tell that to your parents, everybody you work with, the newspapers, your friends, everybody in Melvern, and even yourself. But you can't tell *me* that," said Carl. "I had four children with the woman."

How could Lisa convince a town—better yet members of her immediate family—she was pregnant? This seemed to be the question everyone wanted answered as news about what she allegedly had done continued to spread. Some insisted they never believed Lisa's stories about being pregnant. Others said she wore baggy clothes and maternity wear around town. She even had gained some weight over the six months leading up to the murder. One man who knew her well said she had a knack for being able to swallow air and extend her stomach to make it appear as if she were pregnant. One of her sisters, who said she never believed Lisa when she lied about being pregnant, put her hands on Lisa's swollen stomach one day and swore she felt movement.

Fooling her own kids was one thing; manipulating teenagers was not so hard to do, especially when they lived in the same house and Lisa had all the time she needed to work on them. But

Kevin—the man who slept next to her every night? How could he not know?

Carl Boman couldn't explain it. Didn't she have a menstrual cycle every month? Didn't he ever put his ear up to her stomach and listen for movement? Didn't he put his hand on her stomach and wait for the child to kick?

The problems Lisa faced near the end of 2004, as her fabricated due date approached, mounted. She had a court date in January that would have, Carl was certain, given him full custody of the two children. Moreover, Ryan and Rebecca were beginning to figure her out, along with several other people in town.

"Ryan especially wanted to move back in with me," said Carl. "That was one of the reasons for the court date that month; he had expressed an opinion of wanting to live with me."

Ryan had always been "the quiet one" of the bunch. Fun and loving, he never had a bad word to say about anyone and generally stayed to himself, content with a video game. He liked Kevin and didn't mind living at the house in Melvern. All the kids had moved around a lot while Lisa and Carl were married. Settling down in Melvern hadn't been all that bad, after all. The kids had new friends. A place to call home. Stepsiblings.

As Carl saw it, Kevin was never the problem—it was Lisa. She seemed to be forever chasing another life: the one she left behind as a child and the one ahead that she was apparently making up as she went along. Her behavior leading up to her arrest became more erratic and unpredictable with each passing day and, near the end, began to scare the children.

"Ryan didn't like the situation there," added Carl. "Looking back, his mom was, I believe, worried she was going to be discovered."

63

In Melvern, on Saturday morning, a growing band of television and newspaper reporters and recognizable tabloid television-show hosts were looking for the scoop of the day: an interview with Kevin Montgomery.

In Kansas City, Todd Graves began talking about the next step in the prosecution of Lisa Montgomery. The U.S. Attorney's Office had an unyielding burden of proof to establish. It seemed like a fairly textbook murder prosecution, seeing so much forensic evidence was available and Lisa had, for all intents and purposes, confessed. But when defense attorneys got involved, Graves and his colleagues knew, the fight would truly begin.

Late Friday night, Graves released a formal criminal complaint against Lisa, accompanied by a comprehensive affidavit. For the first time, the gruesome details of Lisa's alleged crimes were made public, fueling the press's impetus to drive the story into Tragedy TV status. The eight-page affidavit, signed by U.S. magistrate judge Sarah Hays, listed names and addresses of people involved: Bobbie Jo and Zeb's neighbor Chris Law, Becky Harper, Dyanne Siktar, along with several others, and explained the actions of the fictional Darlene Fischer and the real Lisa Montgomery during the weeks leading up to Bobbie Jo's murder.

Within hours after the government put the affidavit on its Web site, it spread throughout the Internet.

"This is a heartrending case," Graves said outside the Nodaway County Courthouse in Maryville.

It would be a busy weekend for Todd Graves.

As soon as Lisa was in custody, Graves began working, he said later, "in conjunction with Nodaway County prosecuting attorney David Baird." Then he made a point to say, at least right now, the prosecution, like the initial investigation, was going to be a multi-faceted effort. Every single law that applied to the ultimate charges Lisa would face would be followed correctly, with proper procedure. Now was not the time to butt heads over which office would prosecute the case. Priority number one was filing the correct paperwork so the case could move forward in a timely manner. Some questions, Graves was quick to add, that the affidavit failed to answer would just have to wait. He wasn't prepared to jeopardize such an emotionally charged and important legal case by giving away details prematurely.

"I've also been in contact with my counterpart in Kansas," Graves explained, "and [the paperwork] has been filed in the United States District Court in Kansas City, Missouri, and that's where it will move forward."

The history behind the interstate kidnapping law and how it was written was not only interesting in itself, but applied to the federal case now building against Lisa Montgomery. The law dated back to the 1930s, when pioneering aviator Charles Lindbergh's newborn son was kidnapped from his estate. The Federal Kidnapping Act, which became known more commonly as "the Lindbergh Law," was initiated by Congress shortly after the Lindbergh kidnapping. Its intention was ". . . to let federal authorities step in and pursue kidnappers once they had crossed a state border with their victim."

The idea behind the law was to make sure federal law enforcement agencies assisted in state and local law enforcement investigations when a kidnapping ocurred. Local law enforcement didn't generally have the resources or jurisdiction to pursue kidnappers effectively across state lines. Federal law enforcement officers, such as the FBI and Customs, "have national enforcement authority," Congress noted. Those agencies could actively and expeditiously pursue any suspect at any time in any state. Congress believed the federal investigators could do a more thorough job during kidnapping investigations than state and local authorities, because of the resources they had at their disposal.

* * *

"When there's a kidnapping and someone dies as a result," Graves said, continuing to address reporters, "there's federal jurisdiction." Kansas City, where Graves worked, was no stranger to these types of federal crimes. "We have a state line that divides our city," Graves added. "And so, this isn't the first case that crosses the state line we've dealt with."

The official charge against Lisa was a violation of Title 18, United States Code 1201: kidnapping resulting in death—a fairly straightforward charge, at least from the position of the law.

"And that is a charge that carries a maximum penalty of life in prison without parole, or the possibility of the death penalty in the appropriate case."

The decision to go forward with the death penalty in a case that warranted it was not one Todd Graves could make by himself, or with his colleagues.

Twenty-four hours hadn't yet passed since Lisa was arrested, and many were already saying she deserved capital punishment. Bobbie Jo's body hadn't even been released from the morgue, pending forensics and an autopsy, nor had her family had the time to prepare for her funeral; yet scores of people in both counties affected by the crime—and around the world, for that matter—were prepared to convict Lisa without a trial and send her to meet her Maker. "Monster" became a term associated with Lisa almost immediately; people weren't interested in her side of the story.

"[The death penalty] is something," Graves continued, but then stopped to collect his thoughts, before adding, "We have elaborate procedures. It's not something that's taken . . . lightly. And in the Department of Justice, there's a deliberative process, and that decision will be made. But we have a history of cases like this in this area. The case certainly is unusual, but the nature of the charge isn't really anything out of the ordinary for us."

Almost one year prior to the date of Bobbie Jo's murder, a crime eerily parallel in detail and substance took place in Lamar, Oklahoma, about four hundred miles south of Skidmore. Thirty-seven-year-old Effie Goodson found herself facing two first-degree murder charges and a kidnapping accusation in the death of a local woman, twenty-one-year-old Carolyn Simpson, who was six months pregnant at the time she was murdered.

On December 23, 2003, a biting-cold morning, a hunter working his way through the thick brush in a remote Lamar field, about one hundred miles east of Oklahoma City, came upon Carolyn Simpson's mutilated body. Simpson had been shot in the head, her fetus cut from her womb and kidnapped.

Bizarrely enough, in the Simpson case, Goodson chose her victim and put a plan into effect, one could speculate from the evidence left behind, for the sole purpose of tricking the woman weeks and, possibly, even months, before she carried out the crime.

Simpson was last seen a day before her body was found. She had worked at a tribal casino in Okemah, Oklahoma. Effie Goodson was a casino regular and must have, authorities believed, set her sights on Simpson after meeting her one night and realizing she was pregnant. One report claimed the two women were introduced months before by mutual family members and friends.

On the night before a hunter found her body, Goodson and Simpson were reportedly seen leaving the casino together after Simpson's shift—yet Simpson was never heard from again.

The next day, Effie Goodson showed up at a Holdenville, Oklahoma hospital with a dead fetus that, the hospital reported, "had reached six months' gestation."

"I'm the mother," Goodson told hospital officials, adding that the baby had died during delivery.

After hospital officials determined with a few basic medical tests that Goodson could not have given birth recently, they became suspicious and called authorities.

Minutes later, Goodson was taken into custody.

What happened prior to the murder of Carolyn Simpson mirrored the details surrounding Lisa Montgomery's life leading up to Bobbie Jo's murder. Goodson had "falsely told several people she was pregnant," law enforcement said, "going back as far as ten months." Goodson's own husband, like Kevin Montgomery, believed his wife was expecting. A baby shower had been thrown in Goodson's honor. Some law enforcement officials even said Goodson "lured Simpson . . . into a friendship"—similar to what

Lisa Montgomery evidently had done to Bobbie Jo—"with . . . promises of free baby clothes and a crib." Even more striking, Goodson told her husband, allegedly after murdering Simpson and removing her fetus with a knife, she had given birth to the baby alongside a road near their home.

"I think anybody would agree she wanted a baby," one investigator involved in the case commented, strikingly in sync to what Ben Espey had said probably a half-dozen times since Lisa's arrest. "She already had baby items. She was really set up for a baby."

Despite its gruesome similarity, the Goodson case didn't garner a fraction of the publicity now erupting in Melvern as Lisa Montgomery was booked for kidnapping resulting in death.

64

Sleep was hard to find for Carl Boman. When he finally wrestled his thoughts together, he had one objective in mind: seeing his children.

Because he couldn't get hold of his lawyer, James Campbell, the night before, Carl called him first thing in the morning, hoping he would have some advice regarding what to do next.

Campbell, though, still hadn't returned to his office.

"I'm leaving for Melvern," Carl told Vanessa.

Carl's brother drove from Tulsa, where he lived, to Bartlesville, to pick up Carl. Carl wanted his support and company for the long trip to Melvern. As his brother drove, Carl used his cell phone and called James Campbell again.

"Yeah, Carl? What's happening?"

"I need to have my children here with me," said Carl, "at home, where they belong."

"Well, Carl, I heard about everything last night, and actually tried calling you. I'm on my way back to town now," said Campbell.

Richard Boman, Carl's father, who had been married to Lisa's mother at one time, drove up from Tennessee to meet Carl and his brother as they got closer to Melvern. Richard was well aware of the tenuous situation Carl had been in lately with Lisa and the kids. He knew about the pending child custody court case. The hearing, however, was likely to be postponed now, in anticipation of any legal action against Lisa.

"You're going to get the kids," his brother and father told him. "Relax."

James Campbell said he was going to file a temporary custody order as soon as Carl and his brother made it to his office in Burlington, Kansas.

"Let me take care of the paperwork while you're on your way," Campbell offered.

"Thanks, Jim."

Campbell, a burly man in his early forties, was an experienced lawyer in probate matters. He was certain the court would grant Carl temporary custody, based solely on the events over the past twenty-four hours—which had proved, at least on the surface, Lisa wasn't capable of taking care of the children at this point in her life.

"Drop by my office on your way into Melvern," said Campbell.

"Will do."

Carl and his brother had left Bartlesville about 7:30 A.M. By the time they got to Campbell's office two hours later, the paperwork was waiting for Carl to sign.

Campbell's urgent action was comforting to Carl. "This, of course, I appreciated," said Carl, "even though I knew the case was now going to make a name for him in town and would help him immensely. He's been, gosh, whew—James has been great."

By then, Carl's name had become synonymous with the case. *Good Morning America*, the *Montel Williams Show*, *Larry King Live*, and many other major media organizations were calling, asking Carl to appear with his children on air. Carl, at present, was not about to speak to the world about his relationship with Lisa; he wanted to make sure his kids were taken care of and the press left them alone.

The previous night had been a blur to Carl. Vanessa didn't make the trip to Melvern simply because of "all the emotion involved," recalled Carl. It was too much for her. All the time Carl spent on custody issues and dealing with Lisa and her family had impacted his relationship with Vanessa negatively.

After news of what happened broke, friends stopped by Carl and Vanessa's and called to see if they could do anything for the family. Carl appreciated the support. But now, with the severity of the crime itself beginning to settle on him as he made his way from Bartlesville to Melvern, the entire situation had taken on a new dimension. It was, he said, as if he were leading someone else's life, running on pure adrenaline, not thinking about things thoroughly, just trudging along on autopilot.

"It felt like walking through a cloud. I hate to sound clichéd, but it was like a dream. That's the only way I can describe it."

The plan was for Carl to pick the kids up at the Montgomerys' and bring them to where Judy lived in nearby Lyndon. Carl would stay the night at Judy's and return to Oklahoma the following morning with the kids.

Not long after Carl left Campbell's office, the attorney called with good news.

"The judge is going to sign the ex parte custody order on Monday," said Campbell. "Legally, you can bring the kids home with you."

The long drive to Melvern was cumbersome. Carl and his brother hardly said a word to each other.

"I mean, I had been married to this woman twice and had known her for over twenty years," explained Carl. "She was the mother of my children. When people say, 'These things happen to other people,' we generally take that with a grain of salt. But I know now what that means."

Carl was nervous about seeing the kids. He fretted over what he was going to say. He realized he couldn't gloat about being right—having told every one of the Montgomerys over the course of the past year Lisa was not pregnant. Nor could he put a bow on it and tell the children he'd fix it. It wouldn't be fair to them.

"I was at a loss for what to say and how to handle the situation," Carl remembered thinking while his brother drove. "My brother, whom I love dearly, wasn't much help. He did listen to my rantings along the way, but had no answers."

Carl called Kayla in Georgia. She was a daddy's girl. They had bonded from day one more than any of the other children, according to both. With Kayla being the youngest, Carl knew it was up to him to try to talk her through the situation.

"You okay?"

"I really don't want to talk, Dad."

"Okay, honey. I'm here, though. Let me speak to Auntie M."

Carl told Mary to watch Kayla closely. Kayla was close to Lisa. As soon as what had taken place truly hit her, she was going to implode emotionally.

Mary agreed. "No problem, Carl. Anything you need."

65

While Kayla was in school on Saturday morning, finishing up finals, she made a decision that, as bad as she wanted to leave, she was going to stay in Georgia. She saw no sense in going back home and getting involved in a media frenzy. Still, the brutality of what her mother purportedly had done ate at Kayla as she went about her day.

"By the time I was at school," she said, "I knew my mom had done 'it.'" Kayla had a hard time speaking about the specifics of what "it" was; the reality of the crime was too hard for her to put into words. "I'd had doubts about whether she was pregnant. I mean, it was just a feeling that kept bugging me. But, when Mary told me that day when I returned home from school . . . I knew. I didn't have doubts. I wondered how the person who gave birth to me could do such a thing. You see, sometimes things seem impossible, but they aren't, really."

What about Kevin?

"Did I think Kevin was involved? Not for a second! I know my mom could do something like that. But not Kevin. I didn't think he was involved then, and I still don't. . . . He was (and is) devastated. He loved (and still does) my mom . . . and was really shocked when he found out my mom did it. He really believed Tori Jo was *his* daughter. I feel bad for him."

Part of what hurt the most, Kayla said, was that her mother allegedly had murdered someone she had been close to and was just getting to know. Bobbie Jo and Kayla had corresponded via e-mail, in person, and through instant messages more times than she could count.

"She *murdered* my friend. She left an innocent baby without a mother, a husband without his wife, a mother without her daughter, a little boy without his protective big sister, and a community without a *wonderful* person. I am still so mad about it all.

"I miss talking to Bobbie Jo."

As class came to a close, Kayla began thinking about past events.

"I have always wondered what would have happened if I hadn't gone to live in Georgia. Would my mom still have done what she did? I know that what-ifs aren't good to focus on. But I can't help but wonder what would have happened. I know I can't go back and change things. But I *really* wish I could."

66

A crowd of well over three thousand people gathered to witness the first federal execution in America. It was June 25, 1790, somewhere near Portland, Maine. Thomas Bird, a tall fellow with large muttonchop sideburns and rotten teeth, stood at the gallows, his large hands, rough as rawhide, tied behind his back. Bird was pleading for his life with executioner Henry Dearborn, a U.S. Marshal.

Bird had petitioned the court, asking George Washington, the great general and president himself, for a pardon. His request was denied.

The crowd stood staring at Bird, clamoring for his neck. Bird was, essentially, a pirate, a nuisance to the community, which viewed him as nothing more than a ruffian who took what he wanted without much care for what people thought. He had murdered the captain of the ship he worked on. A man had to pay a price for such violence.

At the time of Bird's landmark execution, maritime law was a major concern for federal courts in America. Bird had violated one of the most cherished laws of the colonies.

Within minutes after he stood at the gallows, the doors below Thomas Bird opened and his feet fell out from underneath him. The fall snapped his neck like a dry twig. In seconds, it was over. History was made: the first federal execution.

Approximately forty crimes recognized by the federal government are punishable by the sentence of death. Most involve murder while in the process of committing a second crime. For example, in Lisa Montgomery's case, the government was alleging Lisa murdered Bobbie Jo Stinnett with the intention (and in the process) of kidnapping her unborn child.

Since the first federal execution, according to studies conducted by the Capital Punishment Research Project, "336 men and 4 women" have been executed under federal guidelines. Thirty-nine percent—134—were carried out on whites, and 118—35 percent—on African Americans; along with 63 Native Americans and 25 Hispanics (or persons of an unknown race).

Nearly every execution since Thomas Bird's in 1790 has been carried out by hanging, electrocution, gas, or lethal injection. A majority of executed inmates were convicted for murder or crimes resulting in murder. Other executions have been carried out for piracy, rape, rioting, kidnapping, and, naturally, espionage.

During the twentieth century, 61 percent of federal executions included minority defendants.

In a sense, these statistics boded well for Lisa Montgomery—if, in fact, the government chose to seek the death penalty against her. Several factors, experts claim, weigh on the side of females facing the death penalty. Number one is that juries sitting on federal cases feel the female murderer is less vicious and more likely to commit a criminal act under extenuating circumstances that ultimately led her to the point where she felt murder was her only option. Another important factor is that most women who face the death penalty are mothers.

"In Missouri," said one local official, "you get a lotta leg outta that—she would only need one vote."

The murder of Bobbie Jo Stinnett, however, was unusual in many ways. Lisa Montgomery was a woman who had confessed to killing another female exclusively for the purpose of kidnapping her child; a child, who, the jury in Lisa's case would no doubt learn, hadn't even been born. If a woman could cut a baby from another woman's womb and present the child to the public, her kids, and her husband as her own, what other crimes was she capable of?

Approximately thirty prisoners were on death row the day Lisa was arrested. Would she be number thirty-one?

As Lisa sat in prison, Todd Graves started laying the groundwork for the government's case.

"There are numerous statutes," Graves said, reflecting on how the government was faring in its decision to pursue the death penalty against Lisa. "We have to have a very specific statute. We have specific jurisdiction, not general jurisdiction. And so there are a number of crimes, but it has to fit within one of those categories."

Speaking a day after her arrest, Graves was specific in the way he viewed what Lisa had reportedly admitted. "I'm not sure any act of violence that results in a death would be considered a normal act."

Graves had grown up in Northwest Missouri and lived there most of his life. He knew a lot of the people in the region where Bobbie Jo was murdered. It was, in every meaningful sense, an indescribable crime, unspeakable. Those images people now had as the affidavit was made public were horrifying. The one person people were talking about most was Becky Harper, Bobbie Jo's mother, who had found her daughter and believed her "stomach had exploded." The words Harper used were, by themselves, appalling. To think a mother would come upon her daughter bleeding to death on the floor of her home and her only grandchild missing—it was inconceivable.

"Well," Graves said after being asked how he personally felt, "it's certainly among the most heartrending, and it is a very unusual case."

Graves had been a state prosecutor before being appointed U.S. attorney.

"And there—believe it or not—there are other unusual cases [I have seen]. But this one definitely kicks you in the gut. . . . This is the heart of America. We are at the geographic and population center of the country. And to have something happen here that gets this kind of attention certainly is something that we don't look forward to."

Representative Sam Graves, who had helped in Ben Espey's fight to get the Amber Alert issued the night Victoria Jo went missing, released a statement on Saturday detailing his plan to introduce legislation that would make it a bit easier to get future Amber Alerts issued for abductions. It wouldn't matter if the child was a newborn, infant, or fetus; this case proved any abduction warranted an Amber Alert, even if issued with a vague description of the child.

Representative Graves was proud to be able to submit legislation in honor of Victoria Jo, who had become a symbol of hope to the entire Skidmore community, if not all of western Missouri. Lisa Montgomery, on the other hand, at least in the eyes of the judicial system from here on out, would be known simply as Case Number 04-00210-01-JTM.

One more number on a court docket.

67

As the town of Skidmore rallied around Zeb, his family, and Becky Harper, comforting them, Pastor Mike Wheatley and the First Church of God became the self-appointed foundation of support for the Montgomery family.

Wheatley told reporters he was "stunned," like the rest of the community, by the events of the past few days. He was "pulling together to . . . surround the Montgomery family with love." He then added, "I've known evil people in my life and you can feel it standing six feet away from them—and Lisa was not that kind of person. It was a horrendous act, but that doesn't make her a bad person."

A few days after Lisa's arrest, Wheatley used harsher words, saying, "If she actually did this crime—it's still alleged—if she doesn't repent of it, yes, she's going to hell."

Carl Boman arrived in Melvern at about 10:00 A.M. and went to the Montgomerys' house. The media were camped at the end of the driveway, waiting for a statement from Kevin.

As Carl and his brother drove past the satellite trucks and local-news vans, kicking up mud behind them, Carl couldn't help but think how far he had come in his life with the woman who was now the center of all this attention.

"When I first met Lisa," he said, "she was a lost teenager. We'd talk for hours about the future, about kids, and normal things two people talk about. Who in their wildest dreams would have thought some day all this interest would be centered on Lisa and such a horrible event, not to mention a young, beautiful woman would be murdered and Lisa responsible?"

Looking at everyone gathered around the end of the driveway, Carl felt overwhelmed.

"My kids, the people I love most in the world—here was their mother being held for this act. She was a woman I had loved at one time and, at the same time, had also lived in hell with."

Although the day was sunny and rather warm for that time of the year, a "heartbroken" Carl felt the "sad and gloomy" sense that the town had taken on. It was as if a pall had been cast over everything, some melancholy blanket of despair.

Having learned in the U.S. Navy the hard way that showing emotion was a sign of weakness, Carl collected himself before he and his brother stepped out of the truck and walked up to the Montgomerys' porch.

Carl knocked on the door. Kevin, disheveled and obviously distraught, answered. Without even thinking about it, the two men, having been foes for a period, hugged as if they were long-lost friends reuniting at an airport.

Rebecca, Alicia, and Ryan were sitting on the living-room floor in shock, Carl remembered, and halfheartedly acknowledged him when he entered the house. Their behavior was odd, he thought, but understandable. They had been sucker punched.

They all sat together in the living room.

"Nice out there today," mentioned Kevin.

"It's warm," said Carl. "Sunny too."

"Not usually this warm, huh," added Kevin.

"No. It's weird."

"How 'bout those Sooners?" They had just put a beating on Colorado and were preparing to take what was an undefeated season to USC. Kevin, however, was more or less just trying to make idle chitchat to pass the time.

"Yeah," said Carl.

Alicia was sitting next to Carl. He had his arm around her. She was quiet while he and Kevin continued talking about the house, the landscaping the Montgomerys had recently done, and more football.

Then, "Why, Dad?" Alicia blurted out.

That one comment changed everything.

Kevin dropped his head and shook it back and forth, fighting tears. "She didn't have to have a baby to keep me," he said. "We could have been happy without a child."

Carl decided to explain he was taking the kids back home to

Oklahoma the following morning. The Montgomerys wanted the children to stay until Christmas, so they could say their good-byes to school friends and enjoy whatever pleasure the holiday was to bring.

Carl ultimately agreed.

"The Montgomerys' house," Carl said later, "was so depressing. I understood why, but it was all I could stand at the time."

When community members showed up with food, Carl felt like an outsider. "I was definitely out of my element."

Among those who arrived was Pastor Mike Wheatley. As if at a funeral, Wheatley and fellow parishioners handed out sandwiches while trying to console everyone. Later that night and the following few days, Wheatley would show up on television speaking on behalf of Kevin, Lisa, and Carl's children.

"No one really asked him," said Carl, "but he just kind of took the reins and started calling himself the family spokesperson."

That creepy sense of numbness Carl felt as he and his brother pulled into town was there again when they left. People appeared traumatized, walking around in some sort of daze.

"I will never understand," said one man in Melvern later. "There are kids in this world nobody wants. Do I hate her? If it happened anywhere else in the country, I'd hate her. But she's from here. I just feel nothing."

Kevin came out of the house Saturday afternoon and released a formal statement to the reporters and television crews. He stood at the end of the driveway with cameras and tape recorders pointed at him. It was clear Kevin had been crying. His eyes were puffy. He looked tired. Worn. He was wearing a baseball cap he kept fidgeting with as he tried to find the right words.

"This has to be as hard, or harder, on them (the Stinnett family) as it is on me," Kevin said through tears a few days later. The sincerity in his voice was evident. What he had to say was, indeed, coming from his heart. "I sure hope they get as much support from their church and community as I have, because we're all going to need it."

Then, he added, "My heart ain't broke just for me and Lisa and her kids. It's them, too. That was a precious baby," he paused, sniffling. "I know. I know."

68

Judy Shaughnessy was at home late Saturday night when the crime her daughter was being accused of settled on her like a death in the family. She felt a sensation of dread. Lisa was being called everything from a sociopath to one of the most vicious killers in American history, sending Internet bloggers into a vengeance-based frenzy, causing Judy to go out of her mind with mixed emotions. She loved Lisa, of course, but she also viewed her as someone who needed professional help.

With the media calling the house for comments and hovering around the end of the driveway, Judy's husband, Danny, drove down to the hardware store in Lyndon and picked up several orange-and-black No Trespassing signs. ("This oughta keep 'em away.")

Danny liked chopping firewood in the forest by himself, hauling it back home, and stacking it. He took pleasure in the simple monotony of everyday tasks. All this attention was overwhelming, an invasion. Before marrying Judy, Danny had been with the same woman for twenty-three years. He'd fathered four children. He did time in 'Nam.

"Danny is strong-natured," Judy said of her fifth husband, "and can only take so much; then he nips it in the bud."

When he returned from the hardware store, six-foot, 215-pound Danny Shaughnessy stopped at the edge of the driveway, took a ball-peen hammer out of the back of his pickup, and tacked one of the No Trespassing signs to an old cottonwood standing guard over the property, facing the street. The others would be posted around the property in back.

"We did make a statement later to the *Kansas City Star*. But all others, 'no comment'; they got the message!" she said.

Judy had traveled around the country and done things most in Melvern and Skidmore had only read about or seen on television. Now she felt her experience could help the family through it all. Yet no one was turning to her for guidance. She felt isolated, as if no one wanted to talk to her.

"The days following Lisa's arrest were hard for me," explained Judy. "I couldn't answer the phone. I didn't want to go anywhere. I stayed here on the farm. I couldn't eat. Sleep. All I did was drink coffee, smoke, and cry."

She'd called the Montgomerys to find out about the kids, but nobody was responding. She left messages.

"I felt that I was their grandmother and the Montgomerys were only step-grandparents. They didn't even have the decency to call me to tell me that the kids were okay or not okay. Not one call from the people in Melvern, not even Kevin. I was *very* hurt."

Judy was never one to choose her words carefully. Some viewed her manner as abrasive, even cold; but Judy was speaking her truth, as she saw it. She felt she deserved better treatment from those involved.

"At the time," she added, "the kids did believe their mother was pregnant, and I do think they had a hard time believing their mother did this. I had a hard time believing it myself. Lisa was capable of a lot of things, but I never thought she would do something like this. But I had to face reality—and it still haunts me."

Judy was also grieving for Bobbie Jo Stinnett and her family, along with the baby. "How could Lisa do this, having four children of her own? Taking a mother away from her baby. . . . Look what she lost."

On the day Lisa was arrested, Judy and Danny had taken Judy's grandson Justin to the Wal-Mart in Topeka to get holiday portraits done. "Right there, Justin, don't move. Smile now, son. Smile." After that mini fiasco, which they thoroughly enjoyed, Judy and Danny drove Justin over to his former foster-family's house. They were having a Christmas party. "I respected them. They needed to see him, too." Then they stopped and had a bite to eat before heading back home.

While Judy and Danny were out with Justin celebrating life, Lisa was reportedly in Skidmore, doing God only knows what. Judy couldn't comprehend how separated she was from the person Lisa had become. It was as if just when Judy thought things couldn't get any worse, something else happened. One kid in prison on a drug charge; another on her way on a possible murder rap. Was there an answer somewhere?

It had been a beautiful day, what with Judy and Justin and Danny just "hanging out" like a family. The sun was bright and powerful. There was a certain *It's a Wonderful Life* spirit in every handshake and "hello," tip of the hat and wave. People were happy and full of that joy only the holidays can bring.

But then everything changed—or, as Judy put it, "the nightmare began."

69

Early Sunday morning, December 19, as Lisa Montgomery sat in an eight-by-ten-foot holding cell in Wyandotte County Detention Center in downtown Kansas City, Sunday services were concluded in Melvern and Skidmore. This morning would be a day of turning to God for answers.

Why had it happened?

In Skidmore, churchgoers sipped coffee, read the morning newspaper, and laid out their Sunday best. Today's prayer, hymns, and Scripture readings would be especially poignant. The supple words of the Bible, so rich in piety and grace, would carry a heavy burden this morning.

The Reverend Harold Hamon had relocated to Skidmore with his wife, Mary Lou, a little over four years ago. At seventy-seven, about five feet, five inches, 133 pounds, Hamon might have seemed to be a frail old man with sagging shoulders and paper-white hair. But Hamon, his congregation confidently knew, was a hulking giant in heart and mind. Hamon was no stranger to giving sermons under ominous circumstances. When he was twenty years old, just out of the navy, the first funeral he presided over was for a victim of suicide. The second, not too long after, was for a stillborn baby. Hamon knew suffering, but more important, he knew how to describe it to the people who looked to him for answers.

Since Bobbie Jo's death, Hamon had been asked by just about every major media outlet to appear on television. They wanted him to talk about the life Bobbie Jo would never have and how Skidmore had been affected by the crime. But Hamon thought it ill-advised to speak of such a beloved community member, who hadn't been buried yet, taking into consideration how Bobbie Jo's family must have been hurting. So he declined.

Hamon's refusal didn't stop the blitz of telephone calls his office had received since the murder—some of which, he pointed out later, were uplifting and consoling: well wishes sent by fellow ministers and pastors throughout the Midwest, offering their support.

"I told them," Hamon described later to a reporter, "to pray. America is a great nation. There's good people here."

Amen.

Harold Hamon's unwavering faith in God would carry him through the next few days. As members of his congregation flocked to the church at ten o'clock Sunday morning, seeking solace and reassurance that life *could* go on in the face of evil, he sensed a collective conviction in town, which couldn't be dispirited in any way. This was significant. For it was a time when many might be asking themselves, if God truly existed, why would He allow a family to experience such an incurable pain? Bobbie Jo was so young. So well-liked and well-deserving. Ahead of her, she had a life many could only dream about. Who could make any sense out of it all?

"These tragedies come not just here," Hamon explained, commenting on how he handled Sunday service and preparations for Bobbie Jo's funeral, "but all over the place, the world. And God *loves* the world."

Over the past twenty-four hours, Hamon had turned to the one source he knew could offer him the answers the town, as well as his own spirit, so eagerly sought. The Bible was where Hamon believed he could find a similar experience and share it with his people. In the words of the Apostles, Hamon would help Skidmore understand that, even during a time of unspeakable tragedy, the Lord was working. Many would have a hard time accepting God's plan; but Hamon was sure, after reading several verses and relating them to Bobbie Jo's death, he could find a way to put it all into meaning and prayer.

The Skidmore Christian Church sat on a small hill just outside downtown. One hundred yards away stood the house Bobbie Jo and Zeb used to call home. Now it was a sad reminder to all who passed by of what had taken place inside.

An unassuming building, no doubt converted from an old house, the Skidmore Christian Church was where many people of Skidmore gathered every Sunday to understand God and all He had to offer. The tannish brown stucco gave the dwelling a gingerbread look, and in winter months, with snow and ice capping the steepled rooftop, covering the shingles like frosting, it looked edible. A flag with baby blue and white, and a red cross where stars should be, hung outside the front door and flapped in the slight breeze. Like the white banner Welcome sign hanging below the north peak, the weathered white trim around the windows spoke to one of the church's core beliefs: the soul is what matters most, not what's on the outside—the heart, the body, the mind.

Hamon had a gift, some explained, for calming people. He could take a situation and make people understand its lesson. As the organ pumped the groan of a tugboat and people proceeded into the small church at a pace of bereavement, here would be Hamon's test.

This was the same church where Bobbie Jo and Zeb had been married, not even two years ago. ("Oh, they were such a lovely couple," said one man in town. "The pride and joy of this little town.") Many of the same people filing in now were there, celebrating the love Zeb and Bobbie Jo shared. After the ceremony, Bobbie Jo had given Hamon a card, thanking him for officiating. Hamon had kept the card. A note stapled to the back of the card was on his mind today: Bobbie Jo thanked Hamon for preaching the service at "my wedding," she wrote, but had crossed out "my" and replaced it with "our." She signed the card "Zeb and Bobbie Jo." Hamon knew, "being a man," he told a reporter, who "wrote that." It was Bobbie Jo, of course, speaking for her and Zeb as a team, a couple—that is, a married couple. She was proud to be able to thank the reverend on behalf of both her and her new husband.

That was Bobbie Jo's spirit, always putting others first. Victoria Jo would know that about her mother one day because people in town would tell the child when she grew up and could understand it.

Gene Day, Bobbie Jo's grandfather, later said, "It's hard most days and the nightmares never seem to go away. Every once in a while, I see someone come down the street, and I think it's Bobbie Jo—then I remember."

The Communion meditation on Sunday morning was based on the premise of forgiveness. A church member, standing in front of the congregation after everyone was seated, spoke of the virtues of forgiving others for their sins.

"There is no life apart from God's love," a verse in the Bible proclaimed. "Therefore, there is no life apart from forgiveness, for forgiveness is the seal, the mark, and the proof of Love. If we say we have love and cannot walk in forgiveness, we deceive ourselves, and our 'love' is only a parody of the real thing."

It was a quiet service, a solemn time of reflection. Hope hovered above the crowd as the pipe organ breathed sweet music. Congregants needed to feel something good, something they could use as means to forgive. After all, they had Victoria Jo back. They could embrace and rejoice. God was the Almighty. He *had* answered prayers already. Look at her. . . . Was there a more beautiful child?

"If you lose hope," someone noted afterward, "you've lost everything."

Optimism was indeed in the blue sky outside the church, in the stubble of the fields that would soon yield a new crop, in the crisp, fresh air, at the Sunday-dinner tables where people would bow their heads for grace.

One church elder got up and mentioned what had happened. "I ask you to pray for the baby and her family," the man said. "We give thanks she is alive and well."

Later in the afternoon came word from the hospital where Victoria Jo was being monitored: she might be able to go home to Zeb that night, or the following morning. It was one of God's little blessings, wasn't it? Bobbie Jo would live on through her own flesh and blood.

70

With the exception of Kayla Boman, Lisa and Carl's children awoke on Sunday morning at Mr. and Mrs. Montgomery's house in Melvern. It was time to sit down and pray in the quiet solitude of the Lord's house.

Pastor Mike Wheatley's job in Melvern was to help his congregation understand how the Lord worked during such trying times. His task would be doubly tough this morning; as the community was facing another loss: a respected local man in his midforties had dropped dead on Friday. "The whole town was hurting over that, too," one of the kids said.

Wheatley wanted the service on Sunday morning to be about "worship," because Christmas was so near, as opposed to "grieving."

"I did the best I could to make it that way," Wheatley said later on television.

Wheatley had written the sermon for Sunday worship "before details of [Bobbie Jo's] death surfaced," he said. Quite prophetically, he had titled his sermon: "A Baby Changed Everything," referring to Baby Jesus, of course.

Now, though, the title seemed to be a fitting foundation for the events of the past four days.

Kevin Montgomery showed up at Wheatley's church with Alicia, Ryan, Rebecca, and his parents. Tears were flowing before the family even sat down and bowed their heads in prayer. Kayla was still in Georgia and had no intention of returning. "Did I want to go home?" she asked herself that morning. "No!" Then, almost in the same breath, "Yes, in a way, I wanted to be around my family. But I did *not* want to go back to Kansas. I didn't want to be around any of that. I just had this feeling that I shouldn't go back, and trust me, I was asked more times than I can count."

Carl and Lisa's other three children sat in Wheatley's First Church of God listening to the organ welcome members. Pastor Wheatley announced he was going to read a statement Kevin had prepared. Kevin would have read it himself, but he was too distressed.

"As everyone here knows well," Wheatley read aloud from a piece of paper in front of him on the podium, "this hasn't been a very good week at all."

As Wheatley articulated Kevin's words, Lisa's oldest, Rebecca, broke down in quiet sobs. She was sitting with friends near Kevin and Alicia. Both Rebecca and Alicia had worked early shifts that morning. The past four days had been a blur. Mom in jail. Bobbie Jo dead. Their baby sister gone. ("What would you do," Rebecca asked later, "if you were told all this stuff? And then your *dad* comes and says he's taking your brothers and sisters away to go live with him. I'd never see my mom again.")

"Our deepest sympathies," Wheatley continued, "also go out to the family of Bobbie Jo Stinnett.'

A hush fell on the church. Many sat without moving or speaking. Some nodded in agreement with Kevin's words; others shook their heads in disbelief. What more could be said? How many tears would lessen the pain?

"This is going to be a long and difficult road for everyone to walk down," Wheatley continued, still speaking for Kevin, "but if we look, and hold out our hands, God is there to lead the way. Please keep Lisa, the kids, and I in your prayers."

As members bowed their heads together in prayer, the choir began a resonating version of "The First Noel." It was a fitting piece of music. Said to be first published in the mid-1850s, the holiday classic carried a new message of comfort in Melvern that morning:

> *The First Noel, the Angels did say*
> *Was to certain poor shepherds in fields as they lay*
> *In fields where they lay keeping their sheep*
> *On a cold winter's night that was so deep.*

Noel, Noel, Noel, Noel.
Born is the King of Israel.

When the congregation reached the song's second verse, Alicia, sitting next to Kevin, started crying. It was all too much.

"Staying at home would have been worse," one church member said later of the children and Kevin. "This is where they get their strength."

After the service, friends surrounded Rebecca, shielding her like bodyguards of a starlet at a film premiere. Flashbulbs popped. Microphones and microcassette recorders were thrust in people's faces. *Over here! Turn, please. Can we get a comment?* Reporters had been hanging around outside the church, asking questions, looking for anyone with the surname Montgomery. "Do you know where the Montgomerys are? Where they live? Were Lisa Montgomery's children in church today?"

Sneaking by, Rebecca laughed to herself. *They don't know who I am.* She made it to her car, and locked the doors, her friends still by her side, without having to answer a single question.

71

By early Sunday evening, the status of Victoria Jo became the topic of conversation for many in the regions affected by the crimes for which Lisa Montgomery had been arrested. No definitive word had come out of the hospital since early morning. By and large, the media had respected Zeb Stinnett's request to keep its distance.

At about six o'clock, Carol Wheeler, the acting spokeswoman at Stormont-Vail Regional Health Center, said, "She is considered a preemie. But neonatal specialists said she is responding as you would expect any child of her gestial age would."

Through Wheeler, Zeb wanted the public to know Victoria Jo was doing "fine" and would be released "soon." No other additional information regarding her condition was made available. The family wanted privacy.

Zeb hadn't left the hospital since Victoria Jo had been found—and wouldn't, he said, until she was released.

72

Monday morning began as a flawless Midwestern winter's day in Melvern. The sun rose in a burst of fiery reds and yellows and, by 10:00 A.M., had burned off an early-morning fog. With the sun shining, people headed off to work, carrying on business as usual.

Along Main Street, shop owners and store clerks opened their doors. Diners, beauty parlors, and coffee shops would soon fill as reports of Lisa's first day in court trickled out through television sets sitting on oak entertainment centers and tag-sale TV stands, as it would in the dark corners of bars and restaurants. Households in the countryside would tune in, too. What would happen to Melvern's most infamous citizen?

The satellite trucks were still parked up and down Main Street. There they sat, broadcasting stories all across the world. Reporters were still scouring the town looking for filler stories, while waiting to learn what Lisa's first court appearance would divulge. The majority of the townspeople made it known they cared not only for Victoria Jo, Lisa's children, and Kevin Montgomery, but for the Stinnett family and the town of Skidmore, too.

Signs were taped to business front doors in downtown Melvern and nearby Lyndon, the county seat. "The Melvern Community Is Collecting Funds for the Bobbie Jo Stinnett Family, Skidmore, Missouri." The Lyndon State Bank, with branches spread across the region, posted similar notices. Understandably, Zeb wouldn't be going back to work for some time. He'd be raising a child on his own. Any contribution—a dime, nickel, dollar—would end up in good hands.

The local school district made counselors available for students and teachers to help them cope with their feelings. Many schools had the next two weeks off in observance of the Christmas holiday, but the school board felt students would somehow view the recent events as a reflection on themselves and the town as a whole. The people of Melvern took pride in their community. "So when tragedy strikes any of its members, the others also are hit hard. The same is true when a community member does something wrong," Ted Vannocker, the superintendent and principal of Marais des Cygnes Valley (High) School, told reporters.

For Kayla Boman, school had always been a release. Not that she enjoyed it all that much, or was glad she had to go. But still, she liked the social atmosphere of being around kids her age. This was probably a day Kayla needed to be in school more than any other—but it wouldn't happen. The holidays were here, school was closed.

Most parents felt that routine was best for kids during times of tragedy. To continue to do the same things as you might on any other *normal* day meant you had some sort of control over your life. Kayla wanted it back, but Lisa had stripped her of any sense of a normal life.

Some kids could be cruel. The story unraveling in Missouri certainly had worked its way into Georgia. If a kid put two and two together and figured out Kayla was Lisa's daughter, name-calling and family-bashing were sure to begin. Internet bloggers were publishing the kids' names on message boards. Any computer-savvy teen could log on and figure it all out.

Home at Aunt Mary's house was a good place for Kayla during those first few days after Lisa was arrested. "At least at Mary's house, I was busy, so I didn't think about 'it' a lot," Kayla asserted.

On Monday, Kayla went to the hospital with Mary to visit Mary's mom, who'd had a brain aneurism a few days earlier. It was a helpful trip in more ways than one. Anywhere but Melvern, Kayla said. To be able to be there for Mary was a gift. It took her out of her own situation, if only for a day. At home, there would have been more reasons to think about everything.

Kayla said she tried talking to her sister Alicia, but Alicia had a completely different opinion about a lot of things, so it was just easier to talk to people who understood her. Ryan wasn't going to be any help, Kayla decided, because, "I don't talk about my mom too much to him. He was pretty sensitive about it, and I didn't want to stir up any emotions. He's a really good person to talk to when I just need to get something off my chest."

Ryan was only ten months older than Kayla, so the two of them had always been in the same grade. "Because of that, we have always been really close."

Carl and Kayla both agreed Ryan had a temper problem when he was younger—"when he would get mad, he would want to hit something"—but as he grew, he learned to manage it. One could speculate the chaotic life Lisa and Carl led as their two marriages imploded around the kids was partly responsible for the issues Ryan struggled with early on. The family had moved a lot, and Lisa and Carl were at odds much of the time during those years.

Rebecca had always been closer to her mom than the other children. "Mom was always the outdoorsy type of person, hiking and camping," she recalled. "She liked her animals; we had lots of animals. She just never took care of them. That was our job. She liked to read—a lot. Once Mom got into a book, you just didn't talk to her. You couldn't get her attention."

Taking care of her siblings was, Rebecca said, her "job" because she was the oldest. "Whenever they needed something, I took care of them."

"Although Rebecca is the bossiest of the four of us," remarked Kayla, "she is the most outgoing. She was in Future Farmers of America for four years, an officer for three, a cheerleader for two years, and I believe the school mascot for a year. She played basketball for two or three years, and was actively involved in journalism, writing articles for the school newspaper right up until her final year."

When their mom wasn't around, Rebecca would watch the other kids.

Kayla recalled, "At the time, it was just me, her, and Mom, who worked two jobs, so she wasn't home much. I was seven-and-a-half. In my opinion, Rebecca had to grow up way too fast. I guess you would kind of have to when you're just a kid (eleven years old) and you're put in charge of another kid."

Carl claimed his oldest daughter bore the brunt of Lisa's manipulation, especially where his duties as a father were concerned.

What hurt Rebecca more than anything was how "we would wait all day and night because Dad said he would be there, and he would never show up. He says it's Mom's fault, but he . . . he faked having cancer one time. He said he had cancer, so Mom drove us all the way down to Oklahoma to see him."

Carl said he was diagnosed with a form of stomach cancer, which, luckily, never materialized.

"I didn't see them as much as I wanted to," recalled Carl. "I lived one hundred fifty miles away and wasn't allowed to take them home. It was Lisa's rule. I was diagnosed with cancer when I first started having stomach problems: one doctor said I had it, one said I didn't. I lost a lot of weight, and I told Rebecca that there was a 'possibility' I had it, and what the doctor said. Lisa made a big issue of it and even went to Social Security to see how much money she would get if I died. I was tested three years ago and didn't have cancer."

Still, Rebecca maintained, Carl rarely called, especially after he met Vanessa and remarried. "He used to call us all the time. But then when he met Vanessa, it stopped. *We* were the ones who were calling him."

"Vanessa and Lisa did *not* get along," explained Carl. "Lisa made it very difficult for me to see the kids, and Vanessa didn't apologize or try to work with Lisa, and me and the kids are the ones who suffered for it. I never didn't call the kids. Lisa made it difficult for me sometimes. It was hard for me to call all the time, but I always called once a week."

If Carl called, Lisa would say he didn't, after not allowing the call to go through to the children. If he wanted to drive over to get the kids for the weekend, Lisa would say no. It was all a carefully framed plan of Lisa's, Carl insisted, to make him look bad in front of his children. What's more, Lisa and Kevin had dial-up Internet service, which, considering the amount of time Lisa spent online, made it nearly impossible for Carl to get through. If he showed up unannounced, "She wouldn't allow me to take them . . . out of the yard."

73

Located in downtown Kansas City, the Charles Evans Whittaker Courthouse building looks more like a high-rise, five-star hotel on the Las Vegas strip than a $90-million federal building. At nearly three hundred feet tall, the six-hundred-thousand-square-foot, ten-story granite structure houses some five hundred government employees. Named after the only Kansas City resident to be appointed to the Supreme Court, the tubular-shaped spiral of this massive structure, from a bird's-eye view, looks like the letter C.

Sixteen courtrooms occupy the building on different floors, where court of appeals, district court, magistrate court, and bankruptcy judges all carry out their trial work. Each courtroom is outfitted with the latest audio-visual technology, which, coupled with the high ceilings and "wedge"-shaped contour of the courtrooms, allows multidefendant trials the working space they often require.

By Monday afternoon, the granite, limestone, and glass corridors inside the rotunda lobby of the courthouse building, where terrazzo floors reflect an assortment of twenty-five-foot-tall sculptures, mattered little to Lisa Montgomery. She would never see any of it. Shuttled into the building via a U.S. Marshal transport, Lisa was whisked by elevator up to the eighth floor and put in a holding cell, where she sat and waited for her first formal arraignment on charges of kidnapping resulting in death.

As Lisa was brought into court—and out in public for the first time since her arrest three days ago—Stormont-Vail Regional Health Center released five-pound eleven-ounce Victoria Jo in good health to her father. Zeb had been given an extended paternity leave from his job at Kawasaki Motors. From the hospital, he drove Victoria Jo to his mother-in-law's house in Skidmore, where he was planning to stay with the baby for a while. Victoria Jo would sleep in the same crib Tyler Harper, Bobbie Jo's little brother, had slept during the early years of his life.

While Zeb Stinnett and Becky Harper made the infant comfortable in her new surroundings, Lisa, wearing an orange prison jumpsuit and her signature oversized glasses, which somewhat shadowed the puffy bags underneath her eyes, was escorted into the courtroom, doing the "paper-slipper shuffle," a term inmates sometimes use in place of the more common "perp walk." With her long brown hair (laced with delicate streaks of blond) hiding her face, Lisa looked down the entire time and seldom made eye contact with anyone. Kevin, fidgeting in a front-row pew, watched his wife as she was led to a mahogany table in front of U.S. magistrate judge David J. Waxse.

And there she stood, head bowed, handcuffs and leg chains clanking every time she moved even the slightest bit, waiting for the judge to begin.

"If convicted, Mrs. Montgomery," Judge Waxse said at one point, after announcing the charges against Lisa, "you could spend the rest of your life in prison or face the death penalty."

Earlier that morning, U.S. deputy attorney Matt Whitworth filed a motion asking the judge to keep Lisa in custody.

"This case involves an act of extreme violence, which resulted in the death of Bobbie Jo Stinnett and the kidnapping of the victim's baby girl, Victoria Jo Stinnett. Further, [the] defendant is now charged with the offense of kidnapping resulting in death, which carries a maximum sentence of life without parole or death."

Whitworth argued that because the government viewed Lisa as a danger to the community, not to mention a flight risk, she needed to be kept behind bars.

"The government respectfully requests that this Honorable Court set a detention hearing to demonstrate that no condition or combination of conditions will reasonably assure the defendant's appearance as required by the court and the safety of other persons and the community, and thereafter detain the defendant without bail pending trial of this matter."

The judge agreed, and set a bond hearing for December 30.

The U.S. Attorney's Office also announced it was bringing in Nodaway County prosecutor David Baird as a special assistant U.S. attorney. Lisa allegedly had committed her crimes in Baird's district. Baird knew the territory and scope of the township. He would be instrumental in investigation and case preparation. But, perhaps most important, Baird would be the go-to man when it came time to pick a jury. Baird knew the people of Missouri. He could add insight and ingenuity to every element of the prosecution.

Baird was an experienced trial lawyer who knew the law well. He was working for the office during the Ken Rex McElroy fiasco in Skidmore, back in 1981, and had a reputation for pressing forward in the face of difficulty in even the most ordinary cases where the law had been breached or broken. Baird was a fighter for the people's rights, often pursuing cases of child porn and rape. He fought hard, right up until the end of any case, high-profile or not. In the coming months, he would be invaluable in the U.S. Attorney Office's case against Lisa.

Todd Graves and David Baird had worked together several times, helping each other where they could, but were also unified in participating in a new drug task force in the Western District. The Northwest Missouri Interagency Team Response Operation (NITRO) had created solid relationships among law enforcement agencies in the district so they could fight together against a growing drug problem.

"I am pleased to be a part of . . . the NITRO endeavor," Baird said after NITRO was formed in 2002. "During my tenure as Nodaway County prosecuting attorney, my office has been actively involved in the vigorous prosecution of those associated with drug activity. . . . My office will be actively involved in the NITRO effort and provide it full support."

On the day of Lisa's first court appearance, she was represented by public defenders Charles Dedmon and Ron Wurtz. Shortly before Lisa's arraignment ended, Dedmon and Wurtz asked the judge to issue a gag order. Every time a new piece of information, no matter how small, was released, the entire history of the case sprang back into the forefront of the media. Some involved were starting to talk. Dedmon and Wurtz wanted a fair shot. They had refused to answer any questions from the media themselves; yet Todd Graves, Ben Espey, and several others, it seemed, were appearing with Larry King and Anderson Cooper on major news shows.

Judge Waxse declined the gag order. "But I remind [everyone involved] to limit their comments to the media."

Assistant U.S. attorney Terra Morehead, who was representing the government, said, "We know what the rules are as it applies to dissemination of information."

Lisa's children were thunderstruck by the image of their mom doing the perp walk on television. They couldn't believe what they were seeing.

"I know it was hard on everyone," said Kayla. "I watched some of the news, but Auntie M didn't want me to watch too much of it, because then I would dwell on it. Instead, she had me talk to her about how I felt . . . and to a psychiatrist (I think that is what he was . . . but he was a friend of hers). It helped, I guess."

As word of Lisa's first day in court spread, members of the Ratter Chatter message board discussed Lisa's alleged crimes. A rumor had started on one of the message boards saying Lisa supposedly had practiced the procedure she allegedly conducted on Bobbie Jo on some of her expecting rat terriers.

"How the rumors about my mom 'practicing' on our champion bitch got started are beyond me," Kayla said in her mom's defense. "That one really makes me laugh, though—because only one of our dogs was shown at dog shows, and I showed *him*. . . . None of our dogs died while having puppies, or were ever missing."

74

A day after Lisa's arraignment, a spokesperson for the U.S. Attorney's Office said no decision had been made about whether the government would seek the death penalty. Such a decision would have to be approved by the Department of Justice.

If the public was yearning for the details of Lisa's admission, or her state of mind at the time Bobbie Jo was murdered, they were going to have to wait. The ten-minute hearing days ago, when the charges against Lisa were read into the record, had failed to yield any particulars about the alleged crimes.

With hardly any assets and little money, Lisa was appointed a public defender, who had spoken on her behalf, telling the judge she "refused to waive her right to a preliminary and identity hearing."

Both hearings were eventually scheduled for Thursday morning, December 23. On that day, the case would officially be transferred to Missouri.

Outside the courthouse, Todd Graves spoke to the press about the case he was preparing. "I'm not aware of any history of mental illness," he said with a serious and direct manner. "But the investigation is, of course, in its early stages. There's a lot of work left for us to do."

Kevin Montgomery was approached by the horde of reporters at the courthouse. "Can you tell us how Lisa's doing?"

"No comment."

"How are you holding up?"

"I'm okay."

"Is there anything you'd like to say, Mr. Montgomery?"

Kevin refused to speak about Lisa, instead offering his thoughts once again to Bobbie Jo's family.

"My family has suffered a tragedy, but I am not the only family."

75

Much of the media left Skidmore by Tuesday morning. Bobbie Jo was going to be laid to rest later in the afternoon. Word was the entire town of Skidmore, in support of the Stinnett and Harper families, was going to attend, as well as people from across the region whose lives Bobbie Jo had touched in some way.

Back at Lisa and Kevin's house in Melvern, a wreath hung from the front door. Red, green and white Christmas lights still dotted the contour of the house, but had not been turned on for days. Lisa and Kevin's goats and chickens were outside, in their pens, bleating and clucking.

A majority of Melvern's residents were standing behind the Montgomery family. "We are filled with sorrow," one small-business owner in town said, "for the Stinnett *and* Montgomery families."

"When one person hurts," another neighbor said, shaking his head in disbelief, "everyone hurts."

Kayla Boman was torn. On the one hand, her mother was in jail facing the worst possible outcome imaginable. On the other, a town was preparing to bury a friend. If it had been proper, Kayla said, she would have made plans to attend the funeral. Then again, considering the circumstances, it just wasn't something she felt she could do, emotionally or honorably.

Since the events of December 16, Kayla had stayed away from the Internet message boards where Bobbie Jo and her mother had communicated—message boards that had become world-famous by this point. They contained too much speculation, rumor, and discussion for Kayla. No one knew her mother, or Bobbie Jo, for that matter, the way she did. To read half-truths and lies would only add to the misery she felt already. But for whatever reason, on the day of Bobbie Jo's funeral, Kayla decided to log on to Ratter Chatter and read some of the memories people were sharing. It would be safe to assume that today the talk would be focused on Bobbie Jo.

Kayla read a few posts and began to get "really upset." Scrolling down the page, she saw pictures of Bobbie Jo. "It all seemed like it couldn't be real."

Part of Kayla longed to "deny it all." But the photographs of Bobbie Jo showing her dogs made denial impossible. One photo showed Bobbie Jo seven months pregnant, about three weeks before she was murdered. She looked at ease, beaming with happiness. Handling her dog, Fonzi, her stomach bulging out of her maternity blouse, her auburn-blond hair flowing below her shoulders, a slight smile on her face, Bobbie Jo seemed elated, Kayla thought, just to be alive.

The photo made Kayla want to cry. Those pictures of Bobbie Jo showing Fonzi, she now knew, were going to be "burned into my memory.

"I think I have looked at them enough. But I can't help it. And then I start to think of what Tori Jo is missing out on. Just thinking about it now, I have tears in my eyes."

76

An impressionist landscape artist could not have painted a more beautiful portrait of the day for Bobbie Jo's funeral. The only drawback to the morning was that temperatures had turned arctic cold over the past few days, bringing that abrupt, bitter air that seeps through layers of clothing and stiffens the joints.

Bobbie Jo's body had been released by authorities late Sunday night and taken directly to the Price Funeral Home in downtown Maryville. Her funeral would begin in late morning at the funeral home and carry on until the afternoon, when she would be laid to rest in a family plot in Skidmore. Ben Espey and his deputies were set to give the funeral procession a full escort to the cemetery and make sure the media kept their distance.

"We promised the family we'd oblige. It was the least we could do."

Maryville is, in a way, the capital city of Nodaway County. Home to Northwest Missouri State University, which educates some sixty-six hundred students at any given time, the town sits about fourteen miles east of Skidmore, one hundred miles north of Kansas City. With a population of approximately eleven thousand, it is one of the larger towns in the county.

Inside the reception area of the Price Funeral Home, it was clear the day was going to be even harder than anyone had anticipated. By noon, mourners began arriving as Reverend Harold Hamon, sitting in a back office, peered out the window. The media kept back, but still had a strong presence across the street, with a few reporters venturing into the parking lot, photographers snapping people as they walked into the parlor, hugging themselves, trying to stay warm.

The last census had found a majority of Skidmore's 342 citizens to be in their early-to-mid thirties, a statistic that was represented on the day of Bobbie Jo's funeral. Many who attended wore dark blue or black suits, while others donned blue jeans, turtleneck sweaters, cowboy boots, and Western ranch coats down to their ankles.

"Pray for me," Hamon said to those around him as he got up from behind the desk. Nodaway County sheriff Ben Espey, whose office was a football toss from the funeral home, was one of the first people Hamon ran into as he worked his way out into the crowd. Many people were still standing in line waiting to get in.

The two men shook hands. "Thank you," Hamon said. He was speaking of Espey's persistence in pursuing the Amber Alert and ultimately getting Victoria Jo back to Zeb—and back into the arms of Skidmore.

"You're welcome, Reverend," Espey said, holding back a storm of emotion.

"I was addressing Christmas cards," Hamon said, "at the moment it was happening. . . . Can you believe it?"

"It's okay, Harold, really," Espey said.

"I was sitting in my kitchen, right around the corner from the house." He shook his head, thinking about it.

Since the crime, Hamon hadn't slept much. He had struggled over the words he would speak during the service. He'd written a four-page, single-spaced sermon to read, but ripped it up over the weekend and decided to start from scratch. He had been losing himself, he said, in Scripture, looking for the proper passage or Psalm to share on such a dire day. It was his job, he knew, to comfort the community.

Yet accepting the responsibility didn't make it any easier.

The theme Hamon would be discussing during the service was how "good people" could be subjected to such tragedy. Why Bobbie Jo? Why would God bring a child into this world, but take her mother? These were thoughts people would have as they sat and pondered the events. Tears would come, surely. That was okay. Perhaps they were God's way of washing away the pain. But anxieties and questions would prevail. It was up to Hamon to put the tragedy into some sort of context and explain it as God's work, no matter how hard it was to accept.

At 2:00 P.M., as the organist played a haunting rendition of "What a Friend We Have in Jesus," Hamon walked into the main sanctuary of the funeral home and approached the pulpit beside Bobbie Jo's casket. He could smell the glorious aroma from what seemed like a field of flowers surrounding her casket.

He bowed his head. The packed room quieted. People who couldn't fit into the home stood outside in the cold, pushing their way forward, hoping to hear Hamon's words of hope.

As he stood by the pulpit, hands folded together, his favorite Bible in one hand, a friend of the Stinnett family read the Lord's Prayer as a chorus of perhaps three hundred echoed the Word of the Lord.

Amen.

"I don't know if I'm up to this or not," Hamon began, after the prayer. "I've struggled to find the right words for today, along with my own grief at Bobbie Jo's passing. I don't know what to say. This is one of those times where you can't figure it out at all and words fail."

Though he started out with a wavering tone, within a few moments, Hamon found his voice. He read three Scriptures, each one more empowering than the previous:

> The Lord is my Shepherd; I shall not want. He maketh me to lie down in green pastures. He leadeth me beside the still waters. He restoreth my soul. He leadeth me in the paths of righteousness for His names' sake. Yea, though I walk through the valley of the shadow of death, I will fear no evil. For thou art with me; Thy rod and Thy staff, they comfort me. Thou preparest a table before me in the presence of mine enemies; Thou annointest my head with oil; My cup runneth over. Surely goodness and mercy shall follow me all the days of my life, and I will dwell in the House of the Lord forever.

In that passage, Psalm 23, David was describing his own experience, because he had spent so much of his early life caring for sheep. For those who took solace from the New Testament, Jesus had also been known as the "Good Shepherd."

After Hamon read the Scripture, he looked at everyone standing in front of him and said, "I don't have the answer. But I know Someone who does."

Later, Hamon said, "I just tried to talk a little bit about how God had created this beautiful world of ours and had designed the home, and how He created man in His own image, and, as such, He created a creature that had the ability to choose, and he could choose for bad or choose for good."

People, Hamon noted, were forever victims of somebody else's *choices*. In this case, according to the government, Lisa had selected Bobbie Jo.

"In a lot of these terrible tragedies that happen, it's impossible for us to understand because we're not big enough in our minds, or our understanding. But there is One that sees the whole picture.

"And that whole picture is presented in His word. . . ."

Following the touching service at the Price Funeral Home, pallbearers carried Bobbie Jo's casket out into a waiting hearse as one of the largest funeral processions in Maryville history, led by the flashing lights on the vehicles of Ben Espey and his deputies, proceeded toward Hillcrest Cemetery, located just south of Skidmore on Highway 113.

77

Cars, trucks, and sport utility vehicles lined Highway 113 for about a mile-and-a-half of roadway running alongside Hillcrest Cemetery. Under a blue tent, mourners huddled near Bobbie Jo's plot in the back of the cemetery. The thin fabric did little to diminish the bite of the stinging wind whipping across thousands of acres of farmland in every direction.

But people managed.

"There was an overwhelming outpouring of concern and sympathy for [Bobbie Jo's] family," Reverend Hamon said later. "It was mind-boggling."

A man in a field, maybe a mile away, stood in silence as the procession came up the blacktop road and slowly stopped. The man, with his three-day-old stubbly beard and stained plaid winter jacket, was in awe at such a sight, something he had never seen in his decades of living in the region.

Bobbie Jo lay in a silver-plated coffin with gold trim, a large bouquet of white-and-yellow daisies dressing the top of it, almost identical to the flowers she had held while walking down the aisle almost two years ago.

Hamon stood at the head of Bobbie Jo's coffin and led the large group in prayer before everyone took a turn paying final respects.

"There are not enough words to tell you what good people they were," one neighbor of Bobbie Jo and Zeb's said, describing the town's feelings for Bobbie Jo and Zeb. "Everyone is one hundred percent behind them. Everybody knew how good they were."

While the wind whistled, throwing his robe and cotton-white hair all over, Hamon told the crowd near the end of a fifteen-minute service, "We have assembled, not for an ending, but a beginning. Bobbie Jo is in a safer place now. It is not a time for anger," he reminded everyone, "but a time of healing."

With Bobbie Jo's funeral behind them, the people of Skidmore could now mourn in private. Not many had slept over the past five days. A part of everyone in town had been murdered. The funeral had brought their feelings to full expression.

In the coming days, as people came out of their shells and began to talk about things, an unsettling tone of grief could be heard in the discussions at PTA meetings and football games, service stations, and diners. For some, the desire for understanding had turned into a burning disgust, as questions about Lisa Montgomery and her past emerged. It was time for justice to run its course, some proclaimed. It had been almost a week since Bobbie Jo was murdered. What was going to happen to her alleged killer? What reparation could Victoria Jo look for when Zeb sat her down one day and told her what had happened to her mother, not to mention the circumstances surrounding her birth?

Like everyone else, the child would want answers.

On the Internet, some were again repeating rumors of how Lisa had practiced the procedure she allegedly used on Bobbie Jo on one of her pregnant rat terriers. Someone else claimed Lisa had tried to buy a baby not long ago. Another woman, still frightened over what could have happened to her, said Lisa had approached her when she was eight months pregnant, asking questions about her due date. The woman claimed Lisa had set her sights on her baby before she found Bobbie Jo.

Pastor Mike Wheatley fueled further speculation when he appeared on television after Bobbie Jo was buried and said Lisa "wanted to have their own child desperately" because "that way she would be attached at the hip with Kevin. There was desperation there."

Beyond the conjecture, many were clamoring for facts. Who was this woman who had supposedly committed one of the most gruesome crimes in Midwestern history? What events in her past had led her down the road to Skidmore? Where did she come from? Lisa had never spoken with a heartland accent or dialect—was she from the region? Where was she born?

Who was Lisa Montgomery?

III

MOTHERHOOD

78

Edgar Mathers was in Korea when his wife went into labor. When the army failed to grant him an extension on his leave, Edgar made sure his mother and father were at the hospital in support of his wife. By February 27, 1968, the day she went in, Edgar had been gone a month already. Sure, she missed him. But that was their life: Edgar was a dedicated military man, he seemingly had spent more time in Asia and Europe than he had in America with her.

"Has her water broke yet?" the doctor asked, while jotting something down on her chart.

She heard one of the nurses say, "No."

"We'll have to break it then. Get things ready."

They gave her a shot in the back, epidural anesthesia, and she didn't remember much pain after that.

A few hours later, Judy sat up best she could in bed.

"It's a girl," someone told her.

She smiled. "A girl. How nice."

Two years earlier, when she was nineteen, Judy had a beautiful baby boy, with blue eyes and no hair, but he died at birth. She felt like God had punished her for being unmarried. But she and Edgar *were* married, and her baby had lived this time.

She was fatigued, of course, groggy and sweaty from all the pushing and breathing. The drugs were still in her blood; she couldn't feel any sensation in the bottom of her body. They had taken Lisa Marie out of the room to wash her up and find a comfortable place for her in the nursery. ("Yes, I did name her after Elvis's daughter," who was born on February 1 that same year,

Judy said "but not because I liked Elvis; I thought the name was pretty.")

"We'll bring her to you," one of the nurses said, "when you're in your own room in a few minutes." She still hadn't held Lisa Marie yet.

Before Judy knew it, there she was, seven-pound, four-ounce Lisa Marie, sitting on Judy's belly wrapped up in a blanket. Lisa looked up at her mother while twisting her pudgy little fingers in her mouth. Judy lifted Lisa's head cap and marveled at her shiny cone-shaped head and the few strands of blond hair.

"She's something."

"Ain't she, though?"

Fort Lewis, Washington, a town of military families living in prefab houses, cookie-cuttered over fifteen square miles of land, was different from where she had grown in Manhattan, Kansas. There, she lived in a two-story farmhouse surrounded by acres of the flattest land one could ever imagine. They had no running water ("We carried water in buckets from the well to the house."), and, forgoing hopscotch and board games and marbles and jacks, she and her five sisters and one brother spent most of their free time working the land. They picked gooseberries and grapes so their mom could can them for winter. ("Mom also fixed grape pudding; it was good.") Dad hunted rabbit, squirrel, and quail. They had chickens, cows, and pigs. ("Mom made the butter out of the cream. We had milk. She made homemade bread and fried chicken on Sundays.")

Save for help from her mother- and father-in-law, Judy was alone in Fort Lewis with two kids. Edgar had brought a child from his first marriage into his new life with Judy. He had received a letter shortly before Lisa Marie was born informing him he had another child in some port he had forgotten he was ever stationed in. The state of Washington wanted him to sign papers so a family could adopt the child, and he gladly did.

At home with the children, Judy was struggling to pay the bills. It seemed Edgar didn't want to be bothered anymore. Pretty soon he stopped sending money. He never said why. Judy's car was repossessed. The lights were shut off. She had little food for the kids. Lisa spent her first twelve weeks sleeping in the top drawer of Judy's dresser because Judy couldn't afford a crib.

"But I'll make it," Judy told a friend. "I'll survive."

If Edgar wasn't going to help, she'd go to her family.

"Daddy," Judy said over the phone one afternoon, "can you send me some money?" Judy's parents still lived in Kansas. She was thinking about moving back there, bidding the Northwest farewell. Then a letter showed up from Edgar, along with $200.

Maybe he does care?

After she opened the letter, however, her mind was made up. Whatever Edgar said had Judy in tears. She gave the letter to Edgar's mother, who was there helping out with the kids: "Read *that!*"

"I'm so sorry, Judy."

During the summer of 1968, Judy, Lisa, and Edgar's daughter took the train from Fort Lewis to Manhattan. "I'm going home," Judy told a friend before she left. "He can find me if he wants me."

Judy's father was waiting at the train depot. Carrying her bags, he said, "It's good to have you home, honey." She knew he meant it.

After spending some time in Manhattan, Judy moved to Rossville. She had a job of sorts waiting there: watching her sister and brother-in-law's children. While the kids were napping one afternoon, Judy sat down and wrote Edgar a letter: "I want a divorce. I'm done with this." There was more. But that's all Edgar would see, anyway: divorce. Why carry on if he wouldn't read it?

Some weeks later, Edgar showed up. "We tried to work it out," she recalled.

Over the next few years, Judy would follow Edgar back to Washington, but a shadow seemed to follow the relationship. She claimed later Edgar was "trying to kill" her and he tried committing suicide. Her word against his: Edgar was never charged with a crime; nor was there any record of his having tried to take his own life.

After giving birth to another child, Judy headed back to Kansas. Edgar followed months later after another tour overseas. They lived together, and things seemed to be going "okay." They had two children now, plus one of Edgar's. They needed to at least "give it a try."

A friend was watching the kids one night. As usual, Edgar was out and about. Judy decided to attend a local party. She'd heard things, but wanted to see for herself. She needed a night out, anyhow. As soon as she walked in, she saw Edgar in the arms of another woman, and that was it—the marriage was over.

The next few days with Edgar were unremarkable. There was no need to discuss the situation any further. ("What's done is done.") And then a friend asked Judy for a ride to Texas. Judy decided the time away would do her some good. She left the children at home with her parents. They were always good about watching the kids, helping out.

Back a few days later, Judy called her mother. "I'm coming over to get the kids, Mom. I'm back."

"Edgar took them, Judy. They're gone."

At the time, Lisa was three years old. Days later, Judy found the kids and filed for divorce soon after. When it went through, Edgar showed up with some gifts—and they never saw him again.

In 1972, Judy was shopping for a car. She went to a local salvage yard because she heard she could get a good deal. After talking to the owner and buying a car, he made a move.

He was an attractive man, well-built, solid, rough around the edges. Just the kind she liked. With his patchouli-oiled, slicked-back hair, he caught her eye. He was much older than Judy, who was twenty-five, but they started dating, anyway. Later, a former relative would describe him this way: "He is an angry little man; he will be drunk when you talk to him; he will curse you and lie and deny."

"I'm in love with you, *Howard*," Judy said to him one night. Of course, she had no idea Howard had a wife and kids at home waiting for him every night he left her arms.

Howard left his wife and kids a while later, and he and Judy moved to Tulsa. Judy got pregnant. She had three kids already. Howard was drinking. He drank a lot, she said. He would stop. Then start again. It was as if the man who drank was someone else.

The only bright spot out of it all was the children, especially Lisa. Soon after she turned four, Lisa was already reading and writing, picking up skills with the natural ease of an artist to paints. As she entered grade school, Lisa excelled. The violin and French horn came easy. Years later, she fancied the mellophone, making first chair in the marching band. She acted in class plays, joined the pep club, and became active in the student council. Anything she put her mind to seemed effortless.

One night, while Howard was drunk, Judy said he hit her and knocked her front teeth out. She was pregnant again. It was awful. She was "living in hell."

But it got worse.

By 1981, after trying to mend things by moving to California and Texas, Judy and Howard ended up in Sperry, Oklahoma, on a piece of land outside town. For a while, life seemed manageable. But Howard, Judy insisted, was dealing in stolen property: cars, car stereos, guns. He was never arrested, but she called the local police chief on him a few times.

"I won't be part of this, Howard. No way. We have a family."

Still, Judy maintained, he continued to drink and carry on with the same behavior.

February 24, 1984, was the day, Judy later swore, she made the decision to leave for good. It was three days before Lisa's sixteenth birthday. The small mobile home they were living in made cramped quarters for the five kids and two adults, even though it had additions on each side. In the middle of the night, Judy was awakened by the sound of what she thought were jars in the kitchen clanking around. It seemed strange.

"What the heck is that?" she asked Howard. She thought he was lying next to her in bed. "Howard? You there?"

Howard was gone.

Judy got up quietly, walking toward the noise. It was coming from Lisa's room, not the kitchen. Approaching the door, she heard some stirring going on inside. ("I opened the door and . . . saw him naked on top of Lisa. He just looked at me and got up.")

Judy was horrified. "Lisa?" she said, walking toward her as Howard left the room.

"Yes . . . Mom." Lisa was crying. She had a terrible look on her face, as if she'd been caught doing something wrong.

Judy sat on Lisa's bed. "Go back to bed, honey. It'll be okay."

Howard went back to sleep as if nothing had happened. Judy went into the room where Howard kept his guns and found a pistol.

"You . . . ," she said, pointing it at Howard's head.

"What are you doing?"

"I couldn't pull the trigger. I tried again, and on the third time, I felt the trigger starting to go, and I heard a voice inside my head . . . *Don't be a fool*," Judy recounted.

Judy simply turned around and put the gun down.

The next day, Judy explained, she learned for "the first time," Howard had been going into Lisa's room for years. She called the doctor. Some would later question why Judy phoned the doctor first, instead of the police, and also why she allowed Howard to stay. Judy answered that by saying she "feared for her life."

Didn't she know her daughter was being sexually abused for all those years? They lived in a trailer. ("I would even say," one family member commented, "that Judy blamed it on Lisa . . . telling her it was all her fault. She knew what was going on. That trailer was the size of a large shed. Judy could see Lisa's bedroom from hers. Lisa told me Judy said it was her fault, and that Lisa encouraged it.")

When Judy got the doctor on the phone, he said, "Bring her in."

Lisa told her mother the next morning her period was late. While examining her, the doctor said, "If you're pregnant, you can't have your mother's husband's child."

Luckily, she wasn't. When Judy got home with the kids from the doctor's office, she "looked Howard in the eye" and told him to "get out."

"If you tell anyone," Judy recalled Howard threatening, "I will kill you and the kids."

Howard eventually moved out and got an apartment in Tulsa. But he wouldn't leave Judy alone, nor was he helping with money for the kids. Alone now with five kids, living in a trailer, Judy went on welfare.

Judy felt she needed protection, so she reached out to the local police chief, Richard Boman—a man she would end up marrying. Howard, she said, had burned everything she owned one afternoon. She believed he was getting ready to kill her and the kids. The situation was escalating.

"I had sent Lisa to counseling. But not once did I ever blame her for anything. I guess in my mind I thought Howard was a grown man and knew better. His drinking became worse over the years. He did try to tell me he didn't remember any of it. I never believed him. He was as sick as a sick man can be for hurting my daughter like that and destroying our family."

After Richard Boman convinced Howard he had better stay away from Judy and the kids, Howard disappeared. Judy had a conversation not long after with a friend. She said it changed her life.

"Look in the mirror and see what you see. When you see *me*, tell me."

"What does that mean? Makes no sense," Judy wondered.

"When you figure it out, let me know."

For three years, Judy wrestled with it. Then one day it hit her. ("Howard had always told me how ugly I was and no man would have me with the kids. He would call me names. I had no self-esteem. I did look into the mirror and realized how wrong he was and I was as good as the next person. When I realized all this, I felt the hate for that man was gone. I felt sorry for him.")

Years later, Howard gave an interview to the *Kansas City Star*, in which he explained that although Judy had made the sexual abuse claim in her divorce filing, he "never molested Lisa in any way, shape, or form." He maintained Judy "concocted" the story to win a favorable divorce. Howard was never convicted of child molestation or sexual abuse, but was reportedly arrested and jailed for failing to pay child support. Furthermore, one of Lisa's half sisters said Lisa claimed Howard never touched her in that way. But Lisa did tell others—Carl Boman and her children—she had been sexually abused.

79

In Carl Boman's opinion, the twenty years he had spent with Lisa Montgomery hadn't always been chaotic. Deep down, Carl was a forgiving person. He gave people second—sometimes third—chances. His father and mother had taught him right: allow people the space they need to make mistakes. Good people don't hold grudges. To the contrary, the way to help someone was to open up your heart.

During his early years in Oklahoma, he was a successful high-school athlete and well-rounded student. After graduation, Carl became "defiant" and angry, letting his hair grow out into a '70s Afro the size and shape of a space helmet. A loner, he started drinking and ended up "confused" about where he wanted to take his life.

It was November 1984 when Carl met Lisa for the first time. She was a fragile sixteen-year-old who spent much of her time lost in the fictional worlds of Stephen King. Lisa loved all his books: *Carrie, Salem's Lot, The Shining.* She read so much, Judy later said, the house could burn down and "Lisa wouldn't even smell the smoke because she was so engrossed in books."

At twenty-three, Carl had been out of the navy for a few years (some said dishonorable discharge; he claimed "other than honorable," whatever that meant) when he set out from his home in Bartlesville to Carthage, Missouri, for a Thanksgiving family reunion of sorts. His grandfather had passed away, and he hadn't seen his grandmother for some time. Carl's father, Richard, was seeing a new woman; she was going to be there, along with her children.

At the time Richard Boman began a relationship with Judy, he was the chief of police in Sperry. Richard had been divorced from Lucy, Carl's mom, for over twenty years by then. In 1966, Richard was in the U.S. Navy, stationed in Boston. Lucy took off one day with Carl and his sister. The kids did not see their dad for almost fifteen years.

"When I came home on leave in 1982, we got to know each other again," Carl said of his dad. "We have a very good relationship. My mother remarried the man she left my dad for and had a daughter."

Carl has no ill feelings toward his mother or father. "They did what they had to do."

The foundation of both families—Lisa's and Carl's—was a complex, mixed bag of remarriages and divorces. After five years of marriage, Judy would leave Richard for another man, marry that man, stay with him for two years, leave him and marry Danny Shaughnessy.

For Carl, the years before he met Lisa consisted of moving around the country, "running from myself." The Navy hadn't done much to harden Carl, or prepare him for life. But leaving three-and-a-half years after he enlisted wasn't a letdown; he had lost interest and knew he didn't have what it took to dedicate his life to the structured, disciplined lifestyle of the military.

When Carl ran into Lisa the first time at his grandmother's house during Thanksgiving, he didn't even notice her. ("Nice to meet you." She shrugged. "Hey.") He was older. By marriage, Lisa would become his stepsister. At the time, Richard and Judy were planning their wedding.

Lisa seemed to take little pride in her looks. She wore no makeup and cared little for the fashion trends set by her peers. She always appeared somewhat reserved and secretive, putting a protective shield around her emotions.

At the Thanksgiving dinner, Richard seemed happy. He wanted to celebrate the beginning of a new life with someone he loved, and share that joy with a son with whom he'd recently reconnected.

There was no attraction whatsoever, Carl insisted, the first time he and Lisa sat together and enjoyed Thanksgiving dinner. He would not have guessed that the taciturn young woman he was sitting next to at the dinner table would be his wife inside the next two years.

80

"To me," Carl said adamantly, "Lisa was kind of, well, she was ugly back then. She wasn't attractive at all. I wasn't paying attention to her. I wasn't looking for anyone. She was a kid. There were no sparks or anything like that. I had no intentions other than meeting my new family, having dinner, and then heading back to Oklahoma to find a life for myself."

After a hot cup of coffee and dessert, Carl returned to his home in Bartlesville. His dad's future wife and family were a strange bunch, Carl thought. Nonetheless, he was delighted to see his dad so happy. He'd finally found someone to love—and perhaps someone to love him back. Judy seemed fun and outgoing. She'd had a horrible experience with her last marriage, had been coping as best she could with a nasty divorce over the past few months, and didn't want to move in with Richard before her previous marriage was behind her legally. Carl respected that decision.

"They seemed like they loved each other, and they did," recalled Carl.

Days later, Carl heard that her divorce had gone through, allowing her, along with the kids, to move into Richard's home in Sperry.

Throughout the past year, Carl had fallen into a deep depression. No single event triggered it, he said. It was more of a "self-imposed, self-pity" thing. He was twenty-three years old and hadn't found any direction in life, bouncing around from state to state, job to job, essentially waiting for life to grab him by the collar and shake some sense into him.

But nothing was happening.

His own behavior over the past few years bothered him. Running with the wrong crowd, "smoking a little weed," getting into trouble—he was a punk. Bartlesville had little to offer; he knew that. But he returned home, anyway, after the navy, and started working at a feed store. The job partly paid the bills, but it did little for his self-confidence.

After Richard and Judy settled down, Richard called one day. "Why don't you move up here to Sperry, son? Maybe live with us for a while, and then think about finding a career."

"Maybe."

Richard had recently been hired as a guard by a prison not too far from his home. It was the perfect job for a former police chief. He felt Carl was just fumbling around trying to figure out where he should root himself, and he knew his son needed to get his priorities in check. Carl was turning twenty-four soon. He wasn't going to school. His life was heading nowhere.

"What are you *doin'*?" Richard asked. He sounded fed up.

"I don't know, Pop."

"I can probably get you a job up in the prison. They're hiring."

Was there much to consider? "Sounds okay."

"You can help out, too, 'round here with them kids."

Richard insisted if Carl moved into the house, he would have to act as a mentor to Lisa and her siblings. They looked up to him in many ways already. But Carl was a grown man. He didn't know these children. It wasn't as if he had grown up with them in the same house. They had just met.

Carl realized he needed some sort of regimented arrangement to keep him focused on acting like an adult. It seemed Richard was offering as much. And now the kids, Richard said, were depending on Carl to be there for them. Judy was looking forward to Carl moving in and setting an example.

"Yeah, sure," Carl told his dad before they hung up. "I'll be up as soon as I close out a few things down here."

81

Lisa Montgomery was presented as scheduled in court on Thursday, December 23, 2004, to face a federal judge in Missouri for the first time. Since her arrest, authorities had released Lisa's booking photograph, which revealed how the past week had weighed on her. If she had let herself go during the past few years, as some opined, not caring much about hygiene or her looks, her mug shot showed a woman who looked ten years older than her thirty-six years.

In one photo, she had the skeletal appearance of an anorexic—her cheekbones high, and pointed—while a double chin she had carried most of her life was almost completely unnoticeable. The second photo—authorities took two: one with Lisa wearing glasses and one without—showed sunken cheekbones and pale, yellowish skin as Lisa stared into the lens of the camera.

She was not talking to many. She wasn't saying much to her lawyers. And she wasn't speaking up for herself in court. Kevin was there at every hearing. The kids were split, confused, and wanted time to work out their feelings. Having all this happen during the holiday season, of course, didn't help. And now here was their mom, looking desolate and empty, plastered all over the world on the Internet and front pages of newspapers from Missouri to California, New York to Bali, Japan to Australia.

One headline, putting a dark twist on a popular film series, said it all: WOMB RAIDER.

Carl was shopping in Wal-Mart one afternoon in Bartlesville with Ryan and Alicia. Just a casual trip to the store for a few domestic items. While standing in line, unloading the shopping cart, Carl noticed Alicia was "visibly shaken and upset."

"What's wrong?"

In front of Alicia, a tabloid was open to an article. Her eyes were teary, fixed on the page.

Carl looked in the same direction and noticed an old photograph of himself, a friend he hadn't seen in a dozen years, and Lisa, who was holding an infant, Kayla.

Carl picked up the popular magazine. It carried a story relating that Lisa supposedly once had discarded in the toilet several hamsters she'd had as pets. Another part of it told a tale of Lisa playing a Halloween trick on people by placing a doll on a chair, and after someone sat on it, she screamed, "My son! You just sat on my son." Everything Lisa had ever done throughout her life now seemed suspect; the press, Carl considered, if it wanted to, could make anyone out to be a monster, turn any situation sinister.

"Don't look at that garbage, Alicia," Carl said, folding it in half and placing it back in the rack. When he looked at it again, he noticed Lisa's mug shot on the cover with WOMB RAIDER underneath.

Leaving the store, Alicia turned to her father and said, "I feel like everyone is looking at us. I feel different. Embarrassed."

"It'll be all right, honey. Don't look at that stuff. They don't know your mother."

82

During the week before Christmas, Lisa was in court twice. Her first appearance, on Tuesday, December 21, was a mere formality. She was in and out of the courtroom within ten minutes as she waived extradition, allowing her case to be transferred to Missouri, where the U.S. Attorney's Office said she would stand trial. She had been arrested in Melvern, Kansas, but was going to be charged in the state where the murder and kidnapping had occurred.

The following Thursday, December 23, was a bit more complicated. Dressed in what had become her normal attire, an orange prison jumpsuit, handcuffs, and leg chains, Lisa, looking somber and withdrawn, was quiet, save for the jingle of the chains binding her as she was led into court. Kevin was sitting in the front row again, looking at her, cracking a comforting smile best he could. It had to be sobering for Kevin to sit and look at the woman he had been married to for the past four years. A week ago, they were making plans for a newborn, looking at baby clothes, getting the child's room ready, discussing baby names. Now Lisa was quickly becoming the most hated woman in America.

U.S. magistrate judge John T. Maughmer began the hearing by asking Lisa if she had read the complaint the government lodged against her.

"Yes, I have," she answered, but her response was nearly inaudible because she spoke so softly.

The purpose of the hearing was to decide whether Lisa could afford her own attorney. If she couldn't, the government was required to provide her with the best public defenders available.

"How frequently did you receive a paycheck?" the judge asked at some point.

"Every . . . every two weeks."

"Do you own your own car?"

"Yes."

"How many children do you have?"

"Four."

At the end of the proceeding, the judge indicated Lisa would likely qualify for public defender assistance, which she was later granted. Anita Burns and David Owen, who were in court beside her, were the best candidates, since they had been working on Lisa's case since her arrest.

For a lawyer, defending Lisa could be a career builder. It would likely become the most high-profile murder case since the Laci and Scott Peterson case in Modesto, California. At trial, television networks and cable shows would run live updates. "Breaking news" and "special report" would set the tone of the coverage. The lawyers involved would be put under a public microscope, their faces piped into the living rooms of millions of people throughout the world.

After the brief court hearing, the U.S. Attorney's Office released its first statement in three days. It hadn't made a determination whether to seek the death penalty, but obviously it was taking the matter seriously.

"We're way too early here in this to make a decision," Todd Graves said, then stated that his office was studying every option, the death penalty being one of many.

At this point, he added, Graves and his office were unsure as to the question on everybody's mind since the crime had occurred.

"Further arrests," Graves told reporters, "remain a possibility."

Lisa herself would complicate matters regarding her possible involvement in Bobbie Jo's murder as she communicated with Carl Boman and her children over the telephone and through letters. One day after her arrest, she called the house, and Carl's wife, Vanessa, "surprisingly allowed the call to go through," Carl remembered.

"What the hell did you do now, Lisa?" Carl asked as soon as he got on the phone. It was the first time he had spoken to her since her arrest.

"I don't have a memory of anything," Lisa said.

"What are you talking about?"

Carl had heard that Lisa confessed to killing Bobbie Jo. He'd read the affidavit. Was she trying to persuade herself that the story she had told authorities wasn't what really happened?

"I didn't kill anyone," she claimed.

"How did you get the baby, then? They found the baby in your arms, Lisa. What is this?"

She stumbled over her words, crying. "I just picked it up," she said. "I have no idea how I got there."

"What?" Carl reacted. "What the *hell* are you talking about?" He was frustrated and upset when Lisa wouldn't admit to being at Bobbie Jo's house. It was as though, to Lisa, it was all happening to someone else. It was so much like Lisa, Carl thought. Every time she got caught doing something wrong, she pushed the blame to someone else or totally denied any involvement. ("It was a ploy," commented Carl. "I know she knows what happened that day, and I know she remembers what she did.")

Lisa was quiet for a time. Carl said, "Lisa, come on now . . . it's all over. You're in jail. Why not admit what you did so we can deal with this?"

"I don't want to be put to death," Carl recalled her saying. "I can't spend the rest of my life in prison, Carl. I can't do it."

"You know what, Lisa, I'm done with this phone call now."

"I know she did it," said Carl, reflecting. "I have never doubted it. That phone call was her way of denying it all to herself. I had heard it for twenty years. Lisa avoided truth at all costs. She never dealt with the actual. She would just talk around things she didn't want to admit or contend with."

Carl said his heart "broke for Lisa" after that call. He couldn't understand why she had such a hard time coming to terms with what she was being accused of: "I can't understand it. Why not finally come clean? I mean, she's caught red-handed. Who does she possibly think she's fooling?"

83

Carl Boman and others have said that Lisa Montgomery projected a social standing in Melvern that wasn't a true portrait of her life. After she married Kevin, as the years passed, Lisa presented herself to the community and her few friends as a devoted homemaker and mother. She told people she used a spinning wheel at home to make yarn from sheep's wool, after which she would knit sweaters and winter hats for the kids.

"Everyone knew she bought the spinning wheel," a former friend remarked, "and never thought twice about her taking it home and using it. But no one knew she really didn't use it. It was just a prop."

Every year, Melvern hosted a large craft show. Lisa would attend, setting up a table and displaying crafts and homemade soaps she claimed she'd made herself.

"I was there visiting the kids one time during a craft show," recalled Carl. "People would come up and watch her knit and look at her crafts." Lisa would talk about crafts to people at the shows as if she were the host of her own show on the Home & Garden Channel. "They assumed that is what she did and how she lived. But in reality, the stuff was only made for the craft shows. She never did dishes, cooked, or cleaned the house. The kids always did it. She spent her time on the computer chatting or whatever, or reading, or watching television. She had very few friends that knew her outside of work, or intimately. Kevin grew up and went to school in Melvern, and yet very few people ever went over to the house to see them."

Her carefully constructed image of motherhood was a figment of her own imagination. As Carl Boman told the press at the time, white lies grew into a dangerous mixture of schemes and faked pregnancies, forcing Lisa to come up with larger lies to cover the smaller ones.

The sacrifices most mothers readily endured were things Lisa turned away from. The "less glamorous" the domestic chore was, according to Carl and some of the children, the more bothersome it was to Lisa.

"If it had no appeal, she wasn't interested," Carl said. "She became basically lazy. When the kids, as babies, cried, it irritated her. She expected me to deal with a lot of the staying up late when they were sick, even though she didn't work. When people were around and we went visiting, the show started. It used to bother me, but it became normal when she pretended to be the perfect mother and housewife. A lot of people knew better, but no one said anything. With the four kids, it became too much for her. She would never admit it, but she relied on me to clean the house and fix meals when I was with her. I couldn't do it all. I worked a lot of hours so we could buy a house. She even told me on several occasions she couldn't handle another child. Lisa's priority was always Lisa. When it came to what was needed in the house, Lisa came first, no matter what."

84

On December 30, during a brief hearing, Judge John T. Maughmer granted a motion filed by the U.S. Attorney's Office the previous week. His decision secured Lisa's pretrial detention, solidifying the government's argument that the best place for Lisa Montgomery was in federal custody at a facility in Leavenworth, Kansas. A trial date hadn't been set yet, but the motion indicated in stark detail just how serious the charges against Lisa were. She had committed a "crime of violence," said one of several "Supporting Suggestions" accompanying the motion: a "felony," involving "an offense where the maximum sentence is life imprisonment or death."

The government had a great concern that Lisa would "flee" if allowed to go free on bond. Additionally, "there is a serious risk," the motion stated, "that the person will obstruct or attempt to obstruct justice, or threaten, injure, or intimidate, or attempt to threaten, injure, or intimidate, a prospective witness or juror."

Apparently, the government was wary of her tampering with its case, if given the opportunity.

During the early part of January 2005, Lisa described, privately, the crimes she allegedly committed as if someone else were there with her at Bobbie Jo's. While talking to certain members of her family, Lisa couldn't recall having struggled with Bobbie Jo or cutting the child from her womb. Instead, she claimed she couldn't remember any of it, saying that the baby was "handed to me" by someone else.

Was she blocking it all out? Or setting the wheels of her defense in motion by trying to implicate someone else? Furthermore, could a $45,000 lump-sum cash payment Lisa and Vanessa had negotiated some years before have been money Lisa needed to hire an accomplice, or purchase a black-market baby?

During the winter of 2002 and the spring of 2003, Lisa claimed that Carl wasn't keeping up to date on child support payments, and for the second or third time since she married Kevin Montgomery, she said she was carrying another baby.

Soon after Vanessa and Carl married, Vanessa started her own envelope-stuffing business. She believed she could make a "great deal" of money in a short period of time. Not only would it help the family, but she thought: *I could give Lisa a large cash payment to get her off our backs and, at the same time, open up the opportunity for Carl to see the kids.* Lisa was holding back Carl's visits with the kids because she was incensed over money she claimed he owed her in back child support. Vanessa, however, said money was taken directly from Carl's paychecks and sent to Lisa for child support.

"Lisa," said Vanessa, when they saw each other one day, "don't take the kids away from Carl. Please. They need their dad as much as their mum."

"What?"

"Why are you being so nasty about it all?"

"Carl hasn't paid me child support since you two got married, Vanessa."

"That's not true, Lisa. You know that's a lie."

From there, "She got in my face," recalled Vanessa, "and we started to argue." Whenever Vanessa and Lisa had problems between them, Lisa would react by keeping the kids from Carl and not allowing them to speak to him.

"I'm sorry," said Vanessa after Lisa continued yelling.

"I want that back child support!"

"Listen," said Vanessa, "I can get you some money in a few months. It'll be enough to pay off the child support."

"How much?"

They talked for a while, according to Vanessa, and settled on $45,000.

But then Lisa started yelling again. "Look," said Lisa at one point, "you have until March and no later. Or else I will go for *more* child support and move the kids so far away Carl will *never* see them again."

Vanessa felt panicked, she said, after she promised the $45,000, because, in reality, she had no way to come up with the money.

Lisa asked, "Where are you getting this money?"

"I have an inheritance coming from Germany—someone in the family I don't even know."

Lisa "lightened up" a bit after that, Vanessa said, and, in the days and weeks that followed, allowed Carl to see the kids more.

Then March came around. When Vanessa's envelope business opportunity failed, she called Lisa with the bad news. The inheritance claim had been a lie. ("I honestly did think I could earn enough to pay her off . . . ," recalled Vanessa.)

"I'm so sorry, Lisa, I can't give you the money. But please don't take the kids away from Carl."

"Carl will never see his kids again, Vanessa." Lisa seemed composed and relaxed about it all. Not the response Vanessa had anticipated.

"I'm sorry, Lisa. . . ."

"I don't need your money. I'll take him to court."

"Let's talk about this, Lisa, come on now."

"I'll ruin you guys," said Lisa, getting louder. "You'll pay for this!"

As Carl and Vanessa would later surmise, Lisa's greatest worry wasn't back child support payments at all. She had been telling people she was pregnant, and so she needed to produce a child. When she realized she wasn't going to get the money from Vanessa and couldn't purchase a child on the black market to cover up "the lie" of being pregnant, she started working on Carl.

"I want forty-five thousand to buy a piece of property," she told Carl a day or so later. "That will take care of all the child support you haven't paid me."

"Are you kidding me?"

He saw her proposal as an insidious request made by a woman who was emotionally unstable, lying about being pregnant year after year, poisoning her children's minds with all sorts of stories until they didn't know what to believe.

"Look, Carl," said Lisa, "I'll forget about bringing you to court if you just come up with the money."

Carl laughed.

"She was faking another pregnancy," remembered Carl. "She was backed into a corner. She told people she was pregnant, hoping she would get the money from us, but when it didn't come through, well, she panicked. What's interesting is, during any one of her faked pregnancies, she never once told me she was pregnant, because she knew I would laugh in her face."

When Lisa realized she wasn't going to get the money, Carl and Vanessa agreed, she developed a story of losing the baby she was carrying.

So what did Lisa actually need the money for?

For Carl Boman, it was appalling, but unsurprising: "I was told she found a woman on the Internet in Alabama who would sell her a baby for forty-five or fifty thousand dollars. If she did get the money and bought the child, she would be able to prove to everyone she wasn't lying about being pregnant."

85

The twenty years Carl Boman spent with Lisa Montgomery were not without good times. Beginning a few months after they met during Thanksgiving dinner, 1984, they felt a connection that was hard to deny.

During the time Carl courted Lisa, he became close to all of Judy's kids, simply because he was always around the house. By this point, Carl lived in Cleveland, just outside Sperry; and after he got off work with his dad at the prison, he ended up spending much of his free time at the house. The one thing that bothered Carl most early on, as he got to know Judy and the kids, was the obvious "absence of love" in their lives.

He and Richard had shown affection for each other as any father and son might. The Boman family, as a whole, had always expressed a certain amount of love. Not to see the same in Lisa's family struck Carl as unusual.

Richard always seemed to be working, often taking on overtime. "It wasn't like there were screaming matches between Lisa, Judy, and the other kids, nothing like that," Carl recalled. "It was just that there was no hugging, talking to one another, no 'I love you.' It was very cold being around them.

"Judy was so judgmental of everyone and all the kids, that it rubbed off on them," Carl said. "You cannot walk into a room and not feel Judy's presence."

Carl had just come out of a period when depression had dominated his life. Now he had a career, his own apartment. He was working with his dad. The cool atmosphere of Judy's home began to weigh on him.

During the winter of 1985, Lisa turned seventeen. She was

"looking for someone to love," someone to care for her. Carl believed she'd never had it.

"Part of her problem was Judy never acknowledged the sexual abuse," Carl claimed, "and Lisa told me time and again, Judy had even said it was Lisa's fault."

Judy Shaughnessy later denied this.

During the time Carl spent at Richard and Judy's house, Lisa would stay in her room and rarely come out. "She would spend twenty hours, literally, if she didn't have to go to school, in her room just reading."

Carl started to notice Lisa, he said, shortly after she turned seventeen. By then, she had changed from an unpretentious teenager who cared little for her looks into a budding young woman who presented herself more attractively. She started combing her hair and wearing it up. She showered regularly, wore makeup and decent clothes. "She started looking good," Carl said. "At least in my eyes back then."

In 1985, Lisa was at a turning point in her life. When she and Carl started getting close, having long talks about life and the future, their connection was instantaneous, and the relationship blossomed into intimacy quickly.

As Carl soon learned, however, it was hard to communicate with Lisa.

"You don't talk to Lisa. You listen to Lisa."

Lisa talked at length about the years she spent with Judy and her stepfather Howard. For the most part, Lisa hated Judy, and despised the life her mother had given her. She felt as if her childhood had been stolen by her own mother.

At this point in her life, Lisa was just starting to deal with the alleged abuse by her stepfather. It had damaged her soul and made her feel irrelevant, unwanted.

"This poor girl," Carl said, "needed some help, and I was glad to be there for her."

86

During the first half of 1985, as Carl stayed busy working at the prison and watching Judy's kids, he had his own small studio apartment in Cleveland. Life, in effect, was going exactly the way his dad had framed it. The dark cloud he had been under the past few years was finally shifting away.

"I felt good about myself for the first time in a long while," remarked Carl. "It was a great proving ground for what was to come in the next year . . . a life change I would have never expected."

On February 27, 1986, Lisa turned eighteen. Carl had been seeing her for almost a year. During the past six months, they had spent as much time as they could together. Through an emotional bond they believed existed between them, sexual intimacy came easy. "We fell in love," Carl recalled.

Every chance she had, Lisa begged Carl to let her move into his apartment. Because she was a minor and still in high school, Carl never considered it. If she felt that way after school, and the relationship was still going strong, he promised he'd give it a shot.

The day before Lisa's eighteenth birthday, Carl found himself sitting in his car outside the front of his father's house holding Lisa in his arms as she cried. Over the past few weeks, she had really poured it on regarding moving into Carl's apartment. It was time to be together, she demanded. "I want to be with you all the time." They had even discussed marriage by then. But Carl was apprehensive, not because of her age, but "she was still in school."

"No," Carl had said when Lisa asked. "Wait until you're eighteen. I love you," he added, "and do want to marry you. But everything is moving way too fast."

Carl didn't want to go through the entire process of living with a woman to "see if it would work out." Five years before he met Lisa, he had been involved with a woman he deeply loved. They'd had a child together (who would later die in an automobile accident). Because he was young and immature, he allowed the relationship to implode, and, he said, "I did a lot of things I wasn't proud of."

Although intimacy wasn't new to him, Carl "wanted true love, you know. . . . I wanted the whole thing. I was just coming out of a crisis in my life and had found myself, I guess you could say. I didn't know that Lisa and I would work out. It scared me."

"Come on, Carl, let's just give it a try?" Lisa pleaded.

Carl stared out the window, shaking his head. "I don't know, Lisa."

"Let's just try it."

"Okay," he said, giving in.

The next day, on her birthday, Lisa packed her things and moved into Carl's apartment.

Carl was working nights at the prison, and Lisa was trying to finish her senior year in high school. Because they never saw each other, the relationship started out "rocky."

Lisa didn't have much incentive after graduation to do anything with her life, Carl said. Reports would later claim Lisa was academically focused on going to college because she was so "smart." But that wasn't the case at all, Carl insisted.

"Lisa never had plans of going to college after high school. She took the SATs, and did very well, but she wasn't *interested* in school."

Lisa had talked about joining the U.S. Air Force, but the idea, like others, came and went. She wasn't cut out for the strict schedule of daily life in the military, and she knew it.

Carl and Lisa talked a lot about what she wanted to do with her life—vocationally speaking. Carl had a solid job he somewhat liked. He was making good money. But Lisa had no direction. Some nights she would stare at Carl and say the same thing over and over: "I want to be a mother, Carl. That's my calling. To mother your children."

"Well, that's a noble thing to want," said Carl. "What is it, where is this coming from?"

Lisa began weeping. "I want to correct the mistakes that were made in my life by my mother."

When school ended in June, Lisa went down and took the physical for the air force to see if it would take her. A week later, she was called into the recruiting office.

"Even if you wanted to join, ma'am," the recruiter told her, "there was no chance we could allow you in at this time."

"Why?" she asked. "What's the problem?"

"Well, ma'am . . . you're pregnant."

87

The first public photograph of Victoria Jo Stinnett was released a few days before Christmas. MSNBC was airing a shot of Victoria Jo that it had sliced from a video clip it captured of Zeb Stinnett holding her. The child appeared to be healthy, and had no visible signs of her violent delivery. The scratches on her face, clear in the photographs taken by Lisa's children, along with the bruises on her chin and right eyelid, had healed. Victoria Jo looked happy, peaceful, and quite spirited. Her cheeks were a rosy red, the color you'd expect to see on any healthy newborn. In another photograph, published later by the *New York Post*, Zeb was smiling, if only slightly. Given the circumstances surrounding the child's birth, it was a lovely snapshot of a newborn and her proud father: two people ready to take on the world together. Here was Zeb, cradling his little bundle, taking delight in her.

Zeb told *Post* reporters, "It's been rough. But I just look at Victoria Jo, pick her up, and that usually does it."

Zeb said he was changing diapers, filling bottles with formula, getting up at all hours of the night, feeding and caring for "Tori Jo," while on paternity leave from Kawasaki Motors. It was clear he was determined to give the child as much care as Bobbie Jo would have.

88

When Lisa returned from the recruiting office and told Carl she was pregnant, Carl figured out the next juncture of his life rather easily.

"Let's get married," he said. He was overjoyed at the prospect of becoming a father.

Lisa smiled. "I'm so happy, Carl," she said, running up and hugging him.

The wedding wasn't elaborate, but it was a celebration with family and friends of the love Carl and Lisa shared and the triumph of bringing a new life into the world. Lisa wore white and made a beautiful bride, while Carl donned the traditional black tuxedo.

Next, with the apartment closing in on them, Carl began looking for a a bigger home. Within a few months, they moved to Hominy, Oklahoma, into a house Carl purchased from a colleague. Hominy was even closer to the prison. The house had three bedrooms. It seemed like the ideal situation.

"Lisa was elated at being pregnant and wore the weight well," remembered Carl. She had no morning sickness. No back pain. No complications whatsoever.

More significantly, there was no doubt in anyone's mind, as Lisa began gaining weight and showing, that she was pregnant. Her appearance during pregnancy would become a major issue later—after she married Kevin Montgomery and claimed to be pregnant several times.

"Like every pregnant woman, Lisa always had a glow," said Carl. "There was never any doubt. It was always obvious." (This comment contradicted a photograph taken of Lisa about four weeks before the government claimed she murdered Bobbie Jo Stinnett and kidnapped her child, when Lisa was telling people in Melvern she was eight months pregnant. In that photograph, taken by one of her children, Lisa wore a sweatshirt, had her hair pulled back and tied in a ponytail, but showed no obvious signs of being pregnant. One would expect a woman eight months pregnant to have a large bulge in her midsection, but it wasn't there. Moreover, any "glow" Lisa displayed during every other actual pregnancy was missing. Her face was oval and emaciated.)

As the months moved forward in 1986, Lisa's impatience about her due date wore on Carl. She mentioned she was interested in drinking castor oil, which, according to an old wives' tale, would hasten the birthing process.

"You're not doing that, Lisa," Carl told her.

"I will, Carl Boman," she said, smiling coyly, raising her eyebrows, "if I want to."

Rebecca, an energetic, healthy baby, quite small, was born on January 11, 1987. Carl and Lisa were beside themselves with pride ("She's gorgeous . . . look at her . . ."). It was as if Lisa had been put on the earth, just as she'd said, to be a mother. She did everything by the book: cleaned the house, kept up with the laundry, made dinner, and always made sure Rebecca was fed properly and had clean diapers. Carl was working nights and days at the prison then, so he depended on Lisa to take care of the home.

"I couldn't have asked for a better wife or caretaker for my daughter."

Perhaps even more important to Lisa's life later on, during those early pregnancies, Lisa was adamant about going to the doctor, taking prenatal vitamins, encouraging Carl to touch her stomach when the baby moved, and allowing him to be involved in every aspect of the nine months she spent carrying the child.

About nine months after Rebecca was born, Lisa went to Carl and told him to sit down at the kitchen table.

"What is it?"

She smiled.

"Spit it out."

"I'm pregnant, honey." She put Carl's hand on her stomach. "We're going to have another baby."

Lisa had never been more attractive. She had freckles and long brown hair that held a shine. She rarely wore glasses and had no trouble dropping the extra weight she put on while pregnant. On some days, Carl would arrive home and she would be waiting for him, all dolled up.

"Dinner is served," she'd say, kissing him on the cheek.

Rebecca would be in her crib, happy, playing.

On the face of it, the perfect life Carl believed he was building with Lisa just kept getting better.

89

As the U.S. Attorney's Office spoke with witnesses, studied "the mountain" of forensic evidence it had collected, and contemplated how it would go about prosecuting Lisa Montgomery, many close to Lisa questioned her behavior leading up to the day Bobbie Jo Stinnett was murdered. Most believed Lisa was smarter than the crime she was being accused of implied. The fact that she reportedly had left behind so much evidence at the crime scene was astonishing to some in her immediate circle of friends and family. In addition, she seemed to have made several overt mistakes leading up to the crime, which seemed entirely out of character. How could someone spend months planning a crime and ignore such obvious evidence left behind: strands of her hair, DNA, a litany of cyber evidence on her personal computer, and the simple, yet inculpating fact of having Bobbie Jo's child in her arms when authorities knocked on her door?

One relative believed that to Lisa, the risk of getting caught was less important than the chance at proving everyone else wrong. "I think Lisa sincerely thought, before embarking on such a terrible crime, it was far better to get caught—if she did—than be labeled a confirmed liar and, essentially, 'found out.' So taking the chances she took and leaving behind so much evidence really made little difference to her. She never looked at it that way."

In 1941, Dr. Hervey Cleckley published an important book, *The Mask of Sanity*, which became a pioneering study of the science of psychopathy as it applied to the criminal mind. Years later, Dr. Robert Hare wrote *Without Conscience*, a book, for the most part, looking at the "psychopath next door." These experts theorized that any mind holds the potential capacity for psychopathic behavior, although not every human being is capable of flipping on those dark switches. In his book, Hare spoke with respect and admiration of Cleckley. Cleckley's work was groundbreaking on several fronts; most notably, for the first time an expert had come forth and talked about insanity as a social problem affecting, perhaps, thousands of Americans who didn't yet know it.

Through these books, antisocial disorder, a mental diagnosis that is often associated with high-profile criminals today, became part of mainstream American thought. Cleckley used case histories of patients to show, by example, how the mind of a mentally ill person worked in everyday situations; and his book has become a textbook for identifying the antisocial psychopath. Based on the work of both men, a checklist of sixteen characteristics of the sociopath emerged. Speaking of Cleckley's work, in *Without Conscience*, Hare wrote, "Half a century ago Cleckley . . . warned us that our failure to acknowledge the psychopaths among us had already triggered a social crisis. . . ."

The Hare-Cleckley sociopath checklist, includes manipulation, superficial charm, pathological lying, shallow emotions, impulsive nature, as well as "glibness, grandiose sense of self, lack of remorse, shame or guilt, lack of empathy, early behavioral problems, and irresponsibility." Although only a trained professional is qualified to make a proper diagnosis of Lisa Montgomery, clearly, she exhibited several characteristics on the Cleckley-Hare checklist, throughout her life—most notably, an "incapacity for love, promiscuous sexual behavior, lack of realistic life plan," and an appearance of being charming, "yet [is] covertly hostile and domineering, seeing their victim as merely an instrument to be used."

"Murder became her only option," stated one relative, "and it was well within any boundaries she put up for her to go through with the crime to get what she wanted."

The alias Lisa chose—Darlene Fischer—was an indication of how little thought went into the actual planning of the fictional person she created online. Darlene was the name of Lisa's favorite aunt, the only member of her extended family who was speaking to her at the time she was arrested; and at one time, she worked with a woman whose last name was Fischer. What's more, the message behind Fischer4kids was perhaps a subconscious desire on Lisa's part to fish for and find a baby: fisher for kids.

There were other warnings. Word was, during the months leading up to Lisa's arrest, she was looking to buy a child. Carl Boman and Lisa's sisters heard from different sources Lisa was asking certain people where she could get a baby on the black market. That was why, Carl insisted, Lisa so desperately wanted his wife Vanessa's $45,000 "inheritance."

After Bobbie Jo's murder, a woman posted a frightening note on an Internet message board Lisa frequented. She related that when she was eight months pregnant, Lisa communicated with her about her child and was still sending her e-mails right up until the time of Bobbie Jo's murder. The woman had been terrified to learn of Bobbie Jo's death, sensing Lisa had sought her out for the same purpose, but Lisa had abandoned the idea after meeting Bobbie Jo.

"Lisa would make friends with people she could get information from and/or use them," Judy recalled. "How do you think she got her second divorce from Carl? She was in New Mexico and had an affair with the lawyer [involved in the divorce]. He faxed her the papers here, and I saw them, and she sent them back. She made it appear as if she wasn't in Kansas. I am telling you, Lisa was *good*. I tried to tell her that wasn't right, nor did I think it was legal. But she didn't care."

Everything had now changed, however. Lisa was in jail facing murder and kidnapping charges. She could claim to have no memory of the crime, but the evidence would condemn or exonerate her, not her own retelling of what had happened. She could say someone else was at the scene of the crime with her, or that a second person had even committed the crime. But if the evidence didn't back up her story, even if she dropped a name, her attorneys would have a tough time convincing a jury she was innocent.

"The forensic evidence against Lisa Montgomery is overwhelming," a law enforcement official who was deeply engrossed in the case said. "Beyond belief. There is no way she wasn't at the scene."

90

Under federal guidelines, for the government to proceed with a felony case of murder against a suspect, a grand jury must first hand down an indictment. An indictment may contain allegations the defendant committed more than one crime, as in Lisa's case. "The separate allegations," says the law, "are referred to as the counts of the indictment."

Todd Graves would have to conduct a grand jury investigation and indict Lisa on charges of kidnapping resulting in death before he could proceed to trial.

On January 12, 2005, Graves called a press conference to confirm he had indicted Lisa Montgomery on charges of kidnapping resulting in death.

The indictment offered little new evidence; however, for the first time, it publicly explained, in graphic detail, what went on inside Bobbie Jo's house back on December 16: ". . . [Lisa] Montgomery strangled Bobbie Jo Stinnett with a rope and then used a kitchen knife to cut her infant daughter from her womb."

Frightening words. People of the heartland now had an image of what Bobbie Jo had gone through as she was being murdered. To think that Bobbie Jo spent her last moments watching a madwoman cut her open and take her child was too terrifying and heartbreaking for some to consider. According to the indictment, not only did Bobbie Jo know she was being killed, but her last thought could well have been the realization that her attacker wanted to take her child.

The indictment replaced a federal complaint, Graves added, his office had filed back on December 17.

Ending the one-page news release accompanying the indictment, the government announced that Graves, "First Assistant U.S. Attorney Roseann Ketchmark, Deputy U.S. Attorney Matt J. Whitworth, Assistant U.S. Attorney Cynthia Phillips, and Nodaway County, Missouri, Prosecuting Attorney David Baird, serving as a Special Assistant U.S. Attorney," would all be on board to prosecute the case. The government was compiling its version of a "dream team" of prosecutors, which had, by themselves, tried some of the most high-profile murder cases the state of Missouri had ever seen.

As Graves stood at the podium, flanked by Kevin Stafford, SA in charge of the FBI's regional Missouri office, and FBI SA Mike Saunders, and read from the four-page indictment, it was clear that this was one of the most serious cases the U.S. Attorney's Office had on its docket. Every resource was going to be used to investigate and prosecute Lisa Montgomery. A list of eight law enforcement investigating agencies was attached to the news release, further proof that an all-out legal effort was being launched.

Every major news outlet broadcast the press conference live, some breaking from regularly scheduled programming to bring the event into outlets around the world. Graves spoke with a calm cadence, a deep baritone, scratchy and sincere, detailing the government's case.

"We're here today to give you limited information—albeit important information—regarding the Montgomery case. Moments ago, a grand jury in Kansas City issued an indictment charging her with one count Title 18, USC, section 1201, which is the same as the previous complaint she had been charged with." He let that statement hang for a moment before adding, "That is a *capital* offense."

He explained that the government had only thirty days to indict a suspect once a federal complaint was issued.

"We are," Graves said, stopping to look up and around the room, "fulfilling that obligation."

Also of importance, Graves wanted to be clear, was that the indictment contained several "special findings," and was in no way to be considered *evidence* against Lisa.

Those special findings, as the indictment read, included that Lisa was "more than eighteen years of age at the time of the offense"; that she "intentionally killed Bobbie Jo; intentionally inflicted serious bodily injury, which resulted in the death of Bobbie Jo; intentionally participated in the act", and so on.

The indictment said Lisa had "committed the offense after substantial planning and premeditation to cause the death of a person, that is, Bobbie Jo Stinnett," that Victoria Jo, "the kidnapping victim, was particularly vulnerable due to her young age," and, surprisingly, "Bobbie Jo, the murder victim, was particularly vulnerable due to her infirmity, that is, at the time of her death [she] was eight months pregnant."

In essence, the indictment was saying the evidence against Lisa was insurmountable; and any plan Lisa's lawyers might have to mount an insanity defense—which, some experts claim, is only successful about 1 percent of the time—was going to be met with a strident, determined clash of legal wits. That is, one cannot plan and premeditatively carry out such a complex act of murder without some sort of knowledge of what one is doing. Lisa, the indictment seemed to insinuate, had acted on her own free will and had gone to great lengths to sketch out and commit the crimes alleged in the indictment.

After reading through each aggravating factor included, Graves said, "That is all the information we have to share today. An arraignment date has not been scheduled yet. But the arraignment will be the first time the defendant has to plead guilty or not guilty."

After a moment, "I'll take a few questions."

Most reporters knew Graves well enough to understand he wasn't going to budge on any part of his case. Still, after a bit of prodding, he admitted Lisa would "be arraigned sometime during the next week."

When asked about the death penalty, Graves said he would "make a recommendation to a Department of Justice committee about whether to pursue the death penalty," which would then "make its own recommendation to the U.S. Attorney General's Office."

"How long will that take?" someone asked.

"That process usually takes several months."

"Will there be any more charges filed against Lisa Montgomery?"

"I don't expect to file any more charges . . . but I won't rule out charges against other people involved in the case."

With that, reporters scribbled in their notebooks. Whispers in the room picked up. It had been on everyone's mind, of course: would Kevin Montgomery be taken in handcuffs any time soon?

Graves wouldn't comment further.

"Do you think, Mr. Graves, that she'll try to use an insanity defense?"

"I can't discuss or speculate about what her defense will do at trial."

After a few more questions, Graves said his good-byes and walked away.

The case of the *United States of America* v. *Lisa Montgomery* was officially set in motion. Lisa was going to get her chance, inside the next eight days, to walk into a federal court and plead her case.

91

Some months after Lisa gave birth to Rebecca, Carl Boman sensed a gradual change in his young bride. It started with subtle things, like breast-feeding. To Lisa, the act became a chore. From there, the normal everyday things most mothers adore doing for their children began to bother Lisa. It was true she loved to dress the kids up and take them out when they were infants, but the older they got, the more she lost interest. In what would soon become a common theme throughout the Boman household—and, later, the Montgomery house in Melvern after Lisa and the kids moved in with Kevin—odd bits of Lisa's character would surface.

Later, Kayla Boman explained: "Something that always bothered me was, at least when my mom would get mad at me, I knew she was paying attention to me. When she would be upstairs on the computer, I would try and talk to her just about anything in general: school, dogs, our animals. Stuff like that. And she wouldn't even look over at me. So I would ask her a question to see if she would respond. Most of the time, I would have to ask the same question about three times before she would finally answer. The only time I can think she would pay attention to me was when she wanted to know something about a dog, if I got a B or C on my report card, or when she wanted something."

Lisa rarely applauded the children for their accomplishments, as if they were expected to do well. Kayla said she first became interested in rat terriers and the dog show circuit because she knew it was "something I could share with my mom, and she would actually pay attention to me. I was always trying to get her attention. Good grades didn't work. Sports didn't work. Spelling bee didn't work. Band didn't work. So ratties it was."

On July 7, 1988, Lisa gave birth to her second child, Alicia. Carl and Lisa were still living in Hominy. The only change in their lives—besides another mouth to feed—was that Carl had been promoted to sergeant at Dick Conner Correctional Center, where he had been working with his dad, who had since quit.

The promotion meant more responsibility—but also more money.

Throughout both pregnancies, Carl went to every prenatal appointment with Lisa. He and Lisa were again elated they'd had another child. The love they had showered on Rebecca was a sign of how much children were a part of the life they had both wanted. Carl had grown from a raucous, unruly punk coming out of the navy, bouncing through life without any direction, to a responsible father of two healthy baby girls. Lisa was by his side at every work function and party, every outing and family picnic. They were a happily married couple talking about having more children. Rebecca, at age two, had become, Carl proudly said, "a daddy's girl."

Other than a few changes in Lisa's behavior that Carl attributed to the hormonal imbalances most new mothers go through, their life together could not have been any better.

92

In the middle of January 2005, Carl and two of the children appeared on a major syndicated talk show. It hadn't turned out the way Carl had hoped; he felt the show's producers made promises they failed to keep, and, in retrospect, going on the show was a mistake. He had not spoken to many reporters by that point, avoiding the media because he was "too emotional." His lawyer, James Campbell, was fielding calls from several major media producers and personalities: Bill O'Reilly, Paula Zahn, Larry King, Montel Williams, Hannity & Colmes, Greta Van Susteren, CBS, NBC, ABC. But Carl kept turning them down. He only ended up on that one syndicated show and a network morning news show, he insisted, because the producers made it sound as though he would be able to tell his side of the story.

Do the shows, he thought, *and maybe the others will go away.*

Carl wasn't paid for his appearance. Only travel and hotel accommodations, along with a small allowance for food, were provided. But the lack of monetary compensation didn't bother him. It wasn't about "the money," he claimed; it was about getting the truth out at a time when rumor and speculation were beginning to smother facts.

Lisa must have seen the show from prison, or been told about it by someone who had, because she was livid. She expressed her anger in a letter written on January 18.

"Are you making enough money . . . ?" she taunted. After that, she accused him of ignoring the children "for years." Interestingly to Carl, the next sentence seemed to, in his mind, imply Lisa was to admit her involvement in Bobbie Jo's murder: ". . . <u>YOU ARE NO BETTER!</u>" she wrote in capital letters, underlining the sentence. Carl believed it was a reference to a rumor she had spread about him years ago—that he had murdered someone while in the navy. The way Carl read it, Lisa was saying since they had both murdered someone, they were playing now on an equal field.

"'You are no better,'" Carl said, "to me, at least, meant she was comparing herself to the rumor she had spread about me killing someone. It's strange, because she knows the FBI and prison officials read her mail. . . . In looking back, nothing had changed with Lisa. It was the same old thing. Classic Lisa."

Farther along in the one-paragraph letter, written on the type of paper a child in kindergarten might use, with dark upper and lower lines and one lightly dotted line in the center, Lisa threatened to expose Carl by putting the old rumor back out there for the public to digest. It might carry new weight, she intimated, taking into account the events of the past month.

Carl sat and looked at the letter. Headlines ran through his mind: COULD HUSBAND OF WOMB RAIDER BE MURDERER, TOO?

Who would believe such nonsense?

Lisa went on to say she had "refused" to grant interviews to the press "to save my kids," and she was disturbed he had dragged them into it all, "missing school . . . for money?"

She then talked about what she viewed as Carl's lack of Christian values, before ending the letter: "You make me sick."

How does one answer a letter with such disregard for reality? Carl wondered. He was beside himself with anger and confusion. To him the letter proved what he had been saying all along: Lisa was more interested in twisting truth than facing it. Here she was, in a prison, still trying to control Carl's life.

Lisa had a hold on Kevin, Carl knew. Carl liked Kevin. He wasn't ready to consider him a friend, but he knew Kevin had been duped by Lisa, and in some way, he felt sorry for him.

When Kevin found out Carl had gone to New York with the kids to appear on television, he started in with the same tone Lisa had used in her letter.

"What'd you do that for, Carl?"

"It's none of your dang business what I do with my kids, Kevin. You got that?"

"The kids, Carl. It's about the kids."

Part of Carl's reason for making the trip was getting the kids out of Kansas for a few days and giving them a break from all the disarray in their lives. Carl didn't have the money to take them to New York himself, and he felt it might be their only chance to see the city.

"Don't tell me about my kids," Carl shot back. Carl was much bigger. He felt Kevin knew he was pushing things too far.

Backing down, Kevin said, "Well, I had always wanted to take them to New York. I'm glad they got a chance to go."

93

A series of e-mails and message board posts written by Lisa had popped up on the Internet during the first few weeks of January, seeming to display a premeditated plan on Lisa's part to meet Bobbie Jo. "Keyboard sleuths," as bloggers are sometimes called, discovered several posts written by Lisa on an unnamed message board, and they were discussing the validity of each message. In one, dated April 19, 2003, Lisa talked about the Melvern house she lived in with Kevin, and listed the ages of all their children. It was an invitation into her life, a way to say hello to everyone on the board. Homey and rustic in tone, the message would have seemed like any other, except Lisa ended the post: "We are also expecting new baby any day."

A week later, she posted again, saying, "Thanks . . . for the warm welcome!" before once again talking about her house.

Lisa appreciated nostalgia and anything having to do with history. She loved visiting historic sites around Kansas and Missouri. In that second message, she rambled on about the house she shared with Kevin, expressing her love for its historic value and significance.

"We started out a couple of years ago," she wrote, noting it was a "second marriage" for both, "with the idea of learning how to do things ourselves. . . ." Then she mentioned that "instead of buying everything," she and Kevin wanted to teach the children how to live like pioneers and depend on the land more than modern conveniences. But, she said, they still had ". . . a lot to learn!"

But the image of her living some sort of *Little House on the Prairie* fantasy was mere propaganda, according to those who knew Lisa best. Kevin's children despised her and refused to go near the house, one of Lisa's children later said. On top of that, her own kids were the first to say Lisa and Kevin hardly ever saw each other because they worked different shifts. During the last year Lisa was a free woman, she worked three jobs. She and Kevin must have passed each other on the way in and out the door.

Yet, the last line of the post was probably what scared people the most when they read it later: Lisa said she and Kevin's "next project" was to "butcher" a "pig."

Lisa and Kevin had a lot of animals at the house in Melvern—except pigs.

Later, after she was arrested and every single word she had written was examined, the second to the last line of the post carried connotations Lisa forever would be known for: "Any suggestions [regarding butchering a pig] would be helpful."

Public discourse surrounding Lisa's case became a cacophony of armchair detectives, cyber sleuths, and psychobabble-spouting Internet serial posters, who were basing much of their opinions on what the newspapers were reporting. No one knew what Lisa was thinking, nor did anyone know if there was a second suspect. Speculation turned to rumor, which became a feeding frenzy for television pundits discussing every statute and mental-capacity law in front of television cameras.

Todd Graves kept a tight lid on his case, and save for the last press conference to announce Lisa's indictment, he had been quiet. Nevertheless, the legal case against Lisa was moving forward. On January 20, 2005, she was once again brought into court to make her plea.

"Not guilty," her lawyers entered into the record.

Lisa never spoke.

After the hearing, the U.S. Attorney's Office indicated it was now leaning toward seeking the death penalty.

"That is the direction we are going," said Todd Graves.

The news of Lisa's not guilty plea inspired a resurgence of media interest in the case. Fox News Channel ran with the headline FETUS-SNATCH SUSPECT PLEADS NOT GUILTY. CNN kept it simple: WOMAN PLEADS NOT GUILTY IN FETUS KIDNAPPING.

After the most recent news, Carl received an e-mail from Judy, which outlined just how confused and conflicted Judy was about the way things had transpired.

The stress factor between the two families was only elevated by Lisa's arrest and the media coverage of the case. Carl was beginning to feel as though it might not be such a good idea for the kids to see Lisa's family for a while. They had too much to deal with already. Carl believed Lisa had not turned out the way she did without help from someone. The last thing he needed was her family confusing the children, as Lisa was trying to do, telling them things they didn't need to know.

In one e-mail, Judy indicated she knew "how hard" it was on Carl, and said she didn't want to "add to the stress."

Without realizing it, Judy seemed to back up what Carl had been saying all along: Lisa had repeatedly abandoned the children, leaving him to pick up the pieces. "I remember how many times Lisa didn't want them. . . ." More pointedly, she also said she felt Lisa had "mentally abused them with all the things she did in the past and now."

According to Carl, Judy never showed any affection toward Lisa or her siblings. Now she was admitting she didn't have any feelings for Lisa as a daughter. "I have no sympathy for her," Judy wrote, adding, "I feel so sad for her for everything she lost," while saying she loved Lisa, "but it's not the love I should have and I feel bad about that."

It was obvious from the e-mail that Judy was having a hard time "forgiving" Lisa. She "struggled with it every day," and didn't want to "see her or talk to her" at this point, "but I know someday I will face her, and I dread it."

Next, Judy said, "I haven't said anything to anyone about the conversation we had about what Ryan told you about Kevin knowing."

Although her syntax was a bit confusing, Carl understood exactly what she meant. Ryan had gone to Carl shortly after Lisa was arrested with some rather disturbing news: he and Kevin discovered that the sonogram Lisa was showing to people was actually downloaded from the Internet. It was not hers.

Lisa's children were talking about their lives with her. The stories they told made their way back to Carl and Judy. Judy was conflicted: she didn't know how much to tell the kids about Lisa's early life and what to leave out. She was seeking some sort of advice from Carl.

"It's hard," she wrote, "because I can't lie to them, and when they ask me, I feel like I have to tell them. I did tell them I don't think she is insane. They asked about my belief about justice and I told them, but I said when it comes to family, am I supposed to change?"

94

The U.S. attorney's Office made an announcement near the end of January. It was going to focus "officially" on pursuing the death penalty against Lisa. All the talk and speculation regarding "weighing their options" was set aside as a formal statement declared the ultimate result of the decision was now in the Federal hands of Attorney General Alberto Gonzales.

More important, the judge in the case had set a trial date of March 14, 2005, a little over two months away.

To most, it seemed too soon. Yet, the Speedy Trial Act of 1974 "mandates the commencement of the trial of a defendant within seventy days from the defendant's first appearance before a judicial officer of the court in which the charge is pending." There could be a delay, but the defendant's lawyers had to prove the "court finds the ends of justice served by the taking of such action outweighed the best interest of the public and the defendant in a speedy trial, provided the court sets forth the reason for such finding."

Although most agreed that the sooner Lisa's case was presented in a court of law, the better off everyone would be, Lisa's lawyers undoubtedly faced long nights in the office if they wanted to delay the trial. Would two months be enough to prepare for what was sure to be one of the most high-profile murder trials the heartland had seen in decades?

Many believed it would take sixty weeks, not sixty days.

95

Many of Lisa Montgomery's friends and extended family had a hard time accepting the fact that Lisa wasn't pregnant, because she had been so convincing in spinning her tale. Lisa, of course, wasn't the first female to feign pregnancy; her case was one more in a growing list in the United States over the past thirty-odd years.

In 1982, *The American Journal of Psychiatry* published a detailed description of the condition pseudocyesis, a term John Mason Good coined in 1923 from the Greek words *pseudes* (false) and *kyesis* (pregnancy). Many claim the condition has been around for thousands of years, as it was first mentioned in 300 B.C. by Hippocrates, who wrote about twelve women who "believed they were pregnant." Every definition of pseudocyesis is, for the most part, the same: a hallucination "pregnancy in women usually resulting from a strong desire or need for motherhood," which clearly defined Lisa Montgomery's behavior. Many women even stop menstruating as their "abdomen becomes enlarged and the breasts swell and even secrete milk, mimicking genuine pregnancy."

Lisa Montgomery, several members of her immediate family agreed, had been irregular with her menstrual cycle most of her life. Whenever she claimed to be pregnant, her stomach was distended—possibly because she swallowed air and made it happen—and she displayed other characteristics that would have led people to have no reason to question her. In some women, the syndrome is so pronounced, the desire to have a child so deeply engrained in their psyche, the uterus and cervix "show signs of pregnancy" and "urine tests may be falsely positive."

No one has suggested that any of Lisa's false pregnancies had gone that far. But some agree that the mind is, indeed, a controlling machine, and a person's will, if powerful enough, can cause the body to react in many different ways.

In 1990, Dowden Health Media, Inc., a company publishing "journals that reach more than 300,000 physicians each month," published an article with supporting research to break down the dynamics of women—and, shockingly, four men—who suffered from pseudocyesis. "There are several theories regarding the cause of pseudocyesis," the article stated. Among the most common included are: (1) the "conflict theory: A desire for or fear of pregnancy creates an internal conflict and causes endocrine changes to explain the signs, symptoms, and laboratory findings in pseudocyesis"; (2) the "wish-fulfillment theory: Minor body changes initiate the false belief in pregnancy in susceptible individuals"; and (3) the "depression theory: pseudocyesis may be initiated by the neuroendocrine changes associated with a major depressive disorder."

"Pseudocyesis," the article went on to explain, "is considered a heterogeneous disorder without a unifying cause. Research to discover the underlying cause of pseudocyesis has been hampered by the relatively low numbers of patients with the illness."

Dowden Health Media's research was substantiated by a study dating back as far as 1890 to 1910, "when one-hundred-fifty-six cases were reported. . . ." By contrast, "only forty-two cases were reported between 1959 and 1979." Interestingly enough, as it pertained to Lisa's life, "the age range of patients with pseudocyesis is six-and-a-half" years old to "seventy-nine" years old. Even more important, the "average age" of a female suffering from the disorder was "thirty-three" years old. (Lisa was thirty-six when she alledgedly murdered Bobbie Jo and kidnapped her child; thirty-two when she began talking about a series of false pregnancies.) "Eighty percent of women with pseydocyesis are married," the article continued, while "14.6 percent [were] unmarried. . . ."

Perhaps most relevant, Dowden's research found that "pseudocyesis is more common in women during their second marriage" and "thirty-seven percent of women with pseudocyesis have been pregnant at least once."

For some women, the belief they are pregnant is rooted so

deeply in their minds that it is hard for them ever to admit the opposite. Friends and family of these women are stunned later when they learn the truth because the argument by the affected person was so powerful.

The night before Bobbie Jo was murdered, Lisa had called a former friend, Brenda Stanford, and told her she'd just had a baby girl. The possibility that Lisa was lying about being pregnant was something Brenda had never considered. Brenda had been over to Kevin and Lisa's house in Melvern for dinner. "Kevin and Lisa loved each other." She knew Kevin from her work in the community. "Great guy. He was really suckered. An innocent victim." A lot of people, Brenda said, believed it as much as she did.

In addition, weeks before Bobbie Jo was murdered, Lisa had talked to Brenda about a home-birthing kit she had purchased online. "I want to have the baby at home," Lisa said.

"Well, call me," Brenda said, "if you need any help when you go into labor. Be glad to help you out."

"Thank you, Brenda; you're the best."

"I know an EMT," Brenda added. "If you need help, Lisa, just call."

"I will."

96

On October 20, 1989, Lisa gave birth to her and Carl's third child, Ryan. They were still living in Hominy. By then, Carl's job at the prison had become a burden. According to him, there were 120 inmates per guard. He was increasingly bothered by the name-calling, spitting, fighting, and aggressive behavior. "I had always told myself that if I woke up in the morning, went to work, and feared for my life, I'm not working there anymore."

During his tenure as a guard, Carl was assaulted several times, receiving stitches, broken bones, cuts, minor bruises. He could, in some way, accept all of that as part of the job. But then one day he arrived home with a rather large welt on his head and two black eyes.

"What happened to you?" asked Lisa. She was holding Ryan. The other two kids were in the playpen.

An inmate had whacked Carl over the head with a two-by-four and knocked him unconscious.

"My, God, Carl." Lisa put her free hand over her mouth.

"It's just not worth it anymore."

With three kids and a wife at home, Carl needed a job with stability that paid well.

By this point, Richard and Judy had moved to San Diego, California, seeking new surroundings for their fractured, dissolving marriage. Richard claimed Judy had cheated on him. In a way, moving to the West was an attempt to save the marriage.

It didn't take long before they were at odds again.

"I left Richard in California," said Judy. "I moved to Ponca City [Oklahoma] and filed for divorce. Yes, I did go with someone, and if you want to call it 'cheating,' fine with me. But I had already filed for a divorce. The man I was going out with was divorced. He helped me a lot. While he was fixing my car, I used his. We knew some of the same people. We went out to eat and didn't hide a thing. So, yes, I had an affair. But I was separated and, at the time, thought my marriage was over with Richard."

Richard and Judy still had feelings for each other, though.

"I divorced Richard on the seventh day of December 1989," Judy recalled. "He called me soon afterward."

"Let's work things out, Judy," she claimed Richard said. "Come back out here."

Judy called the court and got "a paper" she and Richard would have to sign. She told him after he signed it, he would have to send thirty dollars to the court with the paper and their marriage would be reinstated.

"I'll take care of it," Richard told Judy when she arrived in California. "Don't worry about it."

"Okay, Richard."

With Richard and Judy in San Diego, Carl sat one night and thought about it. "Sun and fun was the real reason. The prison was dangerous and I'd had enough of it." Looking at Lisa with a strange, daydreaming look in his eye, as if he were picturing himself on the beach, Carl stated, "San Diego sounds perfect."

97

In January 1990, Carl packed up Rebecca and Alicia and took off for San Diego, while Lisa stayed behind in Hominy with Ryan, who was only a few months old. Carl figured he'd find a house or apartment close to Richard and Judy, move in, and then send for Lisa and Ryan.

On paper, it seemed like a good plan.

While Carl was in San Diego, he developed a sense things weren't right back home with Lisa. "I felt she was either being unfaithful, or was about to be." Carl had never had this type of "strong sixth sense" before, he recalled, and had no real reason to even consider Lisa was fooling around. Since they married in 1986, things had gone well. Work. Baby. Work. Baby. Work. Another baby.

But now it seemed something were terribly out of balance with the relationship. Lisa seemed "distant" when he called her. "No 'I love you,'" said Carl. Lisa wasn't asking when she could "come out there to be with me. Her whole mood was different."

Judy told Carl that Lisa had received a visit in his absence from her former stepfather.

"What are you talking about?" asked Carl. *No way.* The man had been out of her life for so long, what purpose would he have calling on her now?

"He was there, Carl," Judy swore.

Carl never believed it.

Around this same time, Judy and Richard were making plans to drive back to Oklahoma from San Diego. They wanted to bring some of Judy's belongings home so she could eventually move back. After talking to Lisa a few more times, Carl decided that he needed to be home with her. She seemed "different" and with-drawn, the polar opposite to the person he had left just weeks be-fore.

Throughout the ride from San Diego to Oklahoma, Judy bad-mouthed Lisa, said Carl. It was as if Judy were trying to convince Carl he should leave Lisa.

"Yes, many times I would ask [Carl], why do you put up with her?" Judy recalled.

"For the kids," Carl would respond.

"She's no good," Carl recalled Judy telling him. "You can't trust her."

"What are you talking about, Judy? What do you mean by that?"

"She's messing around on you, Carl."

When Carl returned to Oklahoma, he found out Lisa was preg-nant again—in fact, several months pregnant. At first, she claimed the baby wasn't his. But Carl did the math after they received a projected due date and figured out Lisa had become pregnant a few months after she gave birth to Ryan. Carl was working at the prison then, they were still living together. It was well before he took off for San Diego to scout for a place to live.

Even so, Carl said he allowed Judy to influence his decision to leave Lisa when he returned home.

"She was heartbroken. But what I didn't see when I left for San Diego was how much Lisa needed someone to be around her." He believed she was unfaithful while he was gone. "She felt I had abandoned her when I left."

Carl couldn't get over her infidelity. It hurt too much. So, he left her in Oklahoma and drove back to San Diego with Alicia and Rebecca.

98

Judge John Maughmer filed an official order on March 23, 2005, detailing an earlier decision to postpone Lisa's trial until April 24, 2006, about a year after it was first scheduled. "It would be unreasonable to expect defense counsel to prepare adequately for trial prior to [this date]," the judge wrote. Furthermore, the U.S. Attorney's Office continued to say it was "leaning toward seeking the death penalty," but wouldn't—and couldn't—make a formal announcement of its intent until September 2005, after obtaining approval from the Department of Justice.

With a trial date firmly in place and the government likely to pursue the death penalty, Lisa's defense team went to work on her behalf, noting it was "way too early to determine what kind of defense" to pursue. It could be argued, of course, that Lisa was insane at the time of the crime. Yet with the premeditation and careful planning that the evidence seemed to prove, many agreed an insanity plea would be a tough sell to a jury.

A plea of "incompetent to stand trial" was another option, but Susan Hunt, one of Lisa's attorneys, indicated she didn't see it as a viable argument.

Lisa seemed to be developing into her own worst enemy. While searching her cell, guards at Leavenworth uncovered a letter, which purportedly placed Lisa in an entirely new light. When her attorneys found out, they asked the judge not to give prosecutors copies of the four documents. Under a routine search, jailers took several pieces of paper from Lisa's cell, then passed them to the U.S. Marshals Service, who then turned them over to Judge John Maughmer.

In a court filing, Susan Hunt said she wanted the documents

withheld from prosecutors. "Our client asserts the documents must be returned to her, all copies destroyed, and not provided to the government," Hunt wrote. One of the missives Lisa penned was addressed to Anita, who was an assistant federal public defender working on the case, thus making the letter part of the attorney-client privilege act.

"This document," Hunt continued, "was prepared by [Lisa] pursuant to a request of Ron Ninemire, one of the [defense's] investigators on this case. Mr. Ninemire, in one of his visits, requested [Lisa] write down certain information for use by him and the attorneys in preparing [her] case."

Near the end of March, the prison placed Lisa on "suicide watch," because it felt she had implied in one letter that she might take her life if given the opportunity. After finding a letter in which Lisa talked about killing herself, guards searched her cell and found a "handful," one source later said, of Thorazine pills she had been hoarding. Because of the discovery, Lisa wasn't allowed visitors and was put under twenty-four-hour surveillance for about a month.

Deputy U.S. attorney Matt Whitworth explained in a court filing after the incident that a "corrections officer searched Montgomery's cell on March 4 and discovered a letter and drugs" she had been hiding. The letter, Whitworth wrote, had "a strong suicidal theme." Because of it, Lisa was placed on suicide watch and monitored by a psychiatrist, dressed in different clothes, and given a blanket that would be too difficult to use in constructing a noose.

After the suicide watch was lifted in early April, Lisa called the kids. Carl got on the phone with her. He was tired of Lisa and her evident game-playing. He didn't want the children to get dragged—once again—into the problems of a person who, he believed, was struggling with a mental illness.

"What are you doing now, Lisa?" asked Carl.

"That's all nonsense," said Lisa, according to Carl. "I never would have killed myself. The FBI is playing games."

"You are really something else, you know that. You're not bringing the kids into this craziness anymore, Lisa. I am tired of it."

"Carl! That's not what happened. I wouldn't do that. It's all a stage show."

Carl handed the phone to one of the kids, later recalling how he felt: "She accused [the government] of lying. Reality and accountability were not in Lisa. Why would she continue to lie, even after everyone else knew the truth? I honestly believe she would have thought about it, but Lisa is too selfish to take her own life. She still had hope then that she would get out of everything. After she is convicted, it may be a different story."

99

Carl Boman admitted later he wasn't a man who could control his temper well. At times, he would "cuss and raise his voice" to Lisa. Things changed for Carl as he grew older and learned how to deal with situations in a more mature way, but early in the marriage, he sometimes was overcome by anger.

"What are you doing?" raged Carl the day he became convinced Lisa had cheated on him while he was in San Diego looking for a place to relocate the family.

Lisa started crying. "I didn't do it, Carl. I didn't." She was good at denying the obvious, Carl insisted.

"Well, I don't believe you," said Carl. "We're done, Lisa. It's over."

After the conversation, Carl packed his belongings in a van, took Alicia and Rebecca, and drove to San Diego without Lisa and Ryan.

As the spring of 1990 moved along, Lisa had a terrible time making it on her own in Oklahoma. When she realized she couldn't take care of one-year-old Ryan while working enough hours to pay the bills, she moved into her aunt's house in south Texas. She was six months pregnant with her fourth child.

Throughout this time, Lisa and Carl never stopped talking. She still loved him—and, in many ways, he loved her.

By June, Carl wanted Lisa to move to San Diego at once. Yet, he was not ready to have her move into the apartment he had found. At such an early stage, he couldn't face Lisa and act as if nothing had happened between them.

"My father and Judy still had a place down the block from me," recalled Carl. "They were divorced, but nobody knew it . . .

and were still living together, moving things back to Oklahoma when they could so Judy could relocate at some point."

Lisa moved in with her mother and Richard.

"Well," Carl said, "having Lisa move in with her mother was a mistake. Let's just say it didn't work out."

Lisa started telling Carl that Judy was trying behind their backs to get custody of the children. Carl confronted Judy about it—along with the way she was treating Lisa—and ended up having "a major blowout."

"I called her every name in the book. We fought hard that day."

Judy later denied this, saying, "Lisa left Carl and came to Richard and me. We took her in because of the kids. She was pregnant with Kayla. I took her to the Welfare Department, and she got on welfare, but only stayed on it maybe a month or less, and then moved right back with Carl."

It was clear Judy and Carl saw this part of Lisa's life through different eyes. Up until that point, Carl and Judy had always gotten along fairly decently. It wasn't that they played cards together every Saturday night, took long walks with the kids in the park, or sat across form each other at Sunday dinner. But they did appreciate each other's space and knew where the line was.

Carl was slowly integrating Lisa back into the fold of the family by "allowing" her to watch Alicia and Rebecca while he worked long hours at his new job as a Wells Fargo security guard. So, to the kids, Lisa was always around. The recent blowout with Judy, however, convinced Carl he needed to have Lisa back in his home.

Within a month of living together, Lisa gave birth to Kayla, who was born several months premature, on August 18, 1990. During this time, several family crises occurred: Rebecca, only four years old, was in a car accident while riding with her aunt's boyfriend. She had to be airlifted to the hospital. After she recovered from a broken jaw and dozens of bumps and bruises, she was accidentally hit with a softball. The problems, although quite traumatic, seemed to draw Lisa and Carl closer. The children deserved a mother *and* father. "And Lisa deserved a second chance." She was young. Confused. Perhaps even withdrawn, depressed. Judy was, in Carl's opinion, filling her head with all sorts of stories. In Lisa's mind, Carl maintained, he had let her down and abandoned her when he took off for San Diego looking for a place to relocate.

"I couldn't just turn my back on her," said Carl, defending why he took Lisa back. "She deserved more from me. I had, in many ways, acted on the ideas and thoughts Judy had poisoned my mind with. I couldn't live my life based on what Judy was telling me."

IV

GOD IS CALLING

100

The state of Missouri acquired its nickname, the "Show Me" state, official literature proclaims, because of the skepticism residents demonstrate. Some citizens throughout the 69,674-square-mile area of the state have labeled themselves "tough-minded demanders of proof," one document contends. Missourians insist on confirming truth; they want evidence; they want to see facts for themselves before they believe.

By May 2005, Zeb Stinnett released several statements clearly outlining Victoria Jo's health status. If anyone had a doubt about the child's well-being, it was clear from the few photographs Zeb released with his statements she was a happy, healthy baby, who now weighed in at a surprising fifteen pounds eleven ounces.

In just over five months she had gained almost ten pounds.

"She has three great loves right now," Zeb told reporters. "Eating, sleeping, smiling."

A reserved man who believed in keeping family matters private, Zeb spoke out because, mainly, he wanted to thank everyone, from reporters to law enforcement to hospital personnel, for their "contribution to Victoria Jo's safe recovery." It was obvious Zeb was grateful for what he had, as opposed to being angry over what he didn't. It didn't mean Zeb was ready to forgive and forget. But his focus, at least then, was on raising his daughter and providing her with the home she deserved. He had gone back to work at Kawasaki Motors, while Becky Harper and his mother helped with babysitting duties.

Since Bobbie Jo's death some five months ago, Zeb said, he had received e-mails, letters, phone calls, and cards from people all over the world offering their blessings and support. "I want everyone to know that my silence in the press is not meant to be misinterpreted as a sign of ingratitude. We are humbled and awed by the kindness that has flooded our lives. There is no way to thank each person who had reached out to us. But I hope you all know that you have given us a priceless gift."

101

Lisa Montgomery emerged in the spring of 2005 with a complete new outlook on life. In a letter to Carl Boman, dated May 26, it was clear from the opening line that Lisa had found Jesus Christ and was now living under God's word. In the past, she had never expressed a deep-seated belief in God's word, but Carl and the children were about to meet a woman who had been "saved." Faced with the confinement of four walls, barbed-wire, and steel toilets, Lisa turned to God and opened her heart to the Lord. She was running her life now under the guidance of the Bible—and, as the family was about to learn, she was as obsessed with it as she had been with having another baby.

Although Lisa's words contradicted the behavior she had displayed throughout the past few years, it was clear she was preparing herself for the road ahead. Yet, Lisa was apparently willing to be saved—only if it was on her terms. Besides the doilies and paintings she was working on in prison and sending her children, she was still not ready to be accountable for what she was accused of, or even admit having Bobbie Jo's baby in her arms when authorities found her.

Opening the letter, Lisa said she "prayed very hard" for "guidance" on how to "approach" the state of affairs Carl had created.

That statement in itself, Carl thought, was incredible: *I had created this situation? Typical Lisa . . . here she was trying to turn everything around so as to make herself look good.* "She had done it her entire life. The difference now was, I knew what she was doing. Living with her, raising our children, it was hard to see."

Next, Lisa said she opened her Bible to Matthew 18:19, quoting the passage: "If your brother sins against you, go and show him his fault, just between the two of you. If he listens to you, you have won your brother over." There was only one slight discrepancy in the passage; it was Matthew 18:15.

"From the letters she has written to me," Kayla remarked later, "Mom seems like she has found God, but I sometimes wonder. I don't know why, but I just worry about her sometimes. She hasn't really ever been religious, although when we lived in New Mexico, when I was in kindergarten, we used to walk a mile (or something like that) every Sunday to go to church. No, she never quoted from the Bible—she does now, though—around the house; and no, she didn't pressure us into going to church. . . . I think religion *is* her 'crutch' . . . during her darkest hours. I think so much time alone, and the thought that she might get the death penalty, has made her realize she needs God in her life."

"In my opinion," Judy said later, "Lisa did not express hardly anything of the Lord—until she was, like, behind the bars. I know she went to church in Melvern some, but I think it was because of Kevin's parents, Kevin, and the kids. If she had her way, she wouldn't have gone at all . . . that is my opinion."

Further on in the letter, Lisa spoke of the problems she had with Vanessa and the trepidation she had over addressing them. But Jesus had "directed" her to confront Carl "straight" up. It seemed Lisa was under the impression Vanessa was intercepting her letters to the children and "e-mailing them to England." What purpose Vanessa would have to do such a bizarre thing was never broached. Yet, Lisa demanded it "stop at once."

Then again, she maintained, if she had been misguided in any way, she wanted to "apologize" for spouting off about it.

After that, she reacted to what she had heard was Vanessa's "cursing" Alicia and striking her. She wanted to encourage Vanessa, "as the Christian adult role model" in the household, to read James 1:19–20, wherein, Lisa quoted correctly, ". . . Everyone should be quick to listen, slow to speak, and slow to become angry, for man's anger does not bring about the righteous life that God desires."

Concrete walls and the possibility of a death sentence did not dampen the ongoing feud between Vanessa and Lisa. Lisa wanted Carl to make it clear to Vanessa there was no way she could ever replace her as the children's mother, "and . . . attempting to do so" would only "alienate" the kids from her more. She wanted Vanessa to listen to the children and "read God's word" for guidance on how to communicate with them better.

What is this? Carl wondered while reading.

Lisa's newfound piety didn't sit right with Carl. She was sitting in prison facing murder and kidnapping charges. There were larger issues to worry about at the present time. Was the woman out of her mind?

Because of the tension between Alicia and Vanessa, Lisa urged Carl later in the letter to think about allowing Alicia "to be emancipated" on her seventeenth birthday, which was about two months away. She demanded Carl treat Alicia as an adult and give her the opportunity to move out of the house. At the same time, Lisa said she would "not agree" to allow "any of the kids" to move in with Judy.

From there, she went on to advise Carl on the various ways he could "rebuild" his relationship with the kids, especially Alicia.

"Our God is a God," she wrote, "of love. . . ."

Hate wasn't part of God's makeup, she said.

"This is absolutely incredible," Carl said, reading on, staring at Lisa's neatly handwritten words.

Lisa continued praising God's word, explaining that she was going to educate the children to "know God" as she herself had come to "know Him."

She wrote that she felt "persecuted not only by people who do not know me, but my own family," adding that she now lived under God's way, not by "man's word."

After telling Carl that Kevin and his parents were entitled to visits by the children, Lisa encouraged Carl to work with her to "provide a United Christian parenthood" for them.

"She's got to be on drugs. I can't believe this," Carl responded.

At the end, in what could be construed as a viable threat, she instructed Carl to talk to Vanessa and ask her to refrain from using "physical violence" on one of God's children (Alicia), because "she would not want God's anger directed at her the same way."

Nowhere in the letter had Lisa addressed her own behavior, the savage crime she was being accused of, or if and why she had broken one of God's most sacred commandments.

102

For an elected Republican sheriff living in the heartland of America, meeting the president of the United States might be a dream come true. To shake the hand of the man in charge would have to be a crowning moment in any law enforcement official's career. But for Ben Espey, saving Victoria Jo Stinnett's life was enough.

When Espey got word that President Bush wouldn't be in Washington, DC, on the day he and his colleagues would be in the nation's capital to accept an award for their work in the Stinnett case, Espey was disappointed, but not at all upset. He didn't need congratulations and congressional pats on the back. In early May, when he got word he was going to receive an award, along with Jeff Owen, Dave Merrill (both with the MSHP), Investigator Randy Strong, and FBI SA Kurt Lipanovich, for his work in the Bobbie Jo Stinnett case, he simply nodded his head, shrugged, and said, "Okay. Great."

Espey's life already felt full. "I raise horses, mules; we do some horseback riding," Espey recalled. "I got a motorcycle the wife and I like to ride." Sharon Espey is the sheriff's wife of thirty-one years. With a smile, Espey explained that when he isn't working, he and Sharon spend every moment they can together. ("I used to fish and hunt, but mainly it's horseback and motorcycle riding with my wife now.")

Espey grew up in Maryville and never left. The middle son of five boys, he was the captain of the high-school football team who managed to get A's and B's throughout his education and has never been in any trouble ("zero alcohol and zero drugs"). Life has been good to him, he feels.

"Everybody needs to be equal," he asserted, speaking of the sheriff's office he runs. "That's what I have always implemented in the environment we all work in around here."

The reason why Espey had been so successful as sheriff, he said modestly after being pressed about the issue, "is that I know the land and the people. I know what they expect, because I am one of them."

The Department of Justice, along with the National Center for Missing and Exploited Children, honored Espey and those who helped in the Bobbie Jo Stinnett murder investigation with its Officer of the Year Award. In recognition of their work, the men were invited to Washington by Attorney General Alberto Gonzales to receive the honor. *America's Most Wanted* host John Walsh was there, along with members of Congress and state representatives.

Todd Graves announced the award to the press. "These local, state and federal law enforcement officers exemplify teamwork among all levels of law enforcement," Graves said. "Their quick action and resourcefulness transformed what could have been an even worse tragedy into the return of a healthy child to her family. I know they have the profound gratitude of that family, and they have our respect for a job well done and an honor well deserved."

Espey and his crew were among twenty-five honorees from across the nation who had been recognized. Alberto Gonzales, quite proudly, said, "A missing child is every parent's worst nightmare. Every day, the courageous men and women of law enforcement work tirelessly to recover missing and exploited children across our nation. We are grateful for their dedication, and today we recognize their valiant efforts to apprehend would-be predators and keep our communities safe."

Todd Graves explained during the ceremony how the "recovery of Victoria . . . underscored the value of the Amber Alert program."

Back home in Maryville a few days later, Espey was in his office when he received a surprising call.

"George Bush found out about the award and that you guys were out there, but he didn't have time to meet with you then."

"I know," Espey said.

"He wants you to go back out there this week so he can honor all you guys himself personally in the Oval Office."

Espey was speechless.

Whereas Espey and his peers had taken their wives and children to Washington, DC, the first time, this next trip was solely for law enforcement personnel. Each set of officers ("I think there were thirty-two . . . five or six groups . . .") would fly back East and meet with the president separately.

"What an honor."

There were five officers in Espey's group. They walked into the Oval Office together. President Bush was standing in front of his desk waiting for them.

"Hi, how you doin'?" Bush said, shaking each officer's hand. They stood in a half-circle around him at first, and then Bush gathered the men around and talked about the history of the Oval Office, what it stood for in democracy, and some of the decisions made in the room.

"It was just great," Espey said later. "This guy was just super. Outgoing. Very down-to-earth. He took the time to tell us what happened there."

What struck Espey later was how natural it felt for a county sheriff from one of the more rural regions of the country to stand with his colleagues in the Oval Office, just "shooting the breeze" with the president. "And there were people in Washington who had never even seen the guy."

Being escorted around town for the most part by Secret Service, Espey had several conversations with them.

"You must be pretty important to be honored like that," one Secret Service agent had told Espey earlier that day.

"I guess."

"I've worked here in Washington for years now and never even met the guy, or been in the Oval Office."

Espey smiled. "Oh, yeah. How 'bout that."

103

San Diego didn't turn out to be a place for charming moonlit walks along the La Jolla Cove shoreline or romantic hikes up in Mission Trails for Carl and Lisa after they moved back in together during the summer of 1990. The problems they had seemed to be churning inside them like a virus, just waiting to ruin everything again.

When Lisa had given birth to Kayla in August, they had set aside their problems, at least for the time being. But part of the relationship had been severed. Things would never be the same. If anything, the situation was worse. Carl just hadn't realized it yet.

"What was important to Lisa," said Carl, "was never important to anybody else." Lisa lived in her own fantasy, which she constantly tried to transform into some sort of reality. "She believed she could manipulate anyone, and still does," Carl said.

Carl Boman has blamed himself frequently for the problems he had with Lisa throughout their lives. As they got settled in San Diego, Carl said, "I guess I was working too much. She started "having affairs," he later told the press, "with one of our neighbors."

A friend of Lisa and Carl's had driven out to San Diego with them; he had been staying at the apartment for a time. After Carl found out the guy was bisexual, he "kicked him out"; the guy subsequently got his own place right around the corner.

"This guy, our friend, knew Lisa was seeing another man, but he didn't want to tell me."

The proof Carl needed—and he always demanded some sort of confirming evidence, besides someone else's word—came in the form of a phone call one day. Lisa was on the phone with her lover when the evicted friend, who was there gathering some things he left behind, picked up the other phone and handed it to him.

"Here," he said, "you don't believe me . . . see for yourself."

Carl listened.

"Next time," Lisa's lover was telling her, "we need to get us a hotel room. I don't like it on the floor." It appeared they were meeting in an abandoned apartment for which the guy had a key. "I think we left the gas on the last time we were there."

As the conversation between Lisa and her lover continued, Carl slammed the phone down so Lisa could tell he had been listening. On his way out the door, he walked around the corner of the room as Lisa was heading into another section of the apartment. He nearly bumped into her.

"Oh," Lisa said as Carl headed for the door in a huff, "you're leaving already? Have a good night at work, sweetie. I'll see you when you get home."

Carl shook his head. "I was hurt," he remembered. "It was a good thing, looking back now, that I didn't start fighting with her then."

While starting his car outside the apartment, Carl nearly broke down.

Here we go again.

104

By the beginning of summer 2005, the government had filed its suggestions regarding a schedule and trial order. It detailed the trial scheduling conference the lawyers had taken part in back on February 9, when they sat down to discuss certain issues that would come up along the way leading to trial. Among the discovery items, several things came to light, some of which were already public, others that were not.

Lisa's defense, said the government's suggestions, "does not anticipate a competency motion," but the defendant "may rely on a defense of insanity or diminished mental responsibility," and the defendant "does not anticipate an alibi defense," but that she is "relying on the defense of general denial."

In other words, "I didn't do it."

The government was obligated under the order to file its "Notice of Intention to Seek the Death Penalty" on or before September 16, 2005.

The legal case against Lisa Montgomery, at this point, had come down to paperwork and motion filings. The bottom line was, Lisa was scheduled to be tried for kidnapping resulting in death, beginning on April 24, 2006, and the government was going to seek the death penalty.

105

As Carl Boman would later tell the press, on the night he learned his wife had been "having affairs" on him once again, he allowed his feelings to fester inside while he stood watch on his regular midnight to 8:00 A.M. guard shift. He was angry, sure; but he was hurt more than anything. Deep down, he wanted it to work out with Lisa. He still loved her.

With his second job starting at nine o'clock, later that morning, Carl knew he could lose himself in work and try to fight off any thoughts of running home and confronting Lisa.

Is there any way I can ever trust her again?

A few days passed and Carl decided he needed to confront Lisa before he left for work one night. "What the hell, Lisa? Again?"

"What? No, Carl. What are you talking about? You have it all wrong."

By now, Carl knew Lisa's MO: first deny, then cry.

"Come on, Lisa. This is getting old."

"No, Carl, I swear."

"Stop that! Just stop it, damn it."

Then came the tears.

"It was . . . an accident, Carl. I swear it was," Lisa cried. Then she curled up into a ball on the couch. "Please . . . you're working so much. I was lonely. I needed someone."

The one thing Lisa wouldn't have to worry about anymore was the chance of an unwanted pregnancy. In August, after Lisa went into labor with Kayla several months prematurely, doctors gave her "all sorts of drugs," hoping to delay the birth. But after they realized there wasn't much they could do to slow it, they gave

Lisa dose after dose of steroids to try to help Kayla develop her lungs and organs. As a result of the complications surrounding Kayla's birth, Lisa's insides swelled up, mainly her uterus. Because of that, when she had her tubal ligation surgery, doctors couldn't simply "tie" her tubes, as was done in as a popular form of birth control back then; instead, they had to burn them apart. Thus, there would never be a chance for Lisa to have her tubes re-connected.

That was why, Carl said, when she started making claims of being pregnant years later, he knew there was no way it could be true.

"We had always talked about this throughout our marriage. We were only supposed to have three kids and then Lisa would have her tubes tied off and we would go on with life, happy campers. Kayla came along—and believe me, we were both, Lisa and I, happy to have her; it wasn't about not wanting her or any-thing like that—but we weren't going to have a whole house full of kids. We talked it through many times."

After Lisa married Kevin, she never complained to Carl about having had her tubes tied. "She never came to me and said, 'You bastard, you made me tie my tubes, and now I want another child.' It was just never part of the discussion while she was fak-ing all those pregnancies."

In January 1991, Carl approached Lisa. He had done a lot of thinking about the marriage. "Listen, this is *not* working. I cannot do this anymore. The trust is gone."

"Carl, come on," Lisa pleaded, "please try. If not for me, for the children."

Carl thought about it. "Well . . . I'll tell you what, Lisa . . ."

106

Back in January, Kayla Boman's sister Rebecca drove down to Georgia to visit with Kayla. It was time, everyone agreed, for Kayla to return home. She'd been gone since August 2004. Mom was in prison facing trial. Bobbie Jo was dead. Although reporters were still calling the house every once in a while, it was nothing like it had been.

"Do you want to come back home with me?" Rebecca asked as she and Kayla sat and talked about what had happened.

As she had said on the phone several times previously, Kayla repeated, "No, I'm staying here for a while longer."

Georgia offered Kayla what she felt she couldn't get anywhere else: serenity. Back home, she would face reminders everywhere. Staying at Auntie Mary's, she could go about life in surroundings that were still a bit foreign to her. Kids in school didn't bug her to answer questions. She wasn't put on the spot and asked to explain things. Some of her close friends knew what happened, but they didn't push the issue.

So, Rebecca, disappointed, left without her.

Two months later, in March, Kayla was talking on the phone with her brother, Ryan, one night. ("He sounded depressed," Kayla remembered, "and something in his voice just told me that it was time I go home. At first, I was just going to go home for my two weeks of spring break, but then I decided to stay.")

In less than one year's time, Kayla had gone from living in a household with her mom to living with a friend of the family, to staying with her dad and his wife, whom Kayla had never lived with before. ("I didn't like my stepmother, so for the first few days we 'clashed,' so to speak, but then finally, at my dad's request, I apologized to her, and we learned how to get along. It was a lot different being with them, but I was glad to be back around family. Going back to school, I was sorta nervous. I hadn't seen most of the kids in my class for about ten months. . . . I didn't want to switch schools again, and I definitely didn't want to have to try and make new friends. I just wanted some sort of normalcy in my life.")

A normal life was something Lisa Montgomery had stolen from her children, regardless of whether she was innocent or guilty. For the most part, Kayla hadn't been in contact with Lisa since her arrest. "She killed my friend and took her baby."

In late May, Lisa sent Kayla a card and letter. Kayla's fifteenth birthday was approaching in August. Lisa wanted to give her a bit of advice along with a birthday wish. The heading of it read: GOD HAS A *MASTER PLAN*, AND ALL OF US PLAY A SPECIAL ROLE IN IT. Then, in the body, "Today we *celebrate* the part where *you* come in! *Happy Birthday!*"

Lisa quoted Jesus Christ next, "For I know the plans I have for you, plans to prosper you and not to harm you, plans to give you hope and a future. Then you will call upon me and come and pray to me. . . ." Underneath, she made a box out of X's and hearts. Inside the box, she said she was "so glad" Kayla had been a "part of God's plan." She was grateful for "Him" . . . "allowing me to have you."

A one-page, single-spaced letter accompanied the card. After talking about one of their rat terriers, Lisa said if she got a chance to "come home," she was thinking about showing dogs again. She wanted a "toy fox terrier," she wrote. It had to be a small dog, because she was planning on getting a "small apartment." She wanted a cat, too. And perhaps even a "toy poodle" she could dress up with "bows" and "paint" its "nails."

"She's living in some fantasy world," Kayla said aloud while reading. "I cannot believe this."

Later in the same letter, Lisa spoke of her discontentment at the notion Kayla might be dating, which she vehemently denounced. Sixteen years old was the age Lisa agreed her daughters could begin dating. If Kayla didn't abide by this rule, she would be "in defiance of me and God's laws."

"Let me see that," Carl asked when Kayla told him about the letter.

"Here, Daddy, look."

Carl shook his head. "You'd think, by reading this, Lisa had been arrested on a DWI charge."

At the end of the letter, Lisa took a jab at her mother. First, she told Kayla she had "unconditional love" for her and the rest of the kids. Nothing would ever change that. She didn't have to "like" what Kayla did—if, in fact, she was dating—". . . but I will still love you." Then she said she would never "turn" her back on Kayla in the same way, she felt, Judy had on her. "I had enough" of her "'conditional' love," Lisa concluded.

107

From San Diego, Carl, Lisa, and the four kids moved to El Cajon, just northeast of Lemon Grove, maybe twenty miles north of San Diego. When Lisa asked Carl to "please try" for the sake of the kids, Carl thought about it and decided, against his better judgment perhaps, to give Lisa one more chance. ("Actually, things were going a lot better.") It was now well into the spring of 1991. ("Our relationship was working. . . . We started talking again, communicating better.")

According to Carl, he and Lisa "cleared the air" one night about a lot of things and "opened up to each other" for what was the first time in years.

Looking back, Carl said he had to, at times, "allow Lisa to get things off her chest" while he was there "to listen to her." He had never done that before they moved to El Cajon. "I needed to start allowing her to justify her actions," he added. "It was like a game we played."

Lisa often used guilt as her weapon, and started to blame him for things.

"Okay, okay, okay, Lisa. It's my fault."

Carl said, "It got better when we moved because I allowed it to. Not that I let Lisa run over me and stomp on me. But I let her vent and be 'Lisa.'"

Lisa and Carl had different ways of showing affection toward each other. Lisa liked to hold hands and cuddle. Carl didn't. Lisa enjoyed dinner for the two of them alone while the kids slept. Carl didn't. Lisa wanted someone to hold her at night and tell her everything was going to be okay. Carl rarely was willing to do that. To him, working two jobs and taking care of his family financially showed the love he felt.

After they settled in El Cajon, Carl cut back his hours. He took walks with Lisa, while she hung on his shoulder. ("I had never done that before.")

El Cajon didn't turn out to be the best place to fix the marriage. After a few months, as the relationship seemed to stay afloat, they decided it was time to head back to the Midwest—back to Bartlesville.

"The reason we moved back to Oklahoma at that time," Carl said, "was because of Judy. A lot of these things were because of Judy and my father. We moved out to San Diego because my dad wanted us to. During this whole relationship Lisa and I had—and I don't want to sound like I am blaming her for anything—Judy was involved in every way she possibly could. Sometimes, with me in the wrong, I took up Judy's side against Lisa, which caused a conflict."

Carl said at that time he trusted Judy more than Lisa.

As soon as they got settled back in Bartlesville, Carl left his job as an operations manager at Wells Fargo (he had transferred from San Diego) and went to work for a refining company. Although he had cut back on his hours to help in mending the marriage, he and Lisa decided "together" that Carl would once again start working "a lot of overtime in order to purchase a house" of their own. They wanted a two-story Colonial, with big rooms for their large family.

At this point, Lisa neglected her duties as a mother and allowed the kids to live in filth, some later said. She rarely washed dishes, or kept clean clothes on the children. Carl couldn't do much about it because he was always working.

Lisa, Carl would later tell the press, soon met a local Bartlesville man, who was also married, and started an "affair." Carl found out when the guy's wife showed up at the house one day and "kicked Lisa's ass right there on the front lawn."

After the fight, Carl decided he'd seen enough. He moved out and into his sister's house across town. With the marriage over, Carl gathered the paperwork for what he described as a "quickie" divorce. He and Lisa agreed on the terms, filled out the paperwork together, and submitted it. While they waited for it to go through, Carl took the four kids, transferred back to Wells Fargo in San Diego, and moved in with his father and Judy, who were still living together.

On the divorce papers he and Lisa filled out, Carl sought sole custody of the children. But while he was in California with the kids, he decided to return to Oklahoma alone to look for a place to rent so the children could be closer to Lisa.

With the kids in California with Judy and his dad, Carl took off for Bartlesville. But as soon as Lisa got word of his return, she took off for San Diego. Part of the divorce filing they had agreed upon stipulated that the kids were not to move out of the state where either parent was living. If a parent moved and took the kids, the divorce would be nullified before it even went through.

Although Carl said he was "on vacation" in San Diego, just putting some space between him and Lisa while they figured out how to make the divorce legal, he claimed Judy enrolled one of the kids in school out there behind his back, thus violating the quickie divorce they were seeking.

Lisa, while out in California with her new boyfriend, decided she was going to take the kids back to Oklahoma with her.

"She literally tried taking Alicia right out from Judy's daughter's hands," Carl said. "At this time, you have to understand, no one in Lisa's family would have anything to do with her."

Judy was in church when Lisa showed up. Ryan was sitting with Judy, Kayla in the church nursery, while the other two girls were in Sunday school, in the basement of the church.

"I was told Lisa was in town trying to get the kids, so I grabbed Ryan and gave him to my other daughter's husband," Judy recalled. Judy then ran outside, where she spied Lisa coming up the church steps with her boyfriend.

"Stay out of my way," Lisa said, heading toward Judy in a rush.

Just then, Judy's son came out of nowhere and, according to Judy, jumped on Lisa's back and struggled with her.

While Lisa was fighting with her brother, Judy ran and gathered the kids together and put them in the car. ("I took them and hid them where Richard was working.")

After handing off the kids, Judy switched cars, drove to the town house where they were all staying, grabbed some of their clothes, and called Carl. "Meet me at my sister's house in Texas."

"I'll be there, Judy."

Lisa had a legal right to get her kids and bring them home. She believed Carl and Judy conspired to hide the children in California while Carl worked at getting legal custody back in Oklahoma. Seemingly, Lisa figured it out and wanted her children back.

As Judy took off to her sister's house, Lisa went to the police.

En route, Judy called home. Her pastor, who had become involved, answered the phone.

"Judy, if you don't bring the children back, they are going to arrest Richard."

"Pastor," Judy said, "what should I do?"

"Keep going. I'll take care of Richard."

Later, Judy said, "I was told they had a warrant out for me for kidnapping. Oh, well. Lisa should have known better than to come to the church with another man and try to take the kids. She failed."

From California, Judy drove to San Antonio, where she and Carl agreed to meet.

108

September 2005 came and went without the government filing its "Notice of Intention to Seek the Death Penalty." A month later, the case against Lisa Montgomery became major news again after one of the top death penalty lawyers in the country filed paperwork to join Lisa's defense team.

Born in 1953, fifty-two-year-old Judy Clarke grew up in Asheville, North Carolina, "where she dreamt of becoming Perry Mason or the chief justice of the Supreme Court," her bio states.

Clarke had worked on a few of the most high-profile death penalty cases throughout the past few decades. In April 2005, she represented Eric Rudolph, a devoted follower of antiabortion, antigay, and anti-Semitic white supremacist groups, who eluded capture for nearly six years while hiding in the Appalachian Mountains. In 2003, Rudolph was caught in Murphy, North Carolina, and charged with "carrying out a string of bombings that killed several people and wounded over one hundred." Covering the case, the Associated Press called Clarke an "expert at cutting deals." Before saving Rudolph's life, she negotiated a plea for Unabomber Ted Kaczynski that took the death penalty off the table. She had worked on the defense of Zacarias Moussaoui, the only defendant charged in the September 11, 2001, terrorist attacks, before she joined Eric Rudolph's team.

With her short brown hair and tomboyish looks, Clarke has always been open about her core belief that there is no room for the death penalty in American court. She was described as a "one-woman Dream Team" by an associate who helped her defend Susan Smith, the South Carolina mother who avoided a death sentence after being convicted of drowning her two children.

Married for twenty-plus years to Speedy Rice, an attorney and teacher at Gonzaga University in Spokane, Washington, Clarke has developed a reputation over the years for being able to empathize with her clients in a way that convinces them to believe in her.

After successfully sparing Susan Smith's life, Clarke donated her $83,000 fee "to a group that defends the poor in capital cases." Moreover, when she heard that Oklahoma City bomber Timothy McVeigh and Terry Nichols, McVeigh's alleged co-conspirator, were going to be tried separately, Clarke, who rarely spoke to the press, said, "At a time when Congress and the presidential contenders appear willing to do or say anything to seem 'tough on crime,' Judge Matsch's ruling should be commended by all Americans who believe in the United States Constitution. The Constitution says both of these men are innocent until proven guilty, and each of them is to be judged separately and fairly. That way, all, including the victims and survivors of the bombing, can be more certain of the ultimate outcome."

Lisa Montgomery couldn't have asked for a more experienced death penalty lawyer to come forward.

"She is the patron saint of defense lawyers," Gerald Goldstein, the former head of the National Association of Criminal Defense Lawyers, told a reporter in 1996. "Her specialty is impossible tasks that require untold amounts of labor and imagination. There is not anybody I'd rather have at my back in my courtroom."

Many believed that with Judy Clarke now in Lisa's corner, Lisa had a good chance of being able to cut some sort of deal. However, Todd Graves had made it clear the government wasn't interested in cutting a deal that would allow Lisa to escape the death penalty. Sure, she could plead her case out, but insiders said Graves would not waiver on the death penalty—that is, he would accept a plea, but only if Lisa faced a jury on the issue of sentencing.

Statistically speaking, Lisa's chances at getting life in prison were good. According to the U.S. Department of Justice, in 2004, 125 inmates were in prison facing a death sentence, adding to a total number of state and federal death row inmates somewhere in the neighborhood of 3,200. Throughout the past two years leading up to 2004, however, death row admissions declined. Since the latter 1990s, in fact, the actual number of death sentences decreased by nearly 50 percent. Part of the recent change in jurors' minds, some experts claim, is that over the past three decades, "120 innocent people" have been emancipated from death row, many because of DNA evidence and the technological advancements made in science overall.

The question became: would Lisa Montgomery want to gamble with her life?

109

Judy was in San Antonio with the kids when Carl arrived. He wanted them back. A deal was a deal. Lisa was in love with another man now. She was talking about getting married again. It hurt. But Carl felt he could manage. Lisa had agreed, according to Carl, to allow him to raise the kids. If she wanted to end the marriage, that was her decision—but he was getting the kids.

Lisa had apparently changed her mind. But instead of heading to San Antonio herself, Lisa made a beeline for Oklahoma, to a court of law, where she filed paperwork to take the children back legally and, at the same time, divorce the man who had, in her view, kidnapped his own children.

After spending the night in San Antonio, Carl woke up to find out he was being ordered to court later that same morning. "They subsequently awarded Lisa with custody of my kids . . . ," Carl recounted.

The court found Carl had not "gone on vacation" to San Diego, but had taken the children and was planning on staying out there.

The divorce went through and Lisa was awarded custody and child support. But as time moved forward, she started showing up at Carl's house more and more, complaining about her relationship with her new boyfriend. Things weren't going as planned, and Lisa was having second thoughts.

"She actually spent more time with me than she did with him."

Carl sensed that Lisa's visits had little to do with the children and more with her wanting to spend time alone with her new boyfriend. Carl became, essentially, her babysitter. He claimed she used his love and devotion to the kids to open up leisure time with her boyfriend.

With Lisa living with her new beau right down the street, Carl ended up having the children more than if he had gotten custody of them himself. Lisa would drop them off and take off for days at a time without word of where she was going or when she'd be back.

But when the boyfriend figured out he had to pay an exorbitant amount of child support to his wife and he was also going to be responsible for Lisa's four children, he left.

By herself now once again, Lisa did what she had always done when faced with living life on her own: she ran back into the arms of Carl Boman.

110

As her trial date neared, Lisa sat in prison working on drawings and sending letters to her children. Soon she would have to decide whether to fight for her freedom at a full-fledged, high-profile trial, or see what type of plea deal Judy Clarke could cut for her. In either case, it didn't look good for Lisa.

Rebecca, who had moved in with Kevin's parents after Lisa was arrested, was focusing on work and school. She was a firm supporter of her mother, one of only a few left. Every Tuesday, she drove from Melvern up to Leavenworth to sit and talk with her mom. Rebecca had mixed feelings toward Carl. As she saw it, she could overlook the many times her dad promised to visit but failed to show up, or that, in her view, he had faked having cancer. Yet there was one instance, even when she spoke about it later, she couldn't seem to shake.

"The worst was, my dad and his wife moved like two miles from where we lived with Kevin and my mom." Indeed, Carl and Vanessa, shortly after they married, rented a house maybe a mile-and-a-half down the road from Kevin and Lisa's farmhouse. It was, for a while, the perfect situation: the kids would ride their bikes over to the house and visit their dad whenever they wanted. Lisa could drop them off if she and Kevin wanted some time alone, or Carl could even pop in and just say hello to them.

One day, after school, the kids rode their bikes over to the house and sat with their dad for a while just talking.

Everything seemed fine.

After an hour or so, Rebecca recalled, "We had to go home to do a few chores."

When they were finished, they rode back.

"They were completely gone," Rebecca said later, her voice cracking. "They just up and left without saying a word."

According to Rebecca, for years afterward, the kids would only see or hear from Carl and Vanessa sporadically.

Carl viewed the situation differently.

"Lisa was at the house all the time. Lisa and Vanessa fought. It was not a good atmosphere for the kids, or our relationship. Vanessa didn't understand what Lisa was like at that time, but she soon learned. It was my decision to leave and not tell the kids. It was wrong, I know. It has been thrown in my face. I just couldn't face them with this disappointment: *I moved up there just to move out again.* But to me it was an unbearable situation with Vanessa and Lisa. I took the coward's way out, and it has haunted me and hurt the kids and my relationship, especially with Rebecca.

"And believe me, Lisa played it for all it was worth."

Rebecca was quick to say later, "I love my dad to death. . . . I love all of my family." But part of her, still, feels torn between a mother in prison, awaiting trial for murder and kidnapping, and a dad who, she said, hasn't been there for her. She started college in the fall of 2005. No one helped her. She bought all her own books, paid for tuition, and worked two jobs in order to keep up with a mountain of bills. Even her high-school graduation was marred by disappointment when she had to pay for her own cap and gown.

"It's really hard," she said. "I live here in Kansas, and they [my dad and sisters and brother] live in Oklahoma. They never call me. I have to call them. They never come see me. I go see them. It takes two, you know. I tell them: 'You guys have to make the effort, too.'"

111

After Lisa split up with her boyfriend, she was left with a house full of kids and no one to take care of her.

Lisa went back to what she knew—and started working on Carl. Thus, in early 1995, despite everything they had been through, Carl was faced with the notion of taking Lisa back. "I decided to hear her out."

One might wonder why Carl Boman kept reuniting with a woman he knew was eventually going to let him down. How could he allow Lisa back into his life after she routinely disappointed him? Did he expect her to change?

"Why would a woman being abused by her husband keep going back?" asked Carl later, comparing his motives to those of a battered spouse. "My family included Lisa at that time. She had nowhere to go. We didn't jump right back into it in an instant as if nothing happened. We talked about how we could start fresh and see if there was any way to work it out. We didn't sleep in the same room. I worked ten-hour days, six days a week while Lisa took care of the kids. We grew back together naturally. . . . You have to realize my desire to keep my family together. I grew up without my dad. We connected later, but he was gone for a major part of my life. I always longed for my own family. I love my children as much as any father. I guess I had one last try in me."

In the end, Carl said, "I did it for the kids."

Throughout the early 1990s, several large food corporations had built up a presence in Springdale, Arkansas. When Lisa and Carl moved back in together, most were advertising in Tulsa and Bartlesville newspapers, looking for workers. Carl had just gotten laid off from a job he enjoyed at a local food warehouse. Although he and Lisa were now officially divorced, they were talking regularly and trying to work out their differences.

"At the time, there wasn't a lot of work in the area where we lived in Oklahoma. The oil business busted. In Springdale, they were begging for people to come to town and work."

Carl knew Lisa couldn't make it on her own. He also figured new surroundings might help them make a fresh start—Lisa would be taken out of a familiar environment and placed in a setting where she didn't know anyone.

"Who would take care of Lisa the way she was, with her personality and everything?" Carl asked later, defending the choices he made. "Lisa made bad choices and had nowhere to go: I needed the kids as much as she did."

They were talking one day.

"I'm going to Springdale, Arkansas," mentioned Carl, "and I'm taking the four kids with me, and there is *nothing* you are going to do about it." He admitted later there was no way, legally speaking, he could get away with it, but what did he have to lose?

"I'll go with you then," Lisa said without hesitating. "I'll babysit the kids while you work. I'll watch the kids, Carl. It'll work." There was never any discussion at this point of the two of them actually getting back together romantically. "There won't be any child support for you to pay," Lisa added as Carl sat and thought about it.

"Okay, Lisa, let's try it."

After arriving in Arkansas, Carl made sure he and Lisa had separate bedrooms.

Known in some respects as the "Heart of Northwest Arkansas," Springdale is a conservative town insofar as religion is concerned. Faith is strong in Springdale, which lies in the middle of the Bible Belt.

The Church of Jesus Christ of Latter-day Saints—the Mormon Church—had a strong presence in the area. A knock on the door one afternoon opened the way for two Mormon missionaries looking to recruit the new family in town.

"Come on in," Carl said.

Both women sat down and explained to Carl and Lisa that joining the church was the only option they had left.

"You two should be together for the sake of the children," said one of the women. "Your relationship," she went on, "is all wrong under the eyes of God. You're living in sin."

"You are their parents," the other woman added, while Lisa and Carl listened attentively. "You owe them that much."

112

In 1992, author Jim Carrier published a book titled *Hush, Little Baby*. The book detailed the story of Darci Kayleen Pierce, a young, attractive wife from New Mexico, who, on the afternoon of July 23, 1987, showed up at an Albuquerque hospital emergency room "covered in fresh blood."

In Darci's arms was a newborn baby, also covered in blood. "I've just given birth to this child in my car," Darci told hospital officials as the baby wailed.

Doctors rushed Darci and her newborn to an examining room, but Darci "refused all routine medical treatment."

As doctors and nurses became suspicious of the story Darci told, someone in admissions called authorities.

After the police questioned Darci Pierce for a few hours, she admitted the baby wasn't hers. Eventually she said she had kidnapped twenty-three-year-old Cindy Lynn Ray outside a prenatal clinic and driven her to a "remote rural area" in the desert east of Albuquerque. After strangling Cindy Ray unconscious, Darci claimed she "used a car key to perform a crude Cesarean section on her, stole her baby . . . [and] left her to bleed to death."

The child lived.

Cindy Ray didn't.

Twenty-year-old Darci Pierce was tried nine months later for murder, convicted on all counts, and sentenced to thirty years in prison.

Darci's sexual promiscuity as a young child and teenager, set in motion by sexual abuse by a cousin the same age (six years old), became a pivotal defense position during her trial. Darci claimed she was insane at the time of the crime. Some said a "tortured dream of motherhood" while growing up later compelled Darci to commit her crime. She had been pregnant in her late teens, but had lost the child. Every nine months after that miscarriage, Darci Pierce claimed she was going to have a baby. She had put pillows underneath her blouse as a child and paraded around the house as though she were pregnant. As a young teenager, she slept with men four and five times a week. Everything she did throughout her life seemed to be structured around an obsession to have a baby.

The *Journal of Forensic Sciences* published a study in 2002 titled "Newborn kidnapping by Cesarean section," authored by A.W. Burgess, Nahirny C. Baker, and J.B. Rabun. "The female abductors, in essence, become a mother by proxy, by acting out a fantasy of them delivering a baby," the report stated.

A common thread among these women is that they all seem to be "delusional" in some fashion. In many of the cases studied, the women often "show off" the kidnapped child within the first few hours after abducting it, displaying it to the world as "their baby."

Experts claim a mentally unstable mix of "delusion and pride" generally aids law enforcement in its quest to catch the women soon after they commit the crime.

In many ways, Darci Pierce's story ran parallel to Lisa Montgomery's. Could Lisa somehow have taken Darci's story and used it as a road map?

A former acquaintance of Lisa's related that Lisa had become totally absorbed with Jim Carrier's book. One night while Lisa and her friend were watching a forensic television show—an episode about a woman who had faked a pregnancy—Lisa brought up *Hush, Little Baby* and said she had read it.

"Lisa told me about that book. You know what I'm saying? I don't know if she was reading it at the time, or she just wanted to tell me about it. She went into detail and told me about this book. She's read it."

Because Lisa, Carl, and the kids had lived in New Mexico once, and Darci Pierce committed her crime in the same state, Lisa felt some sort of "connection" to the story. Moreover, the acquaintance felt Lisa understood the book, cover to cover.

113

The Mormon church was like nothing Carl Boman had ever seen in his life. Although he spoke highly of the people he met in the church, its rules began to wear on him as he and Lisa were integrated into its core belief system.

The one aspect of their lives the church would not tolerate was Carl and Lisa's living together in the same household without being married.

"I liked the people," Carl said. "I'd never go back to the church. I know it was a mistake."

It started with church members coming into the home and hijacking Carl and Lisa's coffeepot. They weren't allowed caffeine, even tea. At the time, Carl and Lisa smoked. The church said they couldn't. Then it was the money: 10 percent of everything Carl made had to go to the church. If he missed a day of work and didn't get paid for the day, he would have to make up the difference to the church by the end of the month.

During the initiation process, church members took Carl and Lisa to meetings, where they talked comfortingly about family values. Food was served. It was like having an extended family to fall back on. Lisa and Carl enjoyed it. They felt they were doing the right thing for the kids, for themselves.

After they joined, however, Carl began to question things.

"God has a God," church members told Carl one day. Furthermore, "God has a God, who has a God, who *also* has a God." They talked about "different places in Heaven," as if Heaven were some sort of ladder you had to climb in order to reach your final resting place, and on every rung a different God was there to lead you.

Carl and Lisa had always followed the Christian way of thinking, even though they hadn't dedicated their lives to Christ. One God. Jesus Christ. It was easy to grasp.

Now disciples of the church were stopping by the house to "check in" on them.

"I smell coffee," one disciple—or "Mormon police," as Carl called them later—said. "Are you two drinking coffee?"

"You don't smell *coffee*," Carl said. He was appalled.

The man then went into the kitchen and looked around. ("I was offended by that.")

Lisa was addicted to Pepsi. Even though the church preached abstinence, no way was she going to give it up. And cigarettes: Lisa liked to smoke, but they told her she couldn't anymore.

When they moved to Arkansas, Carl and Lisa felt they could rediscover the love they had shared when they were young. And when they agreed to become Mormons, it was a turning point in their relationship; they had finally agreed on *something*. Regardless of what happened afterward, Carl said, it was a "meeting point between us that ultimately brought us back together."

Thus, in June, they remarried.

"We were baptized Mormons one day and the next day married—boom!" Carl recalled, snapping his fingers. "Just like that."

The church had helped them form a new bond, which brought them closer together than they had been in years. They felt they owed it to themselves to give the Mormon way of life a try.

"I remember living in Arkansas as being one of the happiest times of my life," Rebecca said later. She enjoyed being around the Mormon community. "We were happy as a family."

Carl and Lisa, however, weren't.

By the end of 1995, they moved back to Bartlesville.

114

Standing behind a Department of Justice plaque inscribed with a large brass eagle taking flight, and with a United States flag to his right, U.S. attorney Todd Graves held a press conference on Wednesday, November 16, 2005. Wearing his signature dark blue suit, aqua tie, and white shirt, he formally announced the government's intention of seeking the death penalty against Lisa Montgomery.

A reporter asked him how he felt about everything.

"My name is on the document," he said, "and I wouldn't sign anything I wasn't comfortable with."

Regarding the filing itself, and why it took so long, he said, "It's a very organized, methodical process that we go through."

Most had known for at least six months that Graves was planning on going forward with the death penalty, so the press conference wasn't all that surprising. But the television crews on hand, as one reporter said later, were pushing Graves to "throw some red meat out there" for everyone to chew on. Graves didn't do it. "It was fine for me," that same reporter noted, "but television wanted an angry Todd Graves, and they didn't get it."

The waiting and wondering were over. Attorney General Alberto Gonzales had given his consent in the form of a letter for Graves and his office to go ahead and seek the ultimate justice. Judy Clarke was named in the notice of intent, for the first time formally, as one of Lisa's public defenders, with Susan Hunt and David Owen rounding out the team. If they planned on cutting a deal before the government made its final decision, the time to do so had come and gone.

Lisa was thirty-seven years old on the day she heard the

United States government was prosecuting her to the fullest extent of the law. It had been eleven months to the day that Bobbie Jo Stinnett's mother had found her daughter murdered. Todd Graves was sending a message that the crime his office was alleging Lisa had committed deserved the strongest punishment the law appropriated.

In the months since Lisa's arrest, she had gone from being a desolate, desperate woman to a seemingly fragile-minded one, who was still not ready to come to terms with the criminal allegations made against her. Lisa had told some in her family she was going to be set free when the facts of the case emerged. She even mentioned to one family member that Darci Pierce had been let out of prison recently (not true), giving her reason to think maybe the same would happen in her case—that after serving some time, she would be set free.

Her story kept changing. One day it appeared she was coming to grips with her predicament; the next day, she denied having stepped foot in Bobbie Jo's house. When she heard a book was being written about the case, and certain members of her family had been talking to the author about her, she stopped receiving visitors for a time and went into a self-imposed seclusion.

To add to her problems, for the first time since she was indicted back in January, the death penalty was a reality. It wasn't talk from the U.S. Attorney's Office anymore, or speculation on television. It was written in black and white on the "Notice of Intent to Seek the Death Penalty" court filing.

In a press release accompanying the notice, Todd Graves voiced his determination in prosecuting the case.

"We filed notice with the court today," Graves said in the press release, "of intent to seek the death penalty against Lisa Montgomery. . . . In [this] case, [a] federal indictment alleges that murder was committed under circumstances that justify the death penalty." Thirty-six prisoners are "currently under sentence of death in the federal system," Graves noted, "including four from the Western District of Missouri. As the numbers indicate, we intend to prosecute [Lisa Montgomery] to the full extent of the law, and will not shy away from seeking the ultimate penalty for the ultimate crime. Our decision to seek the death penalty . . . is made with careful deliberation so that justice is served."

Several "aggravating factors" became the government's basis for seeking such a severe penalty. Number one was that Lisa "intentionally killed Bobbie Jo . . ."; that she "intentionally inflicted serious bodily injury which resulted in the death . . ."; and she "intentionally participated in an act, contemplating that the life of Bobbie Jo . . . would be taken and that lethal force would be used. . . ."

The filing claimed Lisa had a "reckless disregard for human life," taking into account the brutality and ruthlessness of the crime.

More in touch with the nature of what went on inside Bobbie Jo's house that afternoon, the filing explained how Lisa "killed the victim in an especially heinous, cruel, and depraved manner in that the killing involved torture and serious physical abuse to Bobbie Jo . . . . that is, [Lisa] strangled Bobbie Jo . . . with a rope and then used a kitchen knife to cut her infant daughter . . . from the womb."

When Carl Boman heard the news, it saddened him greatly.

"Phil, the investigator working for Lisa's team, called and informed me," Carl said. "After they officially announced they were seeking the death penalty against Lisa, I thought, there is a side of Lisa no one knows but me—a side no one has ever seen. When we first got together, we spent many hours talking. For years, we would spend hours talking in private. That was the real Lisa. She couldn't talk to her mom. There was no relationship there. She had no father. She never had to pretend with me. There were no secrets."

Carl and the children had, of course, realized the government was likely to seek the death penalty, but it didn't seem real until it was actually on paper. He had since separated from Vanessa, but was rebuilding his relationship with Rebecca. He knew he would play a role ultimately in the defense's case. The government, by late November, hadn't contacted him regarding testifying. He had been in touch with Lisa's lawyers all along the way. He knew the ins and outs of her defense as it was explained to him. But it was always changing, like Lisa. One day it was "insanity." The next, she was going to claim that because of her upbringing, because she had been abused by her stepfather and, in Carl's words, "neglected" by her mother, she was going to blame it on Judy.

"I was the only one she trusted and could confide in," Carl said later in defense of Lisa. "When she talked with Kevin, it was full of lies and deceit. She could still confide in me after she was with Kevin, but only if it was me and her, never if Kevin was in the house, or Vanessa was around. When you asked about why I could still be with Lisa after she messed around on me so many times, it is because I knew the *real* Lisa. I still love the Lisa I first met. She is long gone now. Lies and deceit and manipulations took their toll. She was responsible for the constant friction in her family. She wanted so badly to be normal and accepted. But she couldn't get that from them."

No one in Lisa's family wanted to see her put to death—even Carl, who had said once it might be the best thing for the children, instead of having to watch her waste away in prison. As time passed, it became harder and harder for the family to imagine one day Lisa would be strapped to a gurney and injected with a final solution. After all, her relatives claimed, she truly is sick.

115

From Springdale, Lisa and Carl left the Mormon Church and moved to Bartlesville. But they didn't stay long. Soon they were waking up to glorious New Mexican sunrises, and sinking their toes in sand as soft as velvet.

A friend of Richard and Judy's had asked Lisa and Carl to take care of some acreage he owned. He had a horse. Some cattle. A few dogs. And a house. The only obligation on Lisa and Carl's part was to pay their own bills: water, electric, food. It was an idyllic situation.

The kids recall their stay in New Mexico as one of their family's best times. Their father worked long hours to support the large family, while Lisa was a stay-at-home mom.

Before they arrived in New Mexico, while still in Bartlesville, Carl found out Lisa had run into an old boyfriend. "But I was told she pushed him away . . . and said she was in love again with her husband, had remarried, and was working on rebuilding her family." That sat well with Carl. He felt Lisa was serious about building a new, stronger relationship. "We weren't walking off into the sunset together, or anything like that," Carl remembered. "But I believed she wasn't being unfaithful anymore. As a plus, we heard there was work and cheap real estate in New Mexico."

Soon, those long talks Lisa and Carl had shared when they first met began again. They wanted their marriage to work—not just for the kids, but for themselves.

In what might have been a sign of things to come, Carl woke up one morning, walked outside onto the porch to enjoy the sunrise, and ran into a rattlesnake coiled up like a garden hose.

Soon after they settled, Lisa started working for a local newspaper, delivering inserts. Then she got her own newspaper route.

"That's when the old habits started to emerge. Lisa started to want to be *more* than what she was," Carl recalled.

In fact, Carl said, a few weeks after Lisa started working, she began hanging around a local bar, the Adobe Deli, after completing her paper route. And their troubles returned.

116

As the children grew older, Carl and Lisa continued working on their second marriage, in New Mexico. During the spring of 1997, Carl sensed something, a faint undertone maybe, about the entire family, especially as Lisa started spending time at the Adobe Deli. Putting up with Lisa's old habits wasn't something Carl could do anymore; he had promised himself as much the day they moved to New Mexico. Carl was working long hours contracting mobile homes and delivering newspapers with Lisa. He didn't have time to keep watch on his wife. He had to trust her, or let her go.

As Carl told the press at the time, Lisa started "having affairs" in New Mexico "not long after we made the move."

What hurt Carl most was that the guy was a friend; Carl was helping him do some work on his house. ("I taught him how to tape and texture, put up Sheetrock.")

It wasn't just this one guy, Carl insisted. "There were several. Things got worse than they had ever been."

And now they were married again.

For the kids, New Mexico provided some of their most vivid memories of their mom and dad together.

"*Titanic* was the last movie we all—Dad, Mom, Alicia, Rebecca, and Ryan—saw together as a family," Kayla said. She loved it. She felt close to her siblings and parents.

Around this same time, the kids started calling Lisa "Martha." It was an odd nickname, considering her middle name is Marie. But the kids had good reason for it.

"One day we were all in the car with Mom," Kayla remembered, "and we were talking to her, and we were all trying to get her attention at the same time." With all four of them talking at once, trying to be heard, calling Lisa "Mom" wasn't working. "So we just began calling her 'Martha' when we really, *really* wanted her attention."

Carl ended up moving out of the house into a small apartment nearby. He just couldn't kid himself into believing they would ever have a chance as a couple again.

After three months, Lisa convinced him to move back into the house for the sake of the children.

"She was hanging out in a bar all night long and tagging the kids along," remembered Carl. "I had to move in to make sure my kids didn't grow up inside a bar. They were being neglected."

Carl tried setting some ground rules until he and Lisa could figure out how to end the second marriage and move on.

"I am so out of here," he told Lisa one night. "I'm not going to be your stooge again and again."

"Yeah, right! You're not going anywhere, Carl Boman." She laughed.

"Huh. Is that what you think?"

"You aren't taking the kids . . . and you'll always hang around because of the kids, Carl."

About three days after one of their arguments, Lisa went to Carl and said, "Run down to the pharmacy and get me a home pregnancy kit."

Carl looked at her . . . *What is she talking about now?* "Come on, Lisa. Be real. I'm not wasting money on a home pregnancy kit."

"No, no, no. I'm serious. I haven't had my period in weeks. It's really late."

"No, Lisa! I'm not going to buy you that."

"Carl. Go get it."

"Your tubes were burned. You can't be pregnant."

Lisa became more serious: "Sometimes it *doesn't* work. It doesn't always stay that way."

"Come on, Lisa. You're kidding me, right?"

"You don't know what you're talking about," raged Lisa. She stormed out of the house, slamming the door, and went to the pharmacy herself.

An hour or so later, she returned with the pregnancy test kit.

When it turned out negative, Carl did everything he could to stop himself from saying, "I told you so."

"Damn it, Carl." She shook the thing and started yelling. "These things aren't always right, you know."

Carl believed this episode was the beginning of Lisa's obsession to become pregnant again. Knowing the pregnancy test was negative, she still went back to the bar and told people she had become pregnant by sleeping with Carl's friend.

Word trickled back to Carl, of course, that Lisa was claiming to be pregnant. Carl laughed when a mutual friend stopped by the house and told him what she had been saying.

Carl decided he'd finally had enough. He was taking two of the kids and heading back to Oklahoma. It was over. No more would he be "suckered" into taking Lisa back. He knew he could not drag her into court and get custody of the kids. His only option, to make sure the kids were taken care of, was to leave Lisa in New Mexico, knowing she would follow him northeast to Oklahoma or Kansas, wherever he decided to settle.

117

Judy Shaughnessy received a call from one of Lisa's attorneys on Thursday night, November 17, 2005, but she wasn't home. David Owen left what she described later as an unsettling message: "I'm calling to tell you about the deal yesterday. Call me back."

After hearing Owen's voice, Judy had a hard time sleeping. She wasn't a newspaper reader or television watcher. Lisa wasn't talking to her, nor were many in the family. She wasn't keeping up to date on the status of Lisa's court case, and now worried that something "bad" had happened. Although their lives together had been filled with aberration, anarchy, and unhealthy behavior, not to mention yelling and screaming and fighting, Judy insisted she still cared deeply for Lisa.

"I think it was right after Christmas in 2002, Lisa and I went to Oklahoma to pick up her children, and I also had another granddaughter with me and we all went to Texas to my sister's house."

They spent the day together as a family going to the Alamo, the Boardwalk, and a few other historical landmarks.

"We had a great time. When my sister Ann was in the hospital, Lisa was there for me. The day my sister died, Lisa came to the hospital and stayed with me and helped me cope with the loss. At the funeral, she didn't have much to say, [but] she carried herself very well. Over the last few years, I noticed how she distanced herself when the Montgomery family was around, because I think she was telling them stories I knew to be untrue, and she was afraid I would tell them if they said something to me. So this is why they distanced themselves from me and my new husband. I know the kids love their mother and they should. I know they went a lot of places together, and they did have fun with her. It wasn't all bad."

The next morning, November 18, Judy called David Owen and heard him confirm what she had since found out on the Internet: the government was going to pursue the death penalty. According to Judy, that was the "deal" Owen was speaking about on Judy's answering machine the previous night.

"No matter what, Lisa is my daughter. I do love her. It just hurts so bad. I have to pull myself together. . . ."

When Judy's mother died in 1996, Lisa dropped everything and showed up with two of her children. "She was a big help to me then, too. It's almost like she went in spurts. But all in all, Lisa did have good points, and I just don't want anyone to think she has been evil, or whatever people are saying about her. I know Carl and [his second wife] would say how evil she was all the time. But I don't think Vanessa took the time to know her. I think Carl influenced the way she thought about Lisa. I still have this thing about Lisa having a split personality because it's like she's good and then the opposite happens. Who knows? I don't. I wished I could be stronger now. Back when it all happened, I lost weight, and I couldn't eat and couldn't sleep."

As the Christmas season dawned, all Judy could do, she said, was hope and pray for the best.

118

In February 1998, Carl drove back to Bartlesville with Alicia and Ryan, leaving Lisa in New Mexico with Rebecca and Kayla. Lisa said she would be leaving New Mexico about a month later and moving to Kansas. Judy was remarried and living in Topeka then. At least Lisa would have someone to fall back on when she needed help with the kids. They agreed Carl would get custody of Alicia and Ryan, and Lisa would get custody of Kayla and Rebecca. One weekend, Carl would take all four; the other weekend, they would go to Lisa. It seemed like a fair deal to Carl; after all, he would never take her back again.

"I was finished. For real this time."

According to Carl, the handshake deal he made with Lisa before he left New Mexico was a sham. Lisa finally made it to Kansas and moved in with Judy and her new husband, but not before stopping in Bartlesville to grab the other two children.

"The lawyer she had held on to the papers I sent him to dispute the custody," said Carl, "and I had no chance of being heard."

Lisa was ultimately awarded custody of all four children. Carl claimed she used a friend's address and phone number and lied on court documents to make it appear as if she lived in New Mexico, where she had filed.

By the time Lisa arrived in Kansas, Judy had moved on to another relationship and was living with Danny Shaughnessy, whom she would eventually marry. When Judy left her husband for Danny, Lisa was on her own again.

"She couldn't handle the kids alone," recalled Carl, "so she came and stayed with me for a while." In order to make sure the children were taken care of, Carl once again took her back in. "It was okay, because that meant the kids would be with me, too."

In 1999, Lisa began a job as a security guard in Topeka at a wire manufacturing plant, where she met—and soon became involved with—Kevin Montgomery, who was working at the same plant.

Kevin was a happy-go-lucky divorcé who had spent his entire life in Melvern. When he met Lisa, Kevin had just ended a broken marriage, in which he'd fathered three kids.

Those who knew Kevin during that period claim that when he met Lisa, she viewed him as a pawn she could manipulate without complication. "He was a pushover," one former acquaintance said. "She saw that right away and used it to her advantage."

"Mom always talked bad about Dad to Kevin," recalled Kayla. "Like, she would say she always had to buy our food and stuff . . . but that isn't true. My grandmother [Carl's mom] is the one who did all the cooking, cleaning, and shopping. *Not* my mom."

According to Carl and Kayla, as soon as Lisa moved in with Kevin later that same year, she launched a concerted effort to destroy Carl's reputation as a father. Instead of praising Carl for opening up his home when she needed a place to stay, while she underhandedly filed for divorce and sole custody of the children, Lisa attacked Carl's character behind his back and initiated a series of lies that would have an impact, ultimately, on both their lives.

"It was a pretty rotten and awkward time," remembered Carl. "When she lived with me, but was dating Kevin, she used to write Kevin letters quite a bit. I found a few of them and—being curious, nosy, and maybe even wrong—read them. She told Kevin once that she was pregnant and didn't know if she wanted the baby because they weren't married."

It was another fabrication designed to trick Kevin, Carl insisted. Kevin's parents, Lisa learned quickly, were a churchgoing couple who believed unreservedly in the church and its values. Lisa used the moral fiber the Montgomerys held so closely to their hearts as an asset. Carl believed that if Lisa told Kevin she was pregnant and threatened to go to his parents with the news, knowing they would disapprove, she felt she had Kevin exactly where she wanted him.

"Kevin actually gave her three hundred dollars to have an abortion," confirmed Carl, "according to what I was told."

To add more legitimacy to her argument, and perhaps play on Kevin's sympathies, Lisa named the child Sarah. It was the name Kevin and his previous wife had chosen for their stillborn child, who was buried in Melvern.

Reading the letters proved to be an education for Carl in just how far Lisa was willing to go to wield control over the new people in her life.

"She had even told Kevin she'd had a daughter by [her stepfather after he raped her] and the state had taken the child."

Kevin, like any man, at the mercy of a woman he was falling in love with, "believed it all," maintained Carl.

Moreover, as she became part of the community of Melvern, Lisa played off the town's compassion, positioning herself as a poor little divorcée who'd had a rough go of it with a man she described as a deadbeat dad who didn't want to do anything for his children.

"Lisa began telling everyone in Melvern she had to buy groceries and clean the house when she was staying with me," said Carl. "The kids and I got a kick out of it. She *never* did a *thing*. She told members of my family I was trying to sleep with her while she stayed with me. What a joke! I had to give her money to go back and forth to Kansas to be with Kevin, and let me tell you, it was well worth the investment. We were divorced, and I made sure she knew it. Imagine your ex-wife living with you, and she is making up lies about you, and has a boyfriend that lives one hundred and fifty miles away. It was very uncomfortable, to say the least."

While Lisa was living with Carl during that period, Carl said they talked a lot. "Remember, we had been together for about fifteen years by then, we had four kids. We had a lot to talk about. But still, she felt she had the upper hand."

To put it bluntly, Lisa talked about *Lisa*, and how great Kevin was going to be for the kids.

"I actually felt sorry for Kevin then."

Kevin had gone through what he described to Carl and Lisa as a "bad divorce." Carl saw that he was vulnerable, and Lisa was "filling his head full of garbage."

"I didn't want him raising my kids," Carl said. "Heck, I didn't want *any* man other than myself raising them. The kids and I were extremely close at the time; we were each other's world."

Strangely, for a woman who had often proclaimed her undivided attention and devotion to her kids, after she moved out of Carl's and into her own apartment not far away, Lisa never wanted to have the children over.

On weekends, Kevin would drive up from Melvern and stay with Lisa. To integrate the children into her relationship with Kevin, she would pick them up at Carl's and take off with Kevin, but only for a few hours. "Never for an entire weekend," Carl said.

It was not only a culture shock for the children when Lisa and Kevin moved into their own place in Melvern, but an emotional shock as well. They had adjusted to a way of life with Carl in Bartlesville. Friends. After-school activities. Little League. Soccer. Moving to another state was not easy for thirteen-, twelve-, eleven- and ten-year-olds.

To the kids, it hadn't mattered that Carl and Lisa were in the middle of a divorce; what mattered was that they were all together as a family again before Kevin came into the picture. Now their family was gone—and some new man was taking their dad's place. Lisa's relationship with Kevin was clearly serious. She was already talking about marrying him.

"We actually did things together as a family," said Carl, speaking of the year when Lisa and the kids lived with him. Kayla also recalled the time as one of the more memorable, pleasant periods of their lives together—but also one of the worst.

"When we lived with Dad, whenever he got paid, he would take us to Wal-Mart and let us get a new Barbie, or something like that. On Saturday nights, we would have our 'family night.' We would get all this junk food, get a board game out, and we would all sit together and just be a family."

All of the kids knew the move was inevitable, but when the time came, Lisa showed little sympathy toward the situation, or the children's feelings. One day, without warning, she showed up in Oklahoma and just knocked on Carl's door. Carl's mother was watching the kids.

"I'm taking the kids with me today," said Lisa.

119

It was a marvelous autumn afternoon, eight weeks or more before the new millennium, the kind of day when the two most extreme seasons hung in a state of uncertainty. Midmorning could bring Indian-summer heat, while evenings could turn bitter cold. The leaves, crisp as a paper shopping bag, were a bronze maple-syrup brown, dropping from the Custer Elms, Osage County Cottonwoods, and Post Office Oaks. Lisa and Carl were now officially divorced for a second time. Living with Kevin Montgomery in Melvern, she was planning a spring 2000 wedding.

On this day Carl drove up from Oklahoma to drop the kids off after having them for the weekend. At times, when he and Lisa exchanged the children, Carl met her at a nearby park in Lyndon. To many residents, the park was a symbol of the family unit, a sanctuary of arrowhead-shaped shrubs, manicured grass, merry-go-rounds, monkey bars, and ball fields. But for Carl and Lisa, it had become a suburban drive-through window for broken families, a public stage to swap "property."

The children were running around and playing while Lisa and Carl stood nearby and talked.

"Stop with the lies, Lisa," Carl said. "You're spreading rumors about me. I'm tired of it."

Lisa didn't respond at first. So Carl asked again. "Why are you spreading these lies, Lisa? You better stop it."

Instead of answering Carl, Lisa walked toward the children.

"Come on, kids; it's time to go."

Nine-year-old Kayla ran over and asked why; then she looked at Carl.

"I'm not going, Daddy. I can't leave you," she said, grabbing his legs. She wiped tears from her eyes and reached up for him.

"It's okay," Carl said, picking her up. "I love you. I'll see you soon. Don't worry about anything."

Kayla continued to cry.

"I won't go."

Carl started walking toward Lisa's car as Kayla clung to him tighter.

"You *have* to go," Carl whispered in her ear. "It's okay. I'll see you soon."

Kayla grabbed his jacket and wouldn't let go as he tried to put her in the car. Lisa looked on, held her tongue, and shook her head.

Kayla said later she couldn't "remember" her mother saying anything to her on that day. "But I can say that normally, when I would cry, she would say to me, 'Stop it—or I'll give you something to cry about.'"

"Come on," Carl said, opening the door, trying to lead Kayla into the backseat. "It's okay."

Kayla grabbed hold of the door. "No, no, no."

"I wouldn't let go . . . ," she remembered. "Dad had to pry my fingers off the door and make sure I couldn't grab hold of anything else, so he could shut the door. It wasn't that I didn't like being with my mom; it was just that I wanted to stay with 'daddy' forever."

Watching Lisa pack up the rest of the children, Carl was distressed. He couldn't do anything to diminish their pain. He felt helpless. In their young lives, the Boman kids had gone through their parents' divorce twice. One divorce was torture on a child's emotions. Carl had given it a second chance because of them. But it didn't work.

It would never work.

Kayla sobbed as she watched an image of her dad standing, waving, getting smaller, as Lisa drove away.

"I looked out the back window of the car as we were leaving," Kayla said, "watching my dad until I could no longer see him."

Carl pulled over down the road after leaving the children and cried before returning home. He was troubled and enraged at the same time. The level of uncertainty the kids felt ate at him. They were being yanked, emotionally, in so many different directions, and now they were expected to adapt to new surroundings and a new father figure.

That day was the beginning of the worst years of Carl Boman's life, he later said. But even then, as Lisa moved on with her life, to settle so far away, Carl could not have believed what Lisa would do in order to prove to everyone she hadn't been lying about being pregnant.

120

The town of Skidmore had been quiet since Bobbie Jo's murder. Zeb was spending his time with Victoria Jo and still wouldn't speak publicly about the case.

A few days after Bobbie Jo was murdered, *New York Post* columnist and author Andrea Peyser, in a column titled "Depraved Schemer Deserves No Sympathy," wrote, "Don't hog that lethal injection needle, Scott Peterson. Pass it on down to Lisa Montgomery when you're done." The column sparked some debate over whether death was a severe enough punishment for Lisa, if in fact she was found guilty. Farther down in the piece, Peyser wrote, "Now, people in the Missouri town where Stinnett lived and was murdered lock their doors, fearing the next knock will come from a baby snatcher." Lisa's case came back into the public spotlight as the anniversary of Bobbie Jo's murder approached. Skidmorians were not vengeful people, looking to right a wrong by lynching a woman for the horror she had allegedly committed in the town; they were common folk, waiting patiently for justice to run its course. They got up every day and worked the land. Talked about life and politics, weather and sports. They attended church on Sundays. Many included in their prayers a special plea to God: *May Bobbie Jo rest in peace. . . . May her family be blessed with your love.*

A trial, regardless of the outcome, wouldn't change anything for the people of Skidmore. The town had suffered a devastating blow to the heart—and nothing could alleviate that pain.

About six miles east of Skidmore, heading toward Maryville on the "A" road, Zeb and Victoria Jo had moved to the town of

346 / M. William Phelps

Maitland. Zeb had family there, brothers and sisters who could help him raise his daughter. During the past year, Victoria Jo had grown into a strong, cheerful infant, "active and healthy," with chocolate-pudding brown eyes, big and round, like Bobbie Jo's, and a dynamic, spunky nature.

"She doesn't have much hair yet," Becky Harper told the *New York Post*, "[but Bobbie Jo] didn't grow her hair for a long time either. She seems real content and happy. I think her dad's taking real good care of her. She doesn't take the place of my daughter, but she is a comfort."

Victoria Jo was doing everything any child her age might: crawling, "jabbering," "learning how to walk," and "trying to talk."

Pat Day, Victoria Jo's great-grandmother, told the *Post*, "She's like a little doll. We just enjoy her as much as we can."

December 16, 2005, marked the one-year anniversary of Bobbie Jo's death and was Victoria Jo's first birthday. To memorialize Bobbie Jo, push the need for Amber Alert legislation to close what some were calling "Tory's Loophole," and support grandparents' rights, several Skidmorians held a candlelight vigil at 7:00 P.M. at a park about two blocks from Bobbie Jo and Zeb's former house.

"We know we had someone in Heaven, an angel looking down to save Victoria Jo," someone at the ceremony said as it got under way.

"I spent hours trying to come up with just the right thing to say tonight," Cheryl Huston, a friend of Becky Harper's, said at one point, while people huddled around her trying to stay warm. "But nothing that I say up here is going to do the one thing that would make Becky feel better, and that is to give her back Bobbie Jo. One year ago, a woman from Kansas came here to our community—and from that point on, all she did was take."

After Huston spoke, everyone bowed their heads and prayed, candles in hand, their tiny flames waving and flickering in the wind. They were standing next to a seven-foot-tall brick monument dedicated to Bobbie Jo.

It was a somber ceremony, commemorating the death of a cherished citizen. Many agreed that Bobbie Jo had demonstrated what was so charming about Midwesterners, with her cute drawl, big-boned frame, large brown eyes, and humble demeanor. It had been a rough year for Bobbie Jo's family and friends, especially Becky Harper, who had obviously missed her only daughter dearly. Little things, of course, made it hard: the special way Bobbie Jo spoke, smiled, and always seemed to bring joy to whatever situation she was involved in. Tonight was a tribute to her memory and the child she left behind.

"We're doing this because she is a friend and this is a community," Cheryl Huston told a reporter from the *Kansas City Star*. "We take care of each other."

At the close of the ceremony, Reverend Harold Hamon talked about how the country "rallied together" during the Pearl Harbor and September 11 attacks, before adding, "I saw the same things here a year ago," pointing to the ground below his feet. "When tragedy strikes, you can fall apart, roll over, and play dead—or you can rise to the occasion. I just thank God that we can share together as members of a community such as we are here. Tragedy comes, but we don't have to be defeated by it."

A press release issued a day before the vigil was specific: "A primary purpose of the event is to remember Bobbie Jo Stinnett. It is being held by friends of the family and by caring members of her community. It is being held in support of her family, in an effort to let them know we care about them. A secondary purpose of the event is to raise awareness of legislation regarding 'Tory's Loophole' in the Amber Alert. A final purpose of this event is to bring further awareness to restrictions on grandparent rights of visitation in Missouri. . . ."

To make matters more disheartening for Becky Harper, Zeb Stinnett had cut back on the days she could see Victoria Jo. As of December, Harper was getting the baby only one weekend per month. Zeb seemed concerned over what Harper was telling the child—and would eventually explain as she grew older—about her mother's death and the circumstances surrounding her birth. The situation between Harper and Zeb became so tenuous that Harper filed a petition in Holt County Court so she could legally spend more time with her granddaughter.

Zeb answered by filing an injunction himself, saying he "temporarily cut" Harper's visitation time "because her behavior has become bizarre." Moreover, Zeb indicated that "at no time should Becky Harper discuss any events concerning the death and demise of [Victoria Jo's] natural mother."

As the new year dawned, Harper and Zeb were heading to court. (Under a court ruling weeks later, Harper was allowed visitation with Victoria Jo.)

In spite of the family problems over the past year, *Post* correspondent Jennifer Fermino, in an article published on November 28, 2005, seemed to condense into nine words how the case had impacted the nation, calling Bobbie Jo's murder "a nasty and bizarre killing that broke America's heart."

And that one line seemed to explain everything: America identified with and wept for Bobbie Jo Stinnett and the loss of innocence her murder personified. Bobbie Jo's murder was a gruesome reminder that evil lurks in the most remote and pastoral corners of the rural Midwest. The death of an American sweetheart, in Middle America, exemplifies how uncertain and unpredictable life can be. The painful ripple effects of her death spread throughout the small community and what was once a close-knit family.

121

Her favorite song lately was "Mockingbird," by Eminem. The blond-haired, blue-eyed hip-hop artist had taken an old classic—"And if that mockingbird don't sing . . ."—and rapped an ode to his daughter over it. Lisa seemed to relate to the song's meaning.

"My mom didn't like Eminem when I lived with her," said Kayla. "She listened to some of the same things we did, but not always."

After Lisa ended up in prison, she talked about the lyrics Eminem had written and how they related to the predicament she now found herself in while behind bars, away from her children, awaiting trial. One day Lisa called the house and talked to Rebecca, who was still driving up to Leavenworth to visit her every Tuesday night.

"'I know Mommy's not here right now,'" Lisa sang into the phone, quoting from Eminem's version of "Mockingbird," "'and we don't know why we feel how we feel inside. It may seem a little crazy, pretty baby, but I promise: Mama's gonna be all right.'"

"That really got to Rebecca," remembered Kayla. "It bothered her."

As a Mother's Day gift, Lisa sent Kayla a rather bizarre drawing, considering the charges she faced and the sweet nature of the picture. Artistically speaking, the picture, created with colored pencils, showed talent; the detail and soft use of color displayed an obvious ability.

The picture showed an uncomplicated, cartoonish Laura Ingalls–type character, holding a potted heart-shaped flower plant.

Checkered bows gathered the girl's wisps of blond hair together tightly near her hidden ears. Under a large pink beach hat, with a scarf encircling it like a sash, the girl's blue eyes, purple blouse, and plaid dress, hanging down to her ankles, complement the subtle smile on her pudgy, round face. The character stands on a bed of blue clover, green grass all around her, appearing stress-free and, at the same time, blissfully mysterious.

"It is pretty cool," remarked Kayla, smiling, looking at the picture. "That's Mom," she added before changing the subject.

Accompanying the picture was a doily Lisa had sewn. She said in a note that she hoped Kayla "enjoyed" it as her birthday present.

It was a fine piece of embroidery. From the weblike detail of the item, Lisa was talented in that craft, too. Yet, the doily had soaked up and retained a certain prison stench, as if it had been left in an attic somewhere for years: musty, dank, sour—an eerie reminder of Lisa's daily life.

Three of Lisa's children have been up to Leavenworth to visit her. Kayla has yet to make the trip. The last time she saw her mother was around August 18, 2004, her fourteenth birthday, before she left for Georgia. She has spoken to Lisa a few times on the telephone, but chooses to take a step back and allow the space between them to act as a healer. Lisa writes to Kayla often. ("But I don't always write back.") And she will, once in a while, tell Rebecca "something" to bring back to Kayla, but "I will not go see her.

"As I told Mom in one of my letters," concluded Kayla, "I don't want to have any memories of her in prison. A lot of people have told me I should go see her so I don't have any regrets [if she is put to death]. But I just can't bring myself to do it."

Once, Kayla considered visiting her mother. She thought about it long and hard and almost convinced herself to tag along with her sisters and brother. At the last minute, though, she changed her mind.

"Well, I'm not really sure what else there is to say about that."

Still, Kayla has a photograph Lisa had taken behind bars, copied, and handed out to the kids. It is the exact image of her mom that Kayla doesn't want to see in person. For the first time in her life, said Carl Boman, Kayla is "free" from the restraints Lisa put on her. "She's her own person again. She is happy for the first time in a long while."

"I am," Kayla said later reaffirming what Carl had said earlier about her joy at just being able to be a teenager. "I really am."

EPILOGUE

Lisa Montgomery is in a Leavenworth, Kansas, prison awaiting her trial as I complete this manuscript. The *United States of America* v. *Lisa Montgomery* was slated to begin on April 24, 2006, but was then postponed until October 23, 2006. As of this writing, there has been little indication as to the defense Lisa's lawyers will present. However, I have heard from certain people connected closely to the case that Lisa is going to present a defense claiming that, because of her "abusive" childhood and upbringing, she cannot be held responsible for her alleged actions. She will maintain that the abuse she suffered throughout her life caused her to be unable to decipher right from wrong. Legally speaking, a more appropriate defense might be what is called an "irresistible impulse" defense, which "argues that a person may have known an act was illegal; but, because of a mental impairment, [the individual] couldn't control [his or her] actions." In 1994, Lorena Bobbitt was acquitted of the felony "malicious wounding" when "her defense argued that an 'irresistible impulse' led her to cut off her husband's penis."

Considering the premeditation and substantial planning the government alleges Lisa Montgomery took part in, months before Bobbie Jo's murder, Lisa's lawyers only have so much they can work with. Devoid of any earth-shattering new evidence and surprise witnesses, I don't foresee any groundbreaking relevations coming out at Lisa's trial. From a law enforcement perspective, the case is fairly textbook: the evidence against Lisa is, I was told by several deeply engrained in the prosecution, "overwhelming." As many law enforcement officers said, "Bobbie Jo Stinnett's baby was found in Lisa Montgomery's arms. What more conclusive evidence do you need than that?"

The mass market paperback edition of this book, to be published in 2007, will contain the details of Lisa Montgomery's trial and sentencing.

ACKNOWLEDGMENTS

The people I need to thank for their tremendous work on this project are, first and foremost, the producers. Mainly, Kensington Publishing Corp. as a whole. After editor-in-chief Michaela Hamilton read the outline for the project, she believed, as I did, that this story, as gruesome as it was, could be more than a true-crime book—and certainly more than the horrific elements surrounding the case would have implied. Michaela was behind me from day one; and she saw my vision of using the two towns of Skidmore and Melvern as a narrative thread, through which an important social story would emerge. Michaela's expert editing skills in the beginning shaped this book into the fast-paced narrative it became; she gave me sage advice after reading drafts of the book, sending me back to the canvas with a clearer picture of what I needed to do. Having worked with Michaela now for five years, knowing that she has edited some of the best in the business (Ann Rule among them), I am entirely grateful for the time and care she dedicates to my career.

Kensington publisher Laurie Parkin was instrumental in giving the project legs; without her belief in me as a writer, this project would not have floated. Senior editor Jeremie Ruby-Strauss has always been one of my advocates, and I appreciate his continued advice and consummate understanding of the process.

Copy editor Stephanie Finnegan, in what must have been an exhausting job, did tremendous work.

Equally important on the production side was Jim Cypher, a friend who read and edited an early draft of the book. Jim is a superb editor, smart reader, and perfect gentleman.

Peter Miller, my agent at PMA Literary & Film Management,

Inc., was my biggest supporter from day one. Peter worked a lot of hours for me during the beginning of the year 2004, and continues to. I am indebted to his dedication to my career.

Carl Boman, of course, was helpful to me in many ways. Kayla Boman became my treasure trove of information, helping me with those nuggets of information I needed, and also introduced me to potential sources; she is one of the most intelligent teenagers I have ever met. The other Boman children were helpful in their own ways and I need to thank them for allowing me to infringe on their space.

Judy Shaughnessy, I was told, would be abrasive and rude and no help at all. "You'll be shot if you show up on her property," one misguided man, with an obvious score to settle, told me while I was in Kansas. When I returned to Connecticut, I e-mailed Judy and thus began what turned into two months of conversations that changed this book in many ways. I am sure Judy left a lot of things out of our talks, but I am grateful, nonetheless, she trusted me with what she did.

Sheriff Ben Espey greeted me with a comforting Midwestern charm when I showed up at his office, as did his dispatcher. Ben was forthcoming with so much information about the case, he really turned this book into what I had envisioned from the start. Thank you, Sheriff. I tip my hat to you. I also want to say that although Ben Espey had a problem with a certain member of the FBI, in no way did he play down the FBI's role in the investigation. He spoke highly of Mickey Roberts and Kurt Lipanovich, and wanted me to understand they were instrumental in Victoria Jo's safe return.

Jeff Owen, who did much of the forensics on Bobbie Jo's computer, was extremely helpful in guiding me through the incredibly confusing labyrinth of those critical hours when he and Kurt Lipanovich figured out Darlene Fischer and Lisa Montgomery were the same person.

To those in Melvern, Skidmore, and other parts of the Midwest who stretched out their arms and allowed me to pry into the history of the towns they love so much, I applaud you for your hospitality and warmth while I asked tough questions about the lives you lead.

Those people, spread throughout the little towns I stopped in and gassed up my car, who talked to me about their lives over a cup of coffee, helped give this book its Midwestern feel of reality.

This project took more time away from my family than any of the others. Without the support of Mathew, Jordon, April, and Regina, I could not have done it. They accept my passion for story-telling and the enjoyment I get out of the writing process and allow me the space I need to get things done. I am forever grateful for their love and support, and truly blessed to have it.

SOURCES

A journalist seeks to uncover the truth as thoroughly as he or she can. We develop sources, throw countless questions at them, and then go out and try to back up what is said with additional sources. In doing this, an author can truly uncover the hard facts. Just one little example proves how tedious a task this can be, and how the most basic information can get lost in the shuffle: the FBI's affidavit claims Becky Harper made a 911 call at 3:38 P.M. on the afternoon of December 16, 2004. Sheriff Ben Espey's notes and report have this fact as 3:28 P.M.

For this book, I reached out to every pivotal person involved in the story and offered each the opportunity to speak.

Some did. Others didn't.

Lisa's oldest child, whom I called "Rebecca" in the book, had reservations about talking to me. Mainly, she was concerned about breaking a promise to her mother: Lisa had told her several times not to talk to me. It took a while for Rebecca to be convinced I wasn't out to add more lies to a growing list and wanted everyone's version of the truth. Even so, when she did finally agree to talk, Rebecca was careful about what she said. It was clear she's one of Lisa's dedicated allies. Quite admirably, Rebecca didn't ever seem to judge her mother. Instead, she explained that she wanted to be there for her no matter what happened.

Out of nowhere one day, I received an e-mail from Lisa's only son, whom I have referred to in the book as "Ryan." I had requested an interview with him, but he was apprehensive and rather terse; he said a few things and left it at that. Without being asked, he did send me a concluding remark one afternoon that shows, at least to me, how devoted he is to his mother: "For as long as I have lived with her, she was loving and always tried to push us to better ourselves. She was not always gentle, but she never hurt anyone . . . Also, she could talk and I loved talking to her about a lot of stuff."

There was always an element of Carl Boman's character I felt was missing from our conversations. Although the slice of his life I am referring to was well before he met Lisa, and really didn't have a role in the story I was telling, I felt it was important to explore it anyway, if not to write about it, to at least know he was being completely honest with me. Carl was extremely guarded where certain portions of his life were concerned, even secretive in some respects. This worried me at first—but then I asked him to explain it to me in a more detailed way. As we were finishing up what turned out to be about four months of nearly daily interviews, I asked Carl for a closing comment.

"There is a part of my life I don't speak about," said Carl. "I was young and not very mature. It is my business and is very painful. I have not had a blessed life. I have hurt others in my selfishness and immaturity, and have paid for those mistakes over and again. I have been blamed by Lisa and others, but we will continue to work to rebuild my life in the midst of this family crisis. If the people involved don't wish to offer love and understanding and wish to only cause strife, then I will turn away. This situation isn't the easiest; it is hard for all involved. There is no book you read to prepare. You wake up one morning and it is thrust upon you. I have made decisions. Right or wrong, I made them. I am far from perfect."

In the end, this story, for the most part, is about Lisa Montgomery, her life, and the road that led her to Bobbie Jo Stinnett. I started out wanting to include all I could about Bobbie Jo's short life. But Bobbie Jo's family and some of her close friends, understandably, did not want to talk to me, nor did Zeb. Therefore, I was left to sift through the little bit of information I could find and report it. I greatly regret not giving a more detailed portrait of Bobbie Jo's life that would serve as a legacy to her memory.

*   *   *

In many ways, this story forced me to put all of my journalistic skills to the test. Because I couldn't rely on the comfort of police reports and certain court documents, and there wasn't a trial to cull a lot of those documents from, I had to knock on doors, make calls, and try to find all the pieces of the story I could on my own. So many times throughout my career I have been faced with varying versions of the same scenes involved in the lives of those I write about. That collection of stories allowed me to track people down and ask them questions based on what a police report or piece of trial testimony had said. I couldn't do that here. In a sense, I had to act as a prosecutor and defense attorney, even a cop, and develop my own questions based on what I had learned. This, I believe, forced me to dig deeper than perhaps I would have if given those documents.

In those instances where several people told me varying versions of what happened, I went back and spoke to everyone I could. Some of those people simply would not talk to me, although I did give them the opportunity—and in some instances, multiple opportunities—to do so.

A vast array of sources was used to create this work of nonfiction. The basic structure of the book was based on my extensive interviews with Carl Boman, many members of his family, and several other people closely connected to the story, some of whom have chosen to remain anonymous. I also obtained scores of documents associated with the case, which I used as primary source material. Throughout my research, I also had exclusive access to several additional items, which added an additional layer of truth and quality to the narrative: letters, cards, e-mails, interviews conducted by people close to several of the players and related back to me.

I want to also acknowledge that I relied on previously published accounts—newspaper articles, magazine articles, Internet news articles, videotapes of press conferences, and cable-news network interviews with some of those involved in the story—in some sections of the book to make up for those portions of the story where participants would not speak to me. Most of those sources are clearly identified in the narrative. All of Pastor Mike Wheatley's comments, for example, were taken from interviews he gave to cable-television crime shows and a few of the newspaper articles he participated in. For the most part, I chose these sources carefully, and only used information from what I deemed to be valuable, trustworthy, reputable news organizations: CNN, FOX News Channel, MSNBC, the *New York Times*, the *Kansas City Star*, Associated Press, CBS News, and a few local-news organizations in Missouri, many of which helped to contribute over three thousand news stories about the case.

Some of the quotes were taken directly from television interviews. Several press conferences given by Nodaway County sheriff Ben Espey, U.S. attorney Todd Graves, and several members of the FBI were also used as direct quotes in the narrative, although not always attributed in the narrative itself. Those quotes appear, mostly, in the investigation portion of the book and reflect public statements made at what was a crucial period during the search for Victoria Jo and arrest of Lisa Montgomery. In order to keep the pace of the book moving swiftly, at certain times throughout the text I simply sourced some quotes—not all—with the tag "he (or she) said." A lot of these quotes were repeated by several different news organizations in dozens of newspapers and on television news shows.

I want to be perfectly clear, however: in *no* way is this book written from newspaper accounts of the crime. Eighty-five percent of this book is written from exclusive information, interviews, and research I gathered during a one-year process of full-time investigative journalism. With so many true-crime books today tagged as being "ripped from the headlines" and rushed into print, I want readers to understand that although I used *some* newspaper accounts of the story to lead me along the way of a truthful narrative, I spent a considerable amount of time in Kansas and Missouri, along with other regions where the story took me, and conducted well over one hundred interviews with people from all over the country in order to report the most complete and accurate story I could.

Primarily, the dialogue in the book was reconstructed after carefully piecing together different versions of events and juxtaposing those events with the multitude of interviews I conducted. In some instances, I took it upon myself to speak to as many people involved in a certain scene so as to reconstruct what was said accurately, which was then weighed against published accounts, legal documents, and anonymous sources. Some of the dialogue in the book is based on the memory and recollection of one or more of those involved in the scene.

ABOUT THE AUTHOR

With over three hundred thousand copies of his books in print, M. William Phelps has been called one of the country's most esteemed experts on crime and murder, and has spent years building an outstanding platform to showcase his work. He has appeared on dozens of national radio and television programs as an expert correspondent on crime, most notably on Court TV, the Discovery Channel, Biography Channel, The Learning Channel, History Channel, the *Montel Williams Show,* and Radio America. You can read profiles about his work and life in such noted publications as *Writer's Digest,* the *New York Daily News, Newsday,* the *Albany Times-Union,* the *Hartford Courant, Advance for Nurses* magazine, *Forensic Nursing, The Globe* magazine, the *New York Post, Columbia Daily Tribune,* and the *New London Day,* among others. His Web site is www.mwilliamphelps.com.